W9-ABS-415

Japan's Approach to Legal and Judicial Development in Developing Countries

JAPAN LIBRARY

Japan's Approach to Legal and Judicial Development in Developing Countries

BUILDING TRUST AND PARTNERSHIP

Japan International Cooperation Agency

Japan Publishing Industry Foundation for Culture

This book follows the Hepburn system of romanization. Japanese names are presented in the Western order with exception to this copyright page and the jacket.

Japan's Approach to Legal and Judicial Development in Developing Countries: Building Trust and Partnership
English translation edited by Japan Publishing Industry Foundation for Culture (JPIC)

Published by
Japan Publishing Industry Foundation for Culture (JPIC)
2-2-30 Kanda-Jinbocho, Chiyoda-ku, Tokyo 101-0051, Japan

First English edition: June 2020

This book is a translation of *Sekai o kaeru Nihonshiki hōzukuri: Tojōkoku to tomoni ayumu hōseibi shien* edited by Japan International Cooperation Agency (JICA) and published by Bungeishunju Ltd., 2018.

English publishing rights arranged with Bungeishunju Ltd.

Jacket and cover design: Miki Kazuhiko, Ampersand Works

Printed in Japan
ISBN 978-4-86658-130-9
https://japanlibrary.jpic.or.jp/

Preface

Every country has its own legal system, and Japan prior to the Meiji Revolution of 1868 was no exception. But the legal system at the time was wholly inadequate for enabling Japan to deal with the Western countries with which it established ties in the mid-nineteenth century. The Western powers insisted that Japan enact civil, criminal, and commercial codes and codes of civil and criminal procedure before they would even consider revising the unequal treaties that they had forced on it. Indeed, without such a set of legal codes, it would have been impossible for Japan to maintain stable relations with the outside world.

Japan's leaders in the Meiji period (1868–1912) were well aware of the need to develop a set of modern legal codes. Shinpei Eto, a senior official with the Institutions Bureau and later justice minister, embarked on the task of compiling a civil code in 1871. An admirer of France's Napoleonic Code, he believed that the French civil code could simply be translated into Japanese and put straight into practice in Japan.

Eto resigned from the government in 1873, when he was on the losing side of a dispute over diplomacy towards Korea; he was executed the following year after leading an abortive rebellion in his native Saga. Work on the civil code continued, however, and was completed several years later, in 1878. But the resulting law was so literally translated from the French civil code that much of it was unsuited to Japan's social and cultural values and institutions at the time, and it was scrapped.

The task of overseeing the compilation of a civil code then passed to Gustave-Émile Boissonade, a French jurist hired by the Japanese government. In 1890, after a decade of hard work, a new civil code comprising 1,762 articles was completed under his direction. This, however, was criticized for being at odds with Japanese social and cultural values and institutions, and after heated debate its implementation was postponed; in the end it was never put into practice. It is known as the Old Civil Code. Compilation then resumed and was at long last completed in 1896, although the result was not fundamentally different from the Old Civil Code. Finally, on the third attempt, Japan had its own civil code, 25 years after Shinpei Eto had set to work in 1871.

Criminal and commercial codes and codes of civil and criminal procedure were likewise compiled under Boissonade's direction.

The country also needed a constitution. The study of foreign constitutions commenced in the early Meiji years, and from 1881 Hirobumi Ito, who several years later became Japan's first prime minister, led efforts to draw up one for Japan. Promulgated in 1889, this constitution, the Constitution of the Empire of Japan, was modeled on the Prussian constitution, albeit with considerable differences.

Transcending cultural differences to create a law code that conforms to international standards without clashing significantly with the traditional, locally prevailing legal norms is thus a truly herculean task. Because it has unsurpassed experience in that area, no country is better qualified than Japan to work with developing nations in making their own laws.

That experience, coupled with the dedicated hard work of numerous experts such as Akio Morishima, professor emeritus of Nagoya University, has ensured the success of Japanese technical cooperation for legal and judicial development that cultivates and fosters the rule of law. All concerned are to be commended for their tireless efforts.

Among the crowning achievements of Japan's Official Development Assistance (ODA) has been its success in contributing to legal and judicial development in nearby countries like Vietnam, Cambodia, Laos, and China, as well as more distant lands like Côte d'Ivoire. While paying close attention to local views, Japan's cooperation has contributed to establishing legal and judicial systems that, although respecting tradition, are compatible with the needs of a modern economy, comply with international standards and underpin a peaceful, prosperous existence for all citizens. The publication of this chronicle of how that happened is truly cause for celebration. May it find many readers.

Shinichi Kitaoka
President
Japan International Cooperation Agency (JICA)

A Quick Guide to Japan's Cooperation for Legal and Judicial Development

Basic Facts 1

Major Legal and Judicial Development Projects

Japan's legal and judicial development efforts first got off the ground in Vietnam. They have since expanded throughout Asia and beyond to parts of Africa.

Nepal

- Drafting a civil code
- Improving trial procedures

➤ See chapter 4 for details

Uzbekistan

- Drafting legislation on administrative procedures
- Compiling a commentary on Bankruptcy Law

➤ See chapter 4 for details

Myanmar

- Enhancing functions for drafting and reviewing legislation
- Improving the legal training system

➤ See chapter 4 for details

Laos

- Drafting a civil code
- Compiling flowcharts and handbooks of criminal and civil procedures
- Enhancing the capacity of legal training institutions

➤ See chapter 3 for details

Cambodia

- Drafting and disseminating a civil code and code of civil procedure
- Improving the functioning of the Royal School for Judges and Prosecutors
- Enhancing bar association capabilities

➤ See chapter 2 for details

Côte d'Ivoire

- Improving access to justice
- Strengthening criminal justice functions

➤ See chapter 4 for details

This guide to Japanese cooperation for legal and judicial development is divided into two parts: Basic Facts and Descriptions by Country.

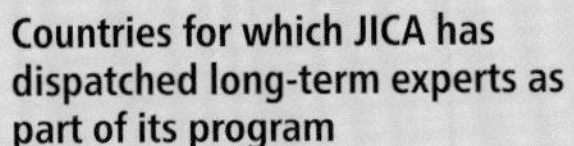

Mongolia

- Strengthening bar association capabilities
- Establishing a judicial mediation system

➤ See chapter 4 for details

China

- Revision of the Company Law
- Revision of the Environmental Protection Law
- Drafting the general provisions of the Civil Code (Support for the compilation of the Civil Code)

➤ See chapter 4 for details

Bangladesh

Vietnam

- Drafting and revising a civil code and code of civil procedure
- Improving the trial and prosecution process
- Enhancing bar association capabilities

➤ See chapter 1 for details

East Timor

Indonesia

- Improving administration of the mediation system
- Enhancing protection of intellectual property rights

➤ See chapter 4 for details

History of JICA's Cooperation for Legal and Judicial Development

- **1960s–present**
  Criminal justice training programs implemented in Japan
- **1996**
  Full-scale cooperation initiated in Vietnam
- **1999**
  Full-scale cooperation initiated in Cambodia
- **2003**
  Full-scale cooperation initiated in Laos
- **2004**
  Full-scale cooperation initiated in Mongolia
- **2004**
  Full-scale cooperation initiated in China
- **2005**
  Full-scale cooperation initiated in Uzbekistan
- **2007**
  Full-scale cooperation initiated in Indonesia
- **2009**
  Full-scale cooperation initiated in Nepal
- **2013**
  Full-scale cooperation initiated in Myanmar
- **2014**
  Full-scale cooperation initiated in Francophone Africa, including Côte d'Ivoire

Basic Facts 2

What Is Cooperation for Legal and Judicial Development?

The aim of cooperation for legal and judicial development

To foster the rule of law

How it accomplishes this

By developing human resources in three areas:

1. Establishing rules
2. Strengthening the functioning of bodies that administer the law
3. Improving access to justice

Capacity development

If a country is to enable its people to live in peace and prosperity, it must build and maintain a society governed by the rule of law: one with fully functioning laws and judicial institutions, in which everyone obeys the rules. JICA's legal and judicial development programs are designed to enable developing countries to make laws and establish judicial institutions, and maintain and enhance them, by developing human resources in three key areas: *establishing rules* by putting legislation in place; *strengthening the functioning of bodies that administer the law*, such as government agencies, the courts, and prosecutor's offices; and *improving access to justice* by making it easier for ordinary citizens to turn to the law for help. The goal is thereby to foster the rule of law in the developing world.

Key Terms Relating to Cooperation for Legal and Judicial Development

Here is a rundown of key terms essential to understanding Japan's cooperation for legal and judicial development.

❶ The rule of law

The principle that everyone, no matter how powerful, must obey the law. The arbitrary exercise of power by those in positions of influence undermines the rights of ordinary people who lack the means to resist them, threatens their ability to live in peace, and prevents them from engaging in economic transactions without fear. Only by building and maintaining a society with fully functioning laws and judicial institutions, where the rules apply equally to everyone, can people live in peace and prosperity.

❷ Capacity development

Enhancing the ability to meet challenges. In the case of cooperation for legal and judicial development, that means empowering people in developing countries to take the steps necessary to achieve the rule of law; namely, establishing rules, strengthening the functioning of bodies that administer the law, and improving access to justice. Specifically, capacity development involves training people to perform those functions. Besides upgrading skills at the individual level, it also entails improving institutional capacity.

❸ Establishing rules

To build a society where people can live in peace and prosperity, the rules that govern it, such as laws and ordinances, must be well designed, and they must evolve in step with social changes. The task of establishing rules can only be done properly if the individuals performing it possess specialized legal knowledge and have developed expertise in other areas, including the ability to identify what rules are required, research laws in other countries and write clear legal prose.

❹ Strengthening the functioning of bodies that administer the law

The bodies that administer the law must possess the ability to enforce the rules justly and fairly, and must ensure that they are not misapplied or abused; otherwise those rules are mere castles in the air. Bodies that administer the law comprise government agencies such as the justice ministry, as well as judicial organs such as the courts and prosecutor's offices. Ensuring that the people who staff these organizations understand the law correctly and are able to execute or apply it fairly is indispensable to building a peaceful, prosperous society.

❺ Improving access to justice

Even if the rules are well designed and applied fairly, they will still not achieve their objective unless ordinary people have a basic knowledge of them and enjoy access to institutions that provide recourse to them. There are several ways to improve access to justice, including conducting public awareness and education campaigns about the law, offering legal consultation, and providing free legal representation services. Enabling agencies in developing countries to take such steps on an ongoing basis is a key aspect of cooperation for legal and judicial development.

Basic Facts 3

How Legal and Judicial Development Projects Are Organized

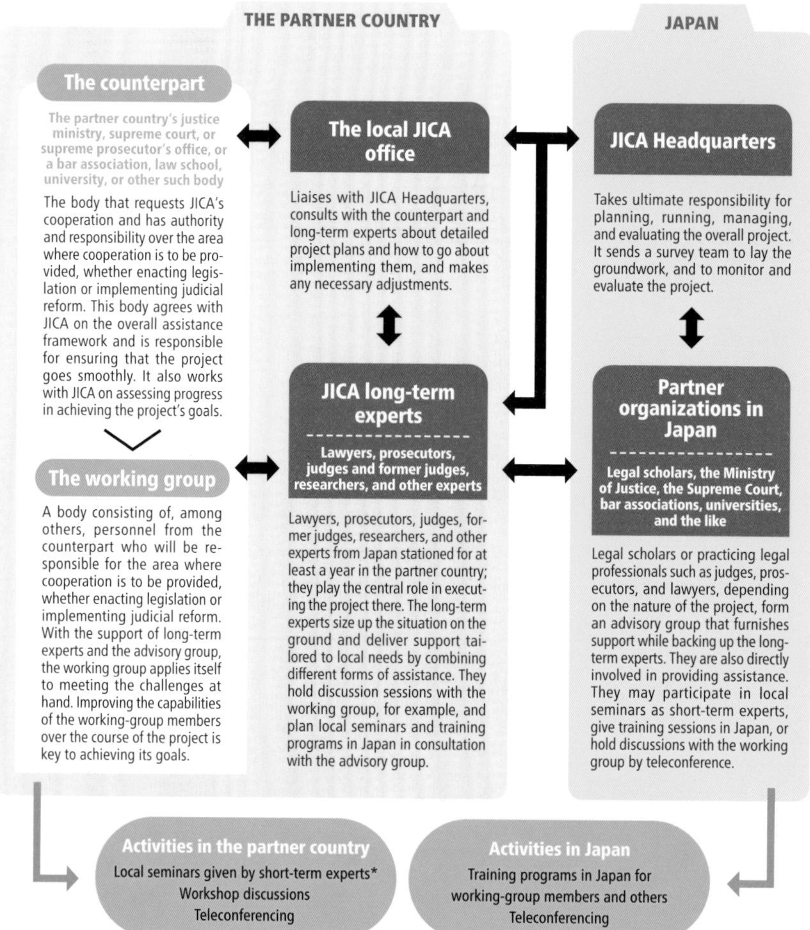

To ensure that cooperation is tailored to local circumstances and needs, long-term experts work closely with the working group on the task it has been assigned, whether drafting legislation or implementing judicial reform. When an issue arises that requires special expertise, the advisory group made up of partner organizations in Japan gives advice. JICA and its counterpart are jointly responsible for the overall project.

*Short-term experts are experts stationed in the partner country for less than one year.

Basic Facts 4

Steps in the Cooperation for Legal and Judicial Development

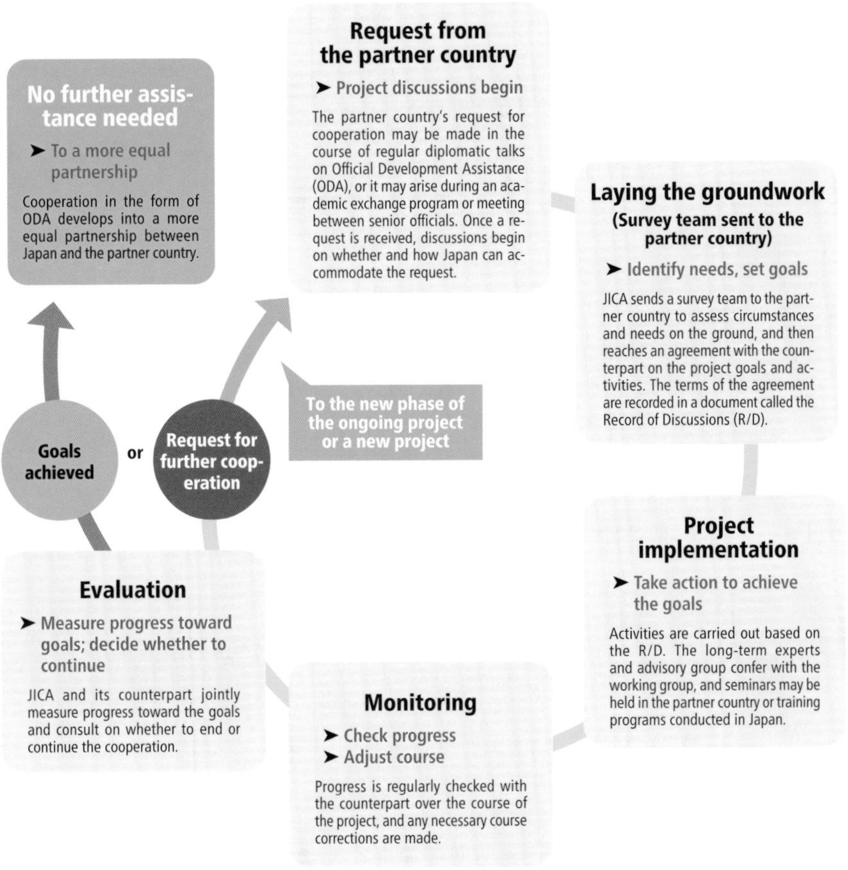

Request from the partner country

➤ Project discussions begin

The partner country's request for cooperation may be made in the course of regular diplomatic talks on Official Development Assistance (ODA), or it may arise during an academic exchange program or meeting between senior officials. Once a request is received, discussions begin on whether and how Japan can accommodate the request.

Laying the groundwork (Survey team sent to the partner country)

➤ Identify needs, set goals

JICA sends a survey team to the partner country to assess circumstances and needs on the ground, and then reaches an agreement with the counterpart on the project goals and activities. The terms of the agreement are recorded in a document called the Record of Discussions (R/D).

Project implementation

➤ Take action to achieve the goals

Activities are carried out based on the R/D. The long-term experts and advisory group confer with the working group, and seminars may be held in the partner country or training programs conducted in Japan.

Monitoring

➤ Check progress
➤ Adjust course

Progress is regularly checked with the counterpart over the course of the project, and any necessary course corrections are made.

Evaluation

➤ Measure progress toward goals; decide whether to continue

JICA and its counterpart jointly measure progress toward the goals and consult on whether to end or continue the cooperation.

Goals achieved or Request for further cooperation

To the new phase of the ongoing project or a new project

No further assistance needed

➤ To a more equal partnership

Cooperation in the form of ODA develops into a more equal partnership between Japan and the partner country.

JICA provides cooperation at the partner country's request on the terms agreed with the counterpart. Project activities are regularly monitored, and at the end of the project JICA and its counterpart jointly evaluate whether the goals have been met. Meeting those goals, and thus moving beyond the donor-recipient relationship to establish an equal partnership, is the ultimate objective of any cooperation program.

Vietnam

OFFICIAL NAME: Socialist Republic of Vietnam
CAPITAL: Hanoi
POPULATION: 92.7 million (2016, General Statistics Office of Vietnam)
ETHNIC GROUPS: 86% Kinh (Vietnamese), with 53 minorities
LANGUAGE: Vietnamese
RELIGIONS: Buddhism, Catholicism, Caodaism, and others
PER CAPITA GDP: US$2,215 (2016, General Statistics Office of Vietnam)
AREA: 329,241 km^2

(Source: Japanese Foreign Affairs Ministry website)

HISTORICAL BACKGROUND

The Socialist Republic of Vietnam was established in 1976, when the north and south of the country were reunited. The Doi Moi (renewal) policy adopted at the Communist Party Congress in 1986 committed the country to a market economy. Since then, Vietnam has been making the transition to a market economy and opening up to the outside world under one-party communist rule.

1996

Japan's first legal and judicial development project is launched.

With the transition to a new economic regime, Vietnam urgently needed to institute a legal system compatible with a market economy and train people to administer it. In 1994, the Vietnamese government requested official development assistance (ODA) from Japan in this field. After two years of preparations, Japanese Technical Cooperation in the Legal and Judicial Field (Phase I), JICA's first project for legal and judicial development, was launched.

2005

The 2005 Civil Code is enacted.

The Vietnamese Ministry of Justice embarked on a complete overhaul of the country's civil code, the fundamental law governing commercial transactions, to bring it more in line with a market economy. Under the Japanese Technical Cooperation in the Legal and Judicial Field agreement, a Joint Research Team for Revision of the Vietnamese Civil Code was set up with the Vietnamese Ministry of Justice to collaborate on rewriting the code. As a result, a revised civil code containing a set of new provisions geared to a market economy was enacted by the National Assembly and became law.

2007

Technical Assistance Project for Legal and Judicial System Reform is launched.

Because there was a considerable gap in knowledge and capabilities between central government and regional officials in Vietnam, the law was not being applied uniformly. The new project went beyond helping central government agencies draft legislation, and assisted regional government offices in applying that legislation as well. It thus ensured that the law was enforced more consistently throughout Vietnam.

The Project for Harmonized, Practical Legislation and Uniform Application of Law Targeting Year 2020 is launched.

This comprehensive project was initiated in the run-up to 2020, which Vietnam had set as the target year for legal and judicial system reforms. It was inspired by the vision of establishing a new partnership between Vietnam and Japan once it was completed, in the hope that the two countries might then move beyond the donor-recipient relationship to interact as equals.

2015

The 2015 Civil Code is enacted.

Vietnam enacted a new civil code in 2015. This was better adapted to the needs of a market economy: it contained provisions on modern forms of commerce and conformed more closely to international standards. Incorporating many of the recommendations made by the Japanese since JICA began assisting Vietnam in 1996, it was the culmination of Japan's cooperation to date.

Cambodia

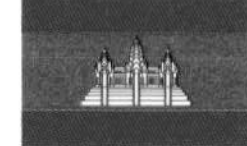

OFFICIAL NAME: Kingdom of Cambodia
CAPITAL: Phnom Penh
POPULATION: 14.70 million (2013, government statistics)
ETHNIC GROUPS: 90% of the population is Cambodian (Khmer)
LANGUAGE: Cambodian (Khmer)
RELIGION: Buddhism, with a Muslim minority
PER CAPITA GDP: US$1,140 (2015 est., IMF data)
AREA: 181,000 km²

(Source: Japanese Foreign Affairs Ministry website)

HISTORICAL BACKGROUND

The mass murder of intellectuals by the Pol Pot regime (1976–1979), coupled with twenty years of civil war, destroyed the old legal system and wiped out virtually the entire legal community. The establishment of the rule of law by enacting legislation and implementing legal and judicial reforms is one of the centerpieces of the Cambodian government's efforts to rebuild the country.

1999

The Legal and Judicial Development Project begins.

The Legal and Judicial Development Project began when Cambodia turned to Japan for help with drafting a new civil code and code of civil procedure, the twin cornerstones of its nation-building efforts in the aftermath of the civil war. A working group was set up in Cambodia and a task force in Japan, and the draft text went back and forth between the two sides and was reviewed by each in turn.

2001

The Legal and Judicial Cooperation for the Bar Association of the Kingdom of Cambodia Project is launched with the JFBA.

From an early stage, certain members of the Japan Federation of Bar Associations (JFBA) had started to help Cambodia rebuild its judicial system on their own initiative. In 2001, JICA and the JFBA teamed up in a partnership project to help the Bar Association of the Kingdom of Cambodia establish and run a Center for Lawyers' Training and Professional Improvement (LTC).

2005

The Project for Improvement of Training on Civil Matters at the Royal School for Judges and Prosecutors begins.

This project was launched in order to help the fledgling Royal School for Judges and Prosecutors train people to be capable of appropriately applying the new Civil Code and Civil Procedure Code. It assisted with putting together a curriculum, producing teaching materials, and training future faculty.

2006

2007

The Civil Procedure Code is promulgated (to come into force in July 2007).

The Civil Code is promulgated (to come into force in December 2011).

Work on drafting a civil code and civil procedure code, which began in 1999, was completed in 2003, and the final versions of both were submitted to the Cambodian Ministry of Justice. These were then reviewed by the Council of Ministers and the National Assembly. The Civil Procedure Code was promulgated in 2006, followed by the Civil Code in 2007. The Civil Code, while respecting Cambodia's traditions and culture, incorporated new concepts geared to a market economy. The Civil Procedure Code expressly guaranteed citizens the right to a trial.

2017

The Legal and Judicial Development Project (Phase V) begins.

This project was inaugurated as the next phase of efforts to embed the Civil Code and Civil Procedure Code in Cambodian society. It had three main pillars: developing related legislation, producing forms to be used for civil procedures, and publishing court judgments.

Laos

OFFICIAL NAME: Lao People's Democratic Republic
CAPITAL: Vientiane
POPULATION: 6.49 million (2015, Lao Statistics Bureau)
ETHNIC GROUPS: 49 ethnic groups, including Lao who make up just over half the population
LANGUAGE: Lao **RELIGION:** Buddhism
PER CAPITA GDP: US$1,947 (2015, Lao Statistics Bureau)
AREA: 240,000 km²

(Source: Japanese Foreign Affairs Ministry website)

HISTORICAL BACKGROUND

After gaining independence from France in 1953, Laos was torn by recurring civil war until a peace agreement was signed in 1973. In 1975, the monarchy was abolished and the Lao People's Democratic Republic was established. In 1986, the government decided to adopt a market economy while maintaining a socialist system and one-party rule by the Lao People's Revolutionary Party. It has since made progress in implementing reforms designed to promote economic growth.

JICA launches Legal and Judicial Development Project in Laos.

In 1998, JICA started providing cooperation at the request of the Laotian government, which was then developing regulations suited to a market economy, in the form of training programs in Japan and seminars in Laos. The first full-scale project for legal and judicial development in Laos commenced in 2003.

2003

2010

The Project for Human Resource Development in the Legal Sector is launched.

A new project building on the achievements and lessons of the one preceding it was launched with a primary focus on human resource development in the legal sector. This took a distinctive approach: the working group consisted of members drawn from a cross section of agencies, and a liaison unit was set up to coordinate the project. In 2012, assistance with drafting a civil code was added to the scope of the project.

2012

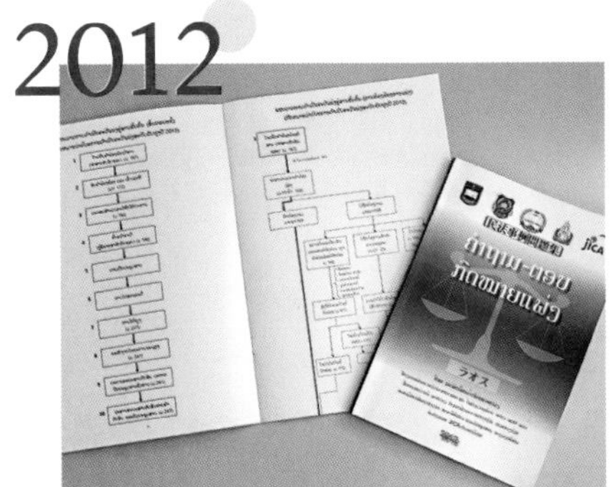

Work is completed on producing a set of exercises on Civil Code cases and civil and criminal procedure flowcharts.

These teaching and reference materials, which emerged from the project, were used not only at schools and law-enforcement agencies but also during deliberations by the National Assembly. During the compilation process, the focus was on stimulating discussion among the Laotian members and improving their understanding of the law. Workshops were held in participatory format, which prompted younger members to speak up; this also got the Laotians, who were used to a top-down approach, thinking in new ways.

The Project for Human Resource Development in the Legal Sector (Phase II) is launched.

A new phase began with the goal of enhancing the skills of a wider range of legal professionals. Participants came not only from the Ministry of Justice, the People's Supreme Court, the Office of the Supreme People's Prosecutor, and the National University of Laos as before, but also from the Lao Bar Association, the Ministry of Public Security, and the Ministry of Labour and Social Welfare.

2014

2015

The National Institute of Justice is established.

The establishment of the National Institute of Justice (NIJ) in Laos was inspired by a visit to Japan's Legal Training and Research Institute when the project participants were on a training program in Japan in 2012. The NIJ offers a specialized training program that equips students who have completed basic legal education with practical skills by emphasizing hands-on experience in trial procedures. Graduates are highly valued for their ability to start working from day one.

Indonesia

OFFICIAL NAME: Republic of Indonesia **CAPITAL:** Jakarta
POPULATION: 255 million (2015, Indonesian government statistics)
ETHNIC GROUPS: Predominantly ethnic Malay (with some 300 subgroups, including Javanese and Sundanese)
LANGUAGE: Indonesian
RELIGIONS: 87.21% Islam, 9.87% Christianity (6.96% Protestant, 2.91% Catholic), 1.69% Hinduism, 0.72% Buddhism, 0.05% Confucianism, 0.50% other (2013, Ministry of Religious Affairs statistics)
PER CAPITA GDP: US$3,876.80 (2017, Indonesian government statistics)
AREA: 1.89 million km²

(Source: Japanese Foreign Affairs Ministry website)

HISTORICAL BACKGROUND Having been in power for three decades, the Suharto regime fell in 1998 after protests calling for democracy erupted in the wake of the 1997 Asian Financial Crisis. Indonesia has taken steps to reform its governance, including the judicial system, as democracy has taken root.

2002–2006

Comparative seminars on judicial systems.

When Indonesia turned to Japan for assistance with judicial reform, JICA organized five seminars comparing the Japanese and Indonesian judicial systems in conjunction with the Research and Training Institute of the Japanese Ministry of Justice.

2007

The Project on Improvement of Mediation System in Indonesia is launched.

Building on the results of the comparative seminars on judicial systems, a full-scale legal and judicial development project was launched with the Supreme Court of Indonesia as counterpart. This project took concrete steps to promote conflict resolution through compromise and mediation.

2008

Training program for judges and court clerks.

As part of the project, a training program was organized to promote understanding of the Supreme Court rules on compromise and mediation and improve mediation skills. Further, as a means of training mediators and encouraging ordinary people to use the mediation system, a DVD on mediation procedures featuring fictional situations was produced. This was sent out to courts throughout the country.

2015

The Project on Intellectual Property Rights Protection and Legal Consistency for Improving the Business Environment is launched.

With the cooperation of the Japan Patent Office, JICA had provided support to the Directorate General of Intellectual Property of the Indonesian Ministry of Law and Human Rights since 1995. Building on those foundations, it now inaugurated a new project with two counterparts, the Ministry of Law and Human Rights and the Supreme Court of Indonesia. This sought to enhance capabilities in the areas of registering intellectual property rights and policing violations. It also aimed to improve the Indonesian judicial system's capacity to handle intellectual property cases.

China

OFFICIAL NAME: People's Republic of China
CAPITAL: Beijing **POPULATION:** 1.376 billion
ETHNIC GROUPS: Han Chinese (92% of the population) and 55 minorities
LANGUAGE: Chinese
RELIGIONS: Buddhism, Islam, Christianity, and others
PER CAPITA GDP: 53,980 yuan (2016, National Bureau of Statistics of China) US$8,113 (2016, IMF)
AREA: 9.6 million km²

(Source: Japanese Foreign Affairs Ministry website)

HISTORICAL BACKGROUND

China decided to reform its economic system and adopt a policy of opening up to the outside world in 1978. It achieved rapid economic growth after bringing in a "socialist market economy" in the 1990s. It amended the constitution in 1999, and its accession to the World Trade Organization (WTO) in 2001 increased the need for legislation conforming to international standards.

2004

The Economic Legal Infrastructure Development Project begins.

This project was initiated at China's request after its accession to the WTO, as it proceeded to enact the relevant legislation. Cooperation was provided in drafting (or drafting amendments to) and enforcing the Company Law, the Anti-Monopoly Law and marketing laws.

2007

The Improvement of Civil Procedure Law and Arbitration Law Project begins.

To deal with the proliferation of civil disputes resulting from the transition to a market economy, the Legislative Affairs Commission of the Standing Committee of the National People's Congress (NPC) requested Japanese assistance with revising China's Civil Procedure Law and Arbitration Law. In response, the Improvement of Civil Procedure Law and Arbitration Law Project was launched. Its defined objective was to establish efficient civil procedure and arbitration systems that were more in harmony with international rules.

2012–2015

The Administrative Litigation Law and other administrative laws are revised.

As the Chinese set about revising the country's Administrative Litigation Law and other administrative laws in a bid to solve the challenges facing administrative litigation in China, JICA provided advice and other forms of support backed up by Japanese knowledge and experience.

2014

The Project on Legal Development for Improvement of the Market Economy and People's Wellbeing begins.

This project provided cooperation in revising China's economic legislation, and laws and regulations governing social security and the environment, to bring them in line with actual social and economic conditions and international standards. By sharing Japan's past experience, the project helped the counterpart—the General Office of the Legislative Affairs Commission of the NPC Standing Committee, which is the NPC's legislative arm—achieve high standards in developing and amending legislation.

2017

The general provisions of the Civil Code are enacted.

Among the legislation that JICA helped draft under the Project on Legal Development for Improvement of the Market Economy and People's Wellbeing were the general provisions of the Civil Code. These provisions, which set out the basic principles regulating private transactions, are also of vital importance to Japanese companies doing business in China.

Mongolia

OFFICIAL NAME: Mongolia **CAPITAL:** Ulaanbaatar
POPULATION: 3,179,800 (2017, National Statistics Office of Mongolia [NSO])
ETHNIC GROUPS: Mongolian (95% of the population), Kazakhs and others
LANGUAGES: Mongolian (official), Kazakh
RELIGIONS: Tibetan Buddhism and others
PER CAPITA GDP: US$3,856.80 (2016, World Bank Atlas method, NSO)
AREA: 1,564,100 km²

(Source: Japanese Foreign Affairs Ministry website)

HISTORICAL BACKGROUND

Mongolia adopted a new constitution in 1992 and renounced socialism, changing its official name from the Mongolian People's Republic to simply Mongolia. Since becoming a democracy, it has implemented a series of structural reforms with support from Japan and other countries, as well as from international agencies, during its transition to a market economy.

2004

JICA starts sending legal advisors.

In March, at the request of the Mongolian Ministry of Justice and Home Affairs, JICA sent a lawyer to work as an advisor in Mongolia. This marked the start of a cooperative relationship rooted in local needs and conditions.

2006

The Enhancement Planning Project for the Association of Mongolian Advocates is launched.

As Mongolian society made the transition to democracy and a market economy, this project aimed to achieve two goals: improving the quality of legal services offered by Mongolia's lawyers to ordinary Mongolians, and strengthening the Association's functions as a bar association for lawyers in private practice. It was implemented by the Mongolian Ministry of Justice and Home Affairs and the Association of Mongolian Advocates.

The Project for Strengthening Mediation System is launched.

In light of the success of the Mediation Center established under the Enhancement Planning Project for the Association of Mongolian Advocates, the Supreme Court of Mongolia began studying the possibility of implementing a mediation system in the courts. It therefore turned to Japan for support. A new project, the Project for Strengthening the Mediation System, began, under which the mediation system was trialed at courts in two pilot regions.

2010

2013

Mediation is implemented at courts nationwide.

With input from project members, a mediation law was drafted as part of Mongolia's judicial reforms and passed by the legislature in May 2012. On November 1, 2013, with the legal foundations of a mediation system now in place, courts of first instance throughout Mongolia began offering mediation.

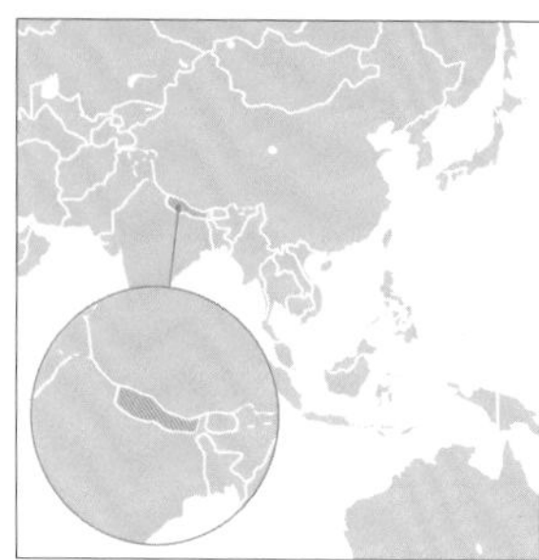

Nepal

OFFICIAL NAME: Federal Democratic Republic of Nepal
CAPITAL: Kathmandu
POPULATION: 26.49 million (2011 population census)
ETHNIC GROUPS: Parbate Hindu, Magar, Tharu, Tamang, Newar, and others **LANGUAGE:** Nepali
RELIGIONS: Hinduism (81.3%), Buddhism (9.0%), Islam (4.4%), and others
PER CAPITA GDP: 90,521 rupees (US$848) (FY2016–2017, Nepalese Ministry of Finance)
AREA: 147,000 km²

(Source: Japanese Foreign Affairs Ministry website)

HISTORICAL BACKGROUND

In 1996, the Communist Party of Nepal (Maoist) began an armed struggle against the government, and fighting continued until a comprehensive peace agreement was signed in 2006. Constituent Assembly elections were held in 2008, and the country made the transition from a monarchy to a federal democratic republic.

JICA begins cooperation on drafting a Civil Code.

Nepal sought Japanese assistance with nation building in the aftermath of the conflict, and as part of the Japanese cooperation effort, JICA began helping to draft a Civil Code. Specifically, a Japanese advisory group commented on drafts of the code prepared by the Nepalese drafting committee.

2010

The draft Civil Code is completed.

The draft Civil Code was completed following discussions between the two sides in various formats: local seminars in Nepal, training programs in Japan, and teleconference calls. It was submitted to the prime minister in August and then presented by the government to the Constituent Assembly in January 2011. The Constituent Assembly, however, was dissolved in 2012 due to political turmoil, and the draft code was scrapped for the time being without being fully debated.

2013

The Project for Strengthening the Capacity of the Court for Expeditious and Reliable Dispute Settlement begins.

In a society where the embers of civil war are still smoldering, it is vital to ensure that conflict resolution mechanisms function effectively, as a trivial disagreement can quickly escalate into a major struggle. A new project was therefore launched to assist the Supreme Court of Nepal in its efforts to enhance conflict resolution capabilities. This sought to improve case-management of civil and criminal cases and also promote conflict resolution through mediation. In June 2017, the Supreme Court published case-management guidelines developed with the project's support.

2014

A revised version of the draft Civil Code, the "2014 Civil Code," is submitted to the Assembly.

A second Constituent Assembly was convened in January 2014. Meanwhile, JICA helped to revise the abortive "2010 Civil Code," and the amended bill was submitted to the prime minister and cabinet in August 2014. This bill, known as the "2014 Civil Code," was tabled before the Assembly in December.

2017

The Civil Code is enacted.

Debate on the Civil Code resumed after the new constitution was adopted in September 2015, and members of the legislative assembly were flown to Japan to facilitate deliberations. Meanwhile, public consultations were held all over Nepal to solicit the views of legal professionals, ordinary citizens, and NGOs. After a lively national debate, the Civil Code passed the Assembly on September 25, 2017.

Myanmar

OFFICIAL NAME: Republic of the Union of Myanmar
CAPITAL: Naypyidaw
POPULATION: 51.41 million (September 2014, figures released by the Burmese Ministry of Labour, Immigration and Population)
ETHNIC GROUPS: Burmese (approx. 70%) and numerous minorities
LANGUAGE: Burmese
RELIGIONS: Buddhism (90%), Christianity, Islam, and others
PER CAPITA GDP: US$1,307 (FY2016–2017, IMF estimate)
AREA: 680,000 km²

(Source: Japanese Foreign Affairs Ministry website)

HISTORICAL BACKGROUND

When President Thein Sein assumed office in March 2011, his government inaugurated a series of legal and judicial reforms in the belief that establishing the rule of law was an important step in building democracy. These reforms have been continued by the new government that took over in March 2016.

2012

A preliminary survey is implemented.

After the transition to civilian rule, Myanmar sought Japan's help in developing institutions and enhancing the skills of the people underpinning the country's economic and social fabric. JICA responded by launching a preliminary survey on the ground in March to determine how it could assist in the legal and judicial fields.

The Project for Capacity Development of Legal, Judicial, and Relevant Sectors in Myanmar begins.

2013

Under this project, three Japanese experts including a prosecutor and a lawyer were stationed in Naypyidaw, the capital, to advise the two project counterparts, the Supreme Court of the Union and the Union Attorney General's Office.

2014

Training programs are held for Burmese government personnel.

Japanese experts gave seminars during regular training programs organized by the Supreme Court of the Union and the Union Attorney General's Office. Training methods that had never been tried before in Myanmar, including case studies and moot court using mock records, were shared by the experts and incorporated into the curriculum.

2015

Efforts to reform the Burmese court system get rolling.

JICA began working with the Supreme Court of the Union on overhauling trial procedures. Both sides cooperated to ensure that laws were properly applied. In anticipation of the enactment of the intellectual property law then being drafted, for example, they took steps to facilitate the efficient resolution of intellectual property cases.

2016

A dialogue begins with the Union Attorney General's Office staff.

To enhance the contract review functions of the Union Attorney General's Office, which reviews all contracts with the government, JICA began a dialogue with the staff of the office. The dialogue resulted in the production of a set of contract-review guidelines. Prompt, accurate reviews of contracts between government and the private sector are expected to foster a better investment environment.

Introduction

The Japan International Cooperation Agency (JICA) is an agency that implements the Japanese government's Official Development Assistance (ODA) programs to developing countries. At JICA, we work to help people in the developing world come up with their own solutions to the challenges their countries face and thus build a better future.

For many people, the term "ODA" brings to mind infrastructure projects like dams and bridges, assistance programs in agriculture and education sectors, and images of young volunteers working overseas. But there is an unusual form of assistance to the developing world that is probably less familiar: helping countries abroad cultivate the rule of law through cooperation for legal and judicial development.

First it is necessary to explain what cooperation for legal and judicial development is about.

One important goal of this type of cooperation is to change the workings of society. It seeks to replace rule by personal whim, which allows those in power to thrive at the expense of the socially disadvantaged, with the rule of law, which requires them to govern in accordance with laws decided by the citizenry. The rule of law is the idea that society should be run according to a set of rules agreed on by everyone—that is, the law. When the bureaucracy and the courts operate on a legal basis, the result is a society where all can live in security.

Imagine, for a moment, what a society without established laws would be like. This might not be easy for those of us who live in a well-governed country like Japan. In such a society, however, in the absence of an established body of laws, your property could be confiscated for no good reason; you might have no recourse if someone failed to honor a contract; and crimes might not be fairly tried and judged. In brief, the very foundations for social development would be wanting.

The fact is that many developing countries are still without a proper body of laws. They lack the requisite legislation. They do not have adequate institutions or human resources to administer the law fairly and embed its principles in society. Their citizens are ignorant of the law and have no means to learn about it even if they want to. People lack easy access to the court system, or they have so little faith in the courts that they distrust trial outcomes.

That situation still prevails in many countries around the world. Cooperation for legal and judicial development focuses on bringing the rule of law to such countries.

We at JICA have been carrying out cooperation for legal and judicial development since the 1990s. Our work in this area commenced in Vietnam and has expanded steadily since. To date we have sent Japanese experts on long-term assignments to ten countries, and we have trained people from 23 countries. This book chronicles how the program has evolved over the past two decades, based on interviews with many individuals involved in it.

Japan is not the only country working on legal and judicial development abroad. Many other governments and international agencies, including the United Nations, do so. But the Japanese approach is very different from theirs. We may introduce the Japanese legal system to our counterparts in the partner country, but we never try to foist it on them. Rather, it is left up to local legal experts to decide what type of legal system will best take root there in the future. In sum, the Japanese approach involves crafting laws tailored to the partner country by respecting its history and culture, and working with the people there to think through how to make those laws useful.

The choice of this unique approach to legal and judicial development has to a great degree been determined by Japan's own evolution as a country. After the Meiji Revolution of 1868, Japan studied and embraced the legal and judicial institutions of the "advanced" Western nations while adapting them to

Japanese society. Japan's experience offers important lessons to countries now seeking to put their own laws in place. Moreover, it has ingrained in the Japanese a belief that it is not possible to force "advanced" laws on a country, for they will never take root that way; rather, the people of that country should be facilitated in making laws suited to their own society as they learn.

Japan's legal and judicial development program was launched by a single legal scholar. Over the past twenty years, it has grown into a massive project involving collaboration among numerous legal experts, universities, and institutions, including the Japanese Ministry of Justice, the Japanese Supreme Court, and the Japan Federation of Bar Associations (JFBA). But it still remains, as much as it was two decades ago, a matter of Japanese and locals steadily working side by side to cultivate the rule of law.

In the process of compiling this book, we interviewed more than a hundred people who have devoted themselves to supporting the rule of law over the past two decades. People's accounts varied widely depending on when they were involved in the project and what role they played. But the stories of their struggles and soul-searching as they worked on legal and judicial development abroad—a task without a rule book—all had one theme in common: a fervent desire to utilize the Japanese experience to support nation building in the developing world.

We also conducted interviews in Vietnam, Cambodia, and Laos. Those interviews offered glimpses of what the program was like on the ground: how experts from Japan and local personnel confided in each other as colleagues, sometimes even like family. We were especially struck by the number of people in those countries who said that they were keen to build on the relationship of trust established with Japan over the course of the legal and judicial development projects.

With the progress of globalization and the growth of international economic activity, Japan has an increasingly important role to play in the international community. The desire to develop legal and judicial systems based on the Japanese model is growing steadily, especially among the countries of Asia. After all, Japan has succeeded in building a stable society by adopting its legal and judicial systems from "advanced" nations while establishing legal and judicial institutions tailored to its own ethos and culture. Never have expectations of Japan's cooperation for legal and judicial development been so high in Asia.

Against that backdrop, cooperation for legal and judicial development has evolved into one of the mainstays of Japan's ODA programs, despite the fact that this type of cooperation did not even exist in Japan twenty years ago. More and more young Japanese who intend to pursue a career in law are, even as students, showing a keen interest in legal and judicial development as a form of international cooperation. But there are few opportunities to find out what the job entails and who does it.

As you read this book, you will learn of the many players working in this fascinating field in Asia and around the world, and you will get a sense of their dedication. Furthermore, you will come to understand what is meant by the book's sub-title: *Building Trust and Partnership*.

This book chronicles the devoted efforts of people in the developing world and the Japanese who have supported them, their trials and tribulations, and the challenges they have faced. It offers insight into how, as a result of their tireless work, Japan's approach to cooperation for legal and judicial development will change the developing world and the world as a whole. Read on to learn more!

Law and Justice Team
Japan International Cooperation Agency (JICA)

December 2017

Contents

Chapter 4

INDONESIA

CHINA

UZBEKISTAN

MONGOLIA

NEPAL

Chapter 1

Japan's First Foray into Legal and Judicial Development—Vietnam

When Vietnam's Minister of Justice asked for advice on drafting a civil code, he inspired a Japanese civil law expert with a mission: to craft enduring legislation for that country. This led Japan to embark on an enterprise the likes of which it had never attempted before.

The streets of Vietnam's capital, Hanoi

PROJECT FACT SHEET Vietnam

Japanese Technical Cooperation in the Legal and Judicial Field (Phase I) December 1996–November 1999 COUNTERPART: Ministry of Justice	JICA's first full-scale legal and judicial development project took place in Vietnam. Case studies of the legal system underpinning the market economy in Japan and elsewhere were shared with the project counterpart, the Vietnamese Ministry of Justice. A broad range of support was provided with legal reforms designed to facilitate Vietnam's transition to a market economy. In addition, social surveys were implemented with the goal of assessing the state of private transactions in Vietnam.
Japanese Technical Cooperation in the Legal and Judicial Field (Phase II) December 1999–November 2002 COUNTERPARTS: Ministry of Justice Supreme People's Court Supreme People's Procuracy	JICA organized a support network in Japan to assist the Vietnamese Ministry of Justice with the task of revising the Vietnamese Civil Code (1995), which had now been fully implemented. It also brought the Supreme People's Court (SPC) and the Supreme People's Procuracy (SPP) on board as new counterparts, and supported judicial reforms by strengthening their ability to function.
Japanese Technical Cooperation in the Legal and Judicial Field (Phase III) July 2003–March 2007 COUNTERPARTS: Ministry of Justice Supreme People's Court Supreme People's Procuracy Vietnam National University, Hanoi	Phase III of the project continued to support the Ministry of Justice's revision of the Civil Code. It also supported its efforts to accelerate the transition to a market economy, including overhauling the legal system as it related to the Civil Code. Meanwhile it assisted the SPC and SPP in making civil and criminal procedures fairer and more expeditious by revising the procedural codes overseen by those bodies, and by developing related manuals. It also provided HR development support to Vietnam National University, Hanoi.
Technical Assistance Project for Legal and Judicial System Reform April 2007–March 2011 COUNTERPARTS: Ministry of Justice Supreme People's Court Supreme People's Procuracy Vietnam Bar Federation	Besides helping to draft legislation, JICA now started to offer full-scale support in applying and disseminating the legislation by engaging with regional agencies. This project assisted the Ministry of Justice with improving Civil Code–related legislation and applying the law at the regional-agency level. It assisted the SPC and SPP in improving the procedural codes and better applying the law "on the ground" in the designated pilot zone, Bac Ninh province. Further, it began helping the Vietnam Bar Federation (VBF) to strengthen its organization.
Technical Assistance Project for Legal and Judicial System Reform (Phase II) April 2011–March 2015 COUNTERPARTS: Ministry of Justice Supreme People's Court Supreme People's Procuracy Vietnam Bar Federation	This project, building on its predecessor, continued to assist the four counterparts—the Ministry of Justice, the SPC, the SPP, and the VBF—in applying and disseminating the law while aiding in amending the 2005 Civil Code and revising the constitution. It helped rework the procedural codes to conform to constitutional changes, and provided extensive support to the four counterparts in their wide-ranging efforts to build a society governed by law, which was the goal of the new constitution.
Project for Harmonized, Practical Legislation and Uniform Application of Law Targeting Year 2020 April 2015–March 2020 COUNTERPARTS: Ministry of Justice Prime Minister's Office Supreme People's Court Supreme People's Procuracy Vietnam Bar Federation	When Vietnam set 2020 as the target year for legal and judicial system reform, JICA responded by launching a new project involving a fifth counterpart, the Prime Minister's Office, alongside the Ministry of Justice, the SPC, the SPP, and the VBF. This was designed to entrench and expand on the accomplishments of previous aid programs. It also aims to lay the organizational groundwork for a new partnership between Japan and Vietnam going forward.

01 An Encounter with Vietnam's Minister of Justice

Landing at Noi Bai International Airport after a flight of some five hours from Haneda Airport, I walked off the plane into a brand-new airport terminal that provides a pleasant welcome to travelers.

After about a twenty-minute drive on the highway from the airport, the Nhat Tan Bridge over the Red River came into view. With a total length of about 3.8 km and a width of 33.2 m, this eight-lane bridge is the longest cable-stayed bridge in Southeast Asia. Perhaps the most memorable feature of this bridge is its five gigantic towers, each shaped like the letter "A." As you pass under one tower after another, your anticipation for arriving at the city builds; it indeed deserves to be the new gateway to Hanoi, the Vietnamese capital city with a history of more than a thousand years.

These three structures—namely Noi Bai International Airport, the highway linking the city center and the airport, and Nhat Tan Bridge—have all been developed with the help of Japanese Official Development Assistance (ODA) loan programs. A lavish ceremony was held on 4 January 2015 to celebrate the simultaneous completion of the three programs. It was an important day that marked the ever-growing "Vietnam-Japan friendship" in this country, which has been achieving dramatic economic growth since the opening up of the national economy under the Doi Moi (renewal) policy.[1]

It was twenty-two years previously that the "seed" of a grand project had been planted in a conference room of the Ministry of Justice of Vietnam in Hanoi. It would lie in wait and grow to support new national development efforts in Vietnam.

Akio Morishima

In the summer of 1993, a seminar on the Civil Code of Japan was held in a conference room of the Vietnamese Ministry of Justice. Akio Morishima,[2]

1 A package of reforms revolving around creating a market economy that was adopted at the 1986 Communist Party Congress.

2 Morishima, a leading jurist in civil and environmental law and professor emeritus at Nagoya University, has taught at universities in Japan and abroad and sat on various Japanese government advisory committees. He pioneered cooperation for legal and judicial development in Vietnam and Cambodia.

an authority on civil law and a lecturer at the seminar, was almost at a loss for words. Morishima was one of the most important figures in the academic study of civil law in Japan. He had taught at many different universities, including Nagoya University, Sophia University, and Harvard Law School. He also served on various government councils and advisory committees, and had been deeply involved in establishing Japanese laws and government policies.

There were about twenty participants in the conference room, including employees from the Department of Civil-Economic Legislation of the Ministry of Justice, Vietnam, and other ministries and agencies, as well as those involved with the National Assembly. Morishima's role at the time was to provide the Vietnamese staff in charge of drafting legislation and developing a civil code for their country with basic knowledge on the civil code. This included giving the definition of a civil code and explaining the fundamental principles of a civil code through specific examples from the Civil Code of Japan. Morishima delivered his lecture in English, with simultaneous interpretation. He spoke in line with a prepared summary and the interpreter translated his words into Vietnamese.

A civil code is a systematic collection of laws designed to deal mainly with the property-related and family-related matters of social life. Of these, "property-related matters" include the buying and selling of goods, the borrowing and lending of money, and accident compensation, while "family-related matters" include spousal relationship issues like marriage and divorce, parent-child relationships, and inheritance between relatives.[3] The civil code of a country stipulates the most fundamental principles governing the social lives of its people, and as such it is closely related to the country's culture and customs. In this country which had little understanding of the concept of the market economy, how much of what Morishima said would they understand? Unable to obtain an answer, he saw that the lecture time given to him was running out, minute by minute. Beads of sweat trickled down his forehead—and it wasn't just due to the hot and humid weather of Vietnam. The thought crossed his mind that this was going to be a tough task.

3 Property- and family-related matters may be governed by a single civil code, or separate laws may be established in each field (e.g., family law).

The events leading up to this moment dated back to 1992, a year before the lecture, when Morishima was the dean of the School of Law of Nagoya University. He had been leading fund-raising efforts for the Foundation for Law and Policy Studies and Education in Asia-Pacific, which had been launched to mark the fortieth anniversary of the school. He was busy planning research projects through the foundation, even for the time after he would step down as dean. On a visit to Hanoi to research the legal and social systems and conditions of Vietnam in his role at the foundation, he met the man who would lead him to deliver the seminar on Japan's Civil Code.

That was Nguyen Dinh Loc,[4] Vietnam's Minister of Justice. He was still waiting for a response to the request he made a few years ago to Japan's Minister of Justice asking for support in developing a civil code.

Vietnam at the time was beginning its transition to a market economy under the Doi Moi policy, which was adopted in 1986. This resulted in difficulties over handling the ever-growing number of economic deals under the existing legal and judicial systems. For this reason, calls were mounting for the establishment of new substantive[5] and procedural[6] laws. Several international organizations, including the United Nations Development Programme (UNDP),[7] the World Bank,[8] and the Asian Development Bank (ADB),[9] as well as the development assistance agencies of various countries, had already offered to support the legislation improvement efforts of Vietnam, but Minister Loc hoped to also receive the support of Japan, a nation in Asia with a civil law system, much like Vietnam's.[10]

Here is Morishima's first impression of Minister Loc, according to Morishima himself:

"He came across to me as a great man with a serious attitude. Loc-san discussed how much Vietnam needed a civil code to implement its Doi Moi policy successfully, and he pleaded with me that Japan support Vietnam in establishing a civil code."

Morishima was proactively involved in research and education about the laws and politics of Asian countries. He was all too aware at that time that the legal systems of developing countries in the Asian region, like Vietnam and Cambodia, were

4 Loc was minister of justice from 1992 to 2002, having previously served as head of the legal affairs department of the National Assembly secretariat. He was also a deputy in the 7th, 9th, 10th, and 11th National Assemblies.

5 Substantive laws govern the substance of legal relationships (rights and responsibilities, legal cause and effect etc.); examples include the Civil Code and the Commercial Code.

6 Procedural laws govern procedures for realizing legal relationships; examples include the Civil Procedure Code and the Administrative Litigation Law.

7 A United Nations agency established in 1966. Headquartered in New York, it supports development in some 170 countries and regions.

8 An international banking organization that provides financing to member states. Headquartered in Washington, DC, it comprises five institutions including the International Bank for Reconstruction and Development (IBRD) (est. 1945).

9 An international banking organization that provides financing to member states in the Asia-Pacific region. Founded in 1966, it is headquartered in Manila.

10 The system of law predominant in continental Europe (France, Germany etc.), in which the courts follow statutory law enacted by the legislature, as opposed to common law, in which the courts follow judicial precedent.

Seminar on drafting a civil code

underdeveloped, despite the fact that laws should be the foundation of each country, and that a lack of these laws constituted a major obstacle hindering their modernization. Furthermore, he had long been questioning the appropriateness of how international organizations and governments of Western nations assisted these countries: he felt that there were many cases in which donors implemented aid projects in order to establish "legal systems that would benefit the donor," rather than "for the good of the recipients."

Morishima communicated Minister Loc's request to the Minister's Secretariat of the Ministry of Justice of Japan immediately after his return home. The Ministry of Justice, however, transferred the matter to the Ministry of Foreign Affairs, saying, "This matter concerns international affairs and is not under the jurisdiction of the Ministry of Justice." The Ministry of Foreign Affairs, in turn, passed it back to the Ministry of Justice, saying, "This is an issue regarding civil code, which relates to internal affairs, not international treaties. As such, it is not under the jurisdiction of the Ministry of Foreign Affairs."

After complicated negotiations, things eventually settled down. The Ministry of Foreign Affairs agreed to budget the necessary amount for the project through the Japan Foundation. It also agreed to host a seminar in Vietnam to introduce Japan's

Civil Code to local participants as "cultural exchange" between the two countries. Morishima was appointed to go to Vietnam as the lecturer. At last he had the opportunity to fulfill Minister Loc's expectations.

02 The Barrier of "State Secrets"

Morishima carefully developed a summary of the seminar in English in preparation for the event, and was fired up about the trip to Hanoi. Once the seminar began, however, he was faced with endless surprise and confusion. He explains,

> Being a socialist nation, Vietnam regarded the laws and legal systems forming the core of state authority as state secrets, which were to be kept secret from foreigners. As such, I was not provided with an overview of the draft of Vietnam's Civil Code. Nevertheless, seminar participants bombarded me with questions between lecture sessions on topics like "households" and "collective ownership by the entire people." If I had understood that "households" were a subject of rights, and "collective ownership"[11] was a concept concerning ownership in Vietnam's Civil Code, I could have answered them properly. In reality, I was just at a loss, since I hadn't seen the Vietnamese draft Civil Code that formed the background to all that. There were often times when I had to try to answer their questions while unsure about what they actually wanted to ask, or what they were getting at.[12]

Morishima did his utmost to share with the participants of this seminar the experiences of Japan, which had been struggling for more than 120 years since the Meiji Revolution to introduce laws from countries with different historical, cultural, and social backgrounds and adapt them to suit the local realities of Japanese society.

11 The concept that assets are owned by the entire people and managed on their behalf by the state.

12 Source: Akio Morishima, "Wagakuni ni yoru kaihatsu tojokoku no hoseibi shien" (Japanese cooperation for rule of law promotion in developing countries), *Gakushikai kaiho* 892, no. 1 (January 2012): 30–36.

03 History of Difficulties behind Japan's Civil Code

The treaties which the Tokugawa Shogunate government had concluded with powerful Western countries toward the end of the Edo period in the mid-nineteenth century were unequal (the so-called Unequal Treaties). They were prejudicial to the sovereignty of Japan in the sense that they denied the country tariff autonomy, while at the same time granting certain foreign powers extra-territorial rights. The Meiji government from 1868 endeavored to make Japan a modern state and an independent member of the international community, so it was its ardent wish to rectify these unequal treaties and establish equal relationships with foreign powers.

Nevertheless, these nations found it problematic that Japan as a country did not have an appropriate, modern legal system, including a civil code stipulating the basic rights and duties of citizens. Under such circumstances, it was urgent for Japan to compile a comprehensive set of civil laws in order to demand abolition of the unequal treaties.

For this reason, the Meiji government decided to translate the French Civil Code into Japanese and adopt it as Japan's civil code. However, the concept of "rights" did not even exist in Japan at that time, and the translation work faced serious challenges. The Meiji government gave up on independently creating a civil code for the time being and opted to compile one with help from France. To achieve this, the government appointed a French jurist, Gustave Boissonade,[13] as a "foreign government advisor."

Gustave-Émil Boissonade (courtesy of the Hosei University History Committee)

Boissonade was invited by the Japanese government to arrive in Japan in 1873; he began to draft a civil code for Japan in 1879 and completed the work over the following decade. The civil code drafted by Boissonade (known as the Old Civil Code) was

13 Boissonade was a French legal scholar who contributed greatly to the development of the modern Japanese legal system, including the drafting of the Old Civil Code.

From left: Masaaki Tomii, Kenjiro Ume, Nobushige Hozumi (courtesy of the Hosei University History Committee)

approved by the Imperial Diet and promulgated in 1890, to be enforced in 1893. However, this civil code was criticized by conservative Japanese people, who specially valued their feudalistic family system, as being "too progressive and individualistic," and its enactment was postponed.

Later, in order to create a civil code drafted by Japanese citizens rather than foreigners, Nobushige Hozumi, Masaaki Tomii and Kenjiro Ume[14] were selected as members of the committee for drafting the new civil code. Their draft was based on Boissonade's Old Civil Code, but they also consulted the civil codes of other countries, including drafts of the German Civil Code. The new civil code drafted by these three individuals was established in 1896 and enforced in 1898. The extra-territorial rights of foreign nationals, one of the main issues in question, were abolished in 1899, and the unequal treaties were completely revised in 1911, including full tariff autonomy.

14 Hozumi, Tomii, and Ume were the three Japanese legal scholars appointed to draft a new civil code in the 1890s.

The Japanese Civil Code under the Meiji Constitution was not significantly revised until 1947, when the New Constitution of Japan was established. The articles of the old Civil Code had ensured the continuation of the feudalistic family system, but this came into conflict with the fundamental principles of the New Constitution, leading to a full-fledged revision of the sections regarding the family and inheritance systems. In 2017, another major amendment was made to the Japanese Civil Code to adapt the articles concerning contracts, etc., to meet changing social and economic situations.[15]

15 The section of the Japanese Civil Code governing obligations, including the validity of contracts, had never been significantly revised until a set of amendments was passed in May 2017 (Act no. 44 of 2017, to take effect on April 1, 2020).

As seen above, Japan has been establishing its own legal system since the Meiji era. Morishima comments:

> The national laws of Japan have stemmed from many different legal systems from various cultural backgrounds and thus

can be compared to a tree grafted onto traditional Japanese society. As such, it is not unusual for our national laws that originate from Western culture to fail to accommodate the social norms that underlie Japanese society. This is not limited to the Civil Code. In fact, the history of practical jurisprudence in Japan is a history of trial and error through which Japan has been exploring how legal concepts and rules developed in other cultures can be adapted to suit Japanese society with its distinctive social structure and social norms. In this regard, I thought, the experiences which Japan had obtained in the course of introducing Western laws would surely be of help to Vietnam.[16]

16 See page 49, note 12.

04 Vietnam Forced to Establish Its Civil Code

When Morishima first visited Vietnam, two different legal systems coexisted there—one that had originated in the French colonial era and the other that had been introduced by the former Soviet Union before the adoption of the Doi Moi policy—and both were outdated in modern Vietnamese society. In other words, Vietnam lagged behind in creating appropriate laws concerning the "rights and obligations of individuals" and "relationships between individuals." At that time, however, Vietnam was aiming to join the World Trade Organization (WTO)[17] in order to successfully transform itself into a market economy, and so it was an urgent task for the government to establish a modern legal system.

The 1980 Constitution[18] enforced after the unification of North and South Vietnam had a new provision that required Vietnam "to be a country ruled by law." In line with this provision, Vietnam set for itself a target of establishing as many as 43 laws in five years, one of which included the country's civil code.

Although a special committee of the Ministry of Justice was set up immediately after the revision of the constitution to draft a civil code, the work did not proceed smoothly. In fact, more than ten years passed without any real progress. This was because, as with Japan in the early Meiji era, the concept of a

17 An international body founded in 1995 to promote free trade. Headquartered in Geneva.

18 A socialist constitution influenced by the Soviet constitution of 1977. This defined the Socialist Republic of Vietnam as a "dictatorship of the proletariat" (Article 2).

"civil code" and an understanding of how civil society should be governed by rules did not exist in Vietnam at that time; the number of experts in this area was also very limited.

Furthermore, the country's "planned economy" system,[19] which Vietnam had been implementing until then, constituted the largest obstacle in the way of establishing a civil code. In Vietnam at the time, people's lives relied mainly on rationing, and government control permeated almost all aspects of life. The Vietnamese people had long been living in a planned economy, and it was a hugely challenging, and even bewildering, task for them to work out how to develop a civil code suitable for a market economy. This was how things were in 1992 in Vietnam, when Nguyen Dinh Loc took office as Minister of Justice and Akio Morishima visited Vietnam for the first time.

19 A system in which all forms of economic activity, including production of goods and distribution of resources, are conducted according to central government plans. The opposite is a market economy.

05 "This Man Will Be of Help."

Morishima's lecture style was unexpected for the Vietnamese participants. As they understood it, a lecture was an event where a stern-looking authority proudly read from a textbook behind a lectern while students silently listened. Moreover, the goal of law education in a socialist nation was to memorize laws clause by clause. By contrast, Morishima's style was like that used in US law schools: he involved the participants as peers, and called on them from time to time to express their views; for example, asking, "This was how Japan failed in the past. What do you think about it?" They had never experienced such a lecture before and were quite nonplussed. He asked questions like, "What specific functions are the concepts and systems of civil codes in market economies, including Japan, designed to perform?" and "What social conditions are required as preconditions for the successful functioning of each system?"

In his lectures, Morishima explained "civil code" from a functional point of view rather than a conceptual one. He was able to provide the Vietnamese with the information they needed, as Vietnam was exploring the extent to which market economy-oriented law could be incorporated while the country continued to stick with socialism as its political system. Participants gradually grew more interested in his lectures, as Morishima passionately spoke about how Japan had gone through hard times but did not give up, rather than about how excellent the laws of Japan were.

Morishima looks back on his experience at that time with a chuckle.

> The great majority of the Vietnamese legal experts involved in drafting the civil code had studied in the former Soviet Union or East Germany, and had virtually no understanding of concepts concerning civil law or a market economy. Given such conditions, I'm not sure how much they understood my lectures at that point in time. One sure thing was that they felt I was somewhat different from other legal consultants sent from non-Japanese aid organizations, as the other entities would propose that Vietnam create their legal system through direct translations of their own laws. Presumably, they thought, "He really cares about the situation in Vietnam. This man will be of help."

Morishima gave lectures from nine o'clock in the morning to five o'clock in the evening for five days, with a lunch break each day. He explained the functions of the civil code system effectively by paying careful attention to the needs of the Vietnamese. This approach won him the trust of Minister Loc, and Vietnam's Ministry of Justice extended him another invitation before his return to Japan, telling him they wanted him to come again soon. Morishima recalls, "Before I left for Japan, the Vietnamese requested that I find some way to extend my stay so I could give more lectures in Vietnam. I was also feeling that I had just begun to get the hang of things there after the five-day seminar."

Regardless of this, the Japanese side replied, "We have already met the request of the Vietnamese by sending over a lecturer," and the Japanese government decided not to organize another expert dispatch program. Morishima, however,

The Vietnamese Ministry of Justice

was eager to fulfill their request. He acquired a grant from the Foundation for Law and Policy Studies and Education in the Asia-Pacific, run by Nagoya University, to visit Hanoi again to give lectures on the Civil Code of Japan.

After giving about a week of lectures, Morishima was speaking to Minister Loc in the minister's office when Dinh Trung Tung,[20] section chief of the Department of Economic-Civil Legislation of the Ministry of Justice, rushed breathlessly into the room with a document in his hand. "I'm so glad I made it in time! This document summarizes our questions. Could you get back to us with your responses when you come to Hanoi next time?"

20 Tung has also served as head of the Ministry's Department of Economic-Civil Legislation and vice minister of justice. As of this writing, he is an advisor to the Ministry.

The sight still remains vivid in Morishima's memory. "Tung-san looked as if he were on the verge of tears, and handed me a document written in Vietnamese. They were giving me 'homework' to complete. By this point in time, I had also made up my mind to do whatever I could for them, as I saw how much they were actually counting on me."

Morishima flew to Vietnam at his own expense from his third visit onward. He asked an acquaintance who was a professor from a university of foreign studies to translate the list of questions in Vietnamese that Tung had handed him, and wrote to them with his answers. He also prepared teaching materials in

Vietnamese by translating his lectures into the language so as to assist understanding on the Vietnamese side. All of this was done out of his own pocket.

On his fourth visit to Hanoi, the Vietnamese had sent him in advance by international mail a draft Civil Code of Vietnam—it had previously been a "state secret"—along with a list of questions. While going over their draft civil code together, Minister Loc and Morishima reached the conclusion that, given the realities of Vietnamese society at that time, their top priority at this stage was to establish a civil code before anything else, no matter how many theoretical problems remained. The two began to confide in each other before they knew it.

In 1994, the drafting of the Vietnamese Civil Code was finally completed. Nearly three years had already passed since Minister Loc had first contacted Morishima for help.

06 | The Beginning of JICA's Cooperation for Legal and Judicial Development

The final (12th) draft of the Vietnamese Civil Code, which had been developed with advice from Morishima, was placed on the agenda for deliberation at the National Assembly of Vietnam, to be enforced in 1995.[21] Around the same time, the Japanese government sent an economic cooperation study team[22] to Vietnam. The Vietnamese government requested of the team that the Japanese government assist in the development of Vietnam's legislation through ODA programs. Japan's Ministry of Foreign Affairs immediately contacted Morishima and the Japan International Cooperation Agency (JICA) to start discussions over a technical cooperation project. Morishima recalls, "The Vietnamese government sent a message through the economic cooperation study team, saying, 'We have two cooperation projects that we would like Japan to provide us.'"

One of these was the Ishikawa Project,[23] which was being implemented under the leadership of Professor Shigeru Ishikawa of Hitotsubashi University. The project was highly evaluated by the Vietnamese for presenting a general direction and

21 In the end, the final draft was released in 1995, and various sectors of the public were invited to comment on it. It was passed by the National Assembly in October 1995 and took effect on July 1, 1996.

22 A survey team sent to identify priority areas of cooperation and set policy on ODA to Vietnam, which had resumed in 1992.

23 This was the informal name of a project implemented between 1995 and 2001, officially called the Economic Development Policy in the Transition toward a Market-Oriented Economy in the Socialist Republic of Vietnam. The results of that project were reflected in Vietnam's next five-year plan.

policy options for the country's economic development, so that it could make a successful transition to a market economy.

The other program was "support for the development of domestic laws" which Morishima had been carrying out since the summer of 1993 through his four visits to Vietnam.

> I was called to the Ministry of Foreign Affairs, where they asked me to give them details of what I had done in Vietnam so far. Personally, I had mixed feelings toward them, as they had turned down my first proposal rather bluntly, saying, "Anything concerning Vietnamese domestic affairs is not the jurisdiction of the Ministry of Foreign Affairs." Even so, it was still a welcome offer of help. I now had the sponsorship of the Ministry of Foreign Affairs to carry out the work which I had had no choice but to do at my own expense until then.

This coincided with the Japanese government's establishment of a new ODA policy to place greater importance on the "development of human resources and institutions" while at the same time continuing with its traditional large-scale infrastructure development activities. Japan resumed ODA to Vietnam in 1992 following the peace settlement in Cambodia,[24] and the new Official Development Assistance (ODA) Charter,[25] which was endorsed by the Cabinet in the same year, stipulated that one of the priorities should be to develop human resources with the aim of ensuring "good governance"[26] through improvement of the socioeconomic institutions of respective countries.

Things began to gain momentum for Morishima. One problem, however, was that no one except for Morishima was experienced in supporting the efforts of another country to improve its legal and judicial system. As the implementing agency, JICA decided to partner with Morishima and the Ministry of Justice of Japan to launch the project.

The Ministry of Justice had an internal organization called the "Research and Training Institute,"[27] which was engaged in providing various kinds of training to related government staff members, in addition to research and studies concerning legal administration, but this body had no experience in proactively

24 Vietnamese forces invaded Cambodia in January 1979, overthrew the Pol Pot regime and installed a new government under Heng Samrin. That led the Japanese government to suspend economic aid to Vietnam from FY 1979, with a few minor exceptions.

25 This policy document setting the basic directions of Japanese foreign aid was endorsed by the Cabinet in 1992 and revised in 2003. A new policy, the Development Cooperation Charter, was adopted in 2015.

26 Governance refers to the mechanisms underpinning the everyday functioning of a country's society (governmental bodies, the legal system, administrative capacity, political participation by the public, and so forth). Good governance means that those mechanisms are maintained in a fashion conducive to the country's stability and growth. Good governance is a prerequisite for sustained growth in developing countries; it is also one of the goals of development assistance.

27 The Research and Training Institute was established in 1959. In 2001, a division dedicated to cooperation for legal and judicial development, the International Cooperation Department (ICD), was established within it. See inset, page 79.

involving itself in the legal and judicial system development activities of other countries.

Morishima sought out researchers who could cooperate on the project. There was a widespread sentiment in the mainstream academic community at the time, however, that developing the legal and judicial systems of other Asian countries was "nerdy." Under such circumstances, Morishima had no alternative but to speak to researchers he knew personally, one by one, to persuade them and increase the number of supporters he had.

In this way, JICA's activities for legal and judicial development were initiated in 1994, and the first two years were allocated to preparations for the full-fledged launch of the project. In 1994, the Ministry of Justice of Japan invited senior officials of the Ministry of Justice of Vietnam and the Vietnam Supreme People's Court to the Research and Training Institute to provide them with training in Japan.[28] In addition, the ministry also sent experts from Japan to Vietnam to host Vietnamese civil code workshops there. Morishima flew to Hanoi and conducted several negotiations with the Vietnamese to design project activities.

> In the course of the negotiations, I visited not only the Ministry of Justice of Vietnam, which was our counterpart,[29] but also all related bodies, including the Supreme People's Procuracy[30] and Supreme People's Court,[31] as well as the Office of Government and the National Assembly, to have them understand that the purpose of Japan's cooperation for legal and judicial development in Vietnam was to help Vietnamese society transition to a market economy. At the same time, we held in-depth interviews with each of these bodies to find out what kind of cooperation was genuinely needed by the Vietnamese.

As a result, it gradually became apparent that the two areas of utmost priority for Vietnam, which was proactively implementing its Doi Moi policy at that time, were the development of market economy-related laws, including a civil code, and the development of human resources in the legal and judicial sectors.

28 Government officials and experts are brought to Japan from the partner country for a set period of time to hold intensive discussions with Japanese academics and experts and visit facilities of interest. In the process, they acquire the knowledge and expertise they need in their own country. See the Quick Guide to Japan's Cooperation for Legal and Judicial Development on page 12.

29 Generally, one of a pair, one's opposite number. In international cooperation, often used specifically of the partner organization in the recipient country (and of its staff); there needs to be an organization overseeing the project in both the donor and the recipient countries. See the Quick Guide to Japan's Cooperation for Legal and Judicial Development on page 12.

30 People's procuracies prosecute criminal cases and oversee the activities of judicial institutions. The Supreme People's Procuracy is the highest procuracy in the country. It is overseen by the National Assembly.

31 The Supreme People's Court is the highest of the people's courts. It is overseen by the National Assembly.

While the 1992 Constitution[32] guaranteed Vietnamese people property rights and freedom of economic activity, and many laws were enforced in the 1990s to cope with the country's transition to a market economy, their basic legal theories and lawmaking techniques remained underdeveloped, and the country was still halfway through its shift from a way of thinking based on a planned economy.

The same problem was also associated with the Civil Code of Vietnam, which had been drafted with support from Morishima. The Civil Code itself had already been promulgated in 1996, but enforcing it was regarded as "easier said than done" at that time, since relevant procedures and systems required to support a market economy were not yet adequately developed. Morishima cooperated with the Ministry of Justice of Japan and JICA to conduct detailed research on what legal and judicial system development work was really needed by Vietnamese society and how Japan's cooperation would be better accepted by them, rather than being imposed on them, and would actually assist the society's transition to a market economy.

The result was the design of Japan's first project for legal and judicial development, in which JICA acted as the implementing agency. JICA, legal scholars, the Research and Training Institute of the Ministry of Justice of Japan, and lawyers worked in cooperation to conduct the necessary research for the implementation of the project, execution of project activities, evaluation of results, and so on. On October 28, 1996, the Record of Discussions (R/D)[33] was signed between JICA and the Ministry of Justice of Vietnam to draw up basic stipulations for the project, Japanese Technical Cooperation in the Legal and Judicial Field.

Nguyen Dinh Loc continued to take position of a member of the National Assembly after reaching the mandatory retirement age in the Ministry of Justice. At the time of writing, in 2017, he was 82 years old. He described, in retrospect, his encounter with Morishima in a lecture at the Nagoya University Tokyo Forum, held in October 2007:[34]

> When I had the opportunity to learn [from a Japanese legal expert] about Japan's experience of establishing its first

32 The new constitution, which was predicated on the opening up of the economy under the 1986 Doi Moi (renewal) policy, enshrined the concept of human rights for the first time.

33 A Record of Discussions (R/D) is an international agreement signed by JICA and the counterpart before the commencement of an international cooperation project. It sets out the details agreed to by the two sides: the project's goals, the nature of the assistance to be provided, the obligations of both countries and so forth. See the Quick Guide to Japan's Cooperation for Legal and Judicial Development at the front of the book, page 12.

34 See Nguyen Dinh Loc, "Betonamu ni taisuru Nihon no hoseibi shien" [Japanese cooperation for legal and judicial development in Vietnam], *CALE Booklet No.2: Daigokai Nagoya Daigaku Tokyo foramu koenshu* (May 2008), 24–41.

> civil code, the Ministry of Justice of Vietnam had just been entrusted by the Vietnamese government to develop a civil code to submit to the National Assembly. This also coincided with when I had just been transferred to the Ministry of Justice after working for over ten years at the Secretariat of the National Assembly. I think it was an amazing twist of fate that I was able to attend Professor Morishima's lectures, which were coincidentally held at that time.

It was this encounter between Akio Morishima and Nguyen Dinh Loc, which cannot be described as anything but serendipitous, that opened the door to Japan's support for the development of Vietnam's legal and judicial system.

Akio Morishima (left) and Nguyen Dinh Loc

07 Shiro Muto, the Lawyer Who Became the First "Long-Term Expert"[35]

At midnight on a day in February 1996, the telephone rang in the Nagoya home of attorney Shiro Muto.[36] The caller was Masanori Aikyo,[37] a professor at Nagoya University. Muto had seen him several times before in meetings concerning Vietnamese laws. Aikyo said, "Given the short notice of this request, feel free to refuse if you're not willing to accept..."

The purpose of the call was unexpected: the Japanese government had decided to use its ODA budget to support the legal

35 This section is based on Shiro Muto, *Betonamu shihosho chuzai taikenki* [A record of my experiences at the Vietnamese Ministry of Justice] (Shinzansha, 2002) and an interview he gave for this book. The material is used with his permission.

36 Muto, a lawyer currently registered with the Tokyo Bar Association and the first long-term expert sent abroad under JICA's legal and judicial development program, was stationed in Hanoi. He practiced law in Japan upon his return from Vietnam, and now works for the Hanoi office of a Japanese law firm.

37 Aikyo, a jurist in Vietnamese constitutional history and Asian law, was chairman of the board of trustees of Aichi Public University Corporation (Aichi Prefectural University and Aichi University of the Arts), professor emeritus at Nagoya University, and former director of CALE (see inset, page 218). He has advanced the study of Asian law and mentored many young scholars.

system development efforts of the Vietnamese government, and was looking for legal specialists willing to be stationed at the Vietnamese Ministry of Justice. Aikyo was offering Muto the job of resident lawyer in Vietnam.

Shiro Muto

The aim of JICA's legal and judicial development project in Vietnam was to work in partnership with the Vietnamese from a medium- to long-term point of view, in order to establish laws and legal systems that would best suit Vietnamese society. Needless to say, it was essential for JICA to receive information from the Vietnamese and evaluate the local situation, rather than just providing information from Japan. This was why JICA was seeking an expert who would stay in Vietnam on a long-term basis and act as a go-between for information exchange and on-site research activities. The problem was, who would be willing to break away from their work in Japan and stay in Vietnam for several years as a resident legal expert? Morishima and Aikyo searched around for the right person, and Muto emerged as a likely candidate. At that time, Muto, who had been registered as a lawyer in Nagoya, was 32 years old and only in his third year as a lawyer. But the recruiters thought that he seemed like a young man of action who might accept this offer, which came out of the blue.

Bewildered, Muto answered Aikyo, "Let me sleep on it," and hung up. But he couldn't help but feel there was something fateful about the call. He had traveled as a backpacker in the monsoon countries of Asia, such as Thailand and Nepal, as a university student. Furthermore, he had joined the Japan-Vietnam Friendship Bar Association immediately after his registration as a lawyer. This association, an organization formed mainly by lawyers based in Osaka and Kyoto, provides civil and commercial law-related lectures and other programs to legal specialists in Vietnam. In 1994, it hosted the Vietnamese Investment Law Seminar in Hanoi, in which Muto had participated as lecturer.

It was shortly before the Asian Financial Crisis of 1997–1999,[38] and the economic growth of Asia was attracting lots of worldwide attention. Japan was also in the midst of the "Vietnam Boom" at the time. On his vacations, Muto visited Vietnamese law specialists he had become acquainted with through the Japan-Vietnam Friendship Bar Association, as well as Japanese companies investing in Vietnam, to study and collect information on Vietnamese laws and ask about how they were actually used.

38 The 1997 economic crisis was triggered by a sudden drop in the Thai baht, which sent currencies and stocks into a nosedive across Asia, including the Philippines, Malaysia, Indonesia, and South Korea. It left Asia's previously booming economies on the verge of collapse.

He visited Vietnam frequently, making friends and becoming acquainted with an increasing number of law specialists there. Wanting to communicate with them in their own language, Muto took time out of his busy schedule as a lawyer to take private Vietnamese-language lessons with a woman who had come to Japan from the former South Vietnam to study, and who later became a naturalized citizen of Japan. In fact, Muto had already begun to learn to read the Vietnamese Civil Code in the original Vietnamese.

Looking back on those days, Muto, who is currently stationed in the Hanoi office of a major Japanese law firm, recalls, "At the time, I was just going where my curiosity took me. In retrospect, however, I suppose I was preparing myself to work in Vietnam, guided by the 'invisible hand of God.' I thought, 'If I turn this down, I'll regret it for the rest of my life.'" He had already made up his mind. On December 24, 1996, Muto took up his post in Hanoi as a long-term expert for the Japanese Technical Cooperation in the Legal and Judicial Field. This was the birth of the first "long-term expert"[39] in JICA's cooperation for legal and judicial development.

39 When JICA implements an international cooperation program in a particular field, it sends experts with knowledge and expertise in that field to the partner country. These experts play the central role in providing support on the ground. Experts stationed in the partner country for more than a year are termed "long-term experts." See the Quick Guide to Japan's Cooperation for Legal and Judicial Development on page 12.

Soon after arriving at his new post, Muto was called by the department head in charge of his project at the Ministry of Justice of Vietnam. When he visited the office, the department head told him, pityingly, "The Ministry of Justice of Vietnam doesn't require an expert stationed in the ministry on a long-term basis. It would be better if you didn't come to the ministry every day. If you work five days a week in Japan, you can work half of that at the Ministry of Justice, two or three days per week. On the remaining days, you can work at the JICA office." Muto's spirits sank, as he thought to himself, "Not again..."

At the same time, this reaction by the Ministry of Justice was not a total surprise to Muto, who had been witnessing the history of negotiations between the two countries before arriving at his new post. It could even be considered inevitable for the Vietnamese to react like that when looking objectively at the nature of legal and judicial development work. Muto explains,

> This is because when a country develops laws and a legal system for itself, what it does is nothing other than the "exercise of state sovereignty." When an outside country supports those legislation development efforts, it means that the "haves" from overseas—the country providing assistance—intervene in the exercise of state sovereignty by the "have-nots"—the country receiving the assistance. Especially given that Vietnam has a history of repeated invasions by foreign powers, it was all too natural that they should be wary and suspicious of foreign experts stationed in their Ministry of Justice, which is essentially the core of state sovereignty.

Although things like this made it far from easy, Muto's work as a long-term expert finally started in earnest. His main duty was to do his best to provide the Vietnamese with the information required to draft auxiliary laws necessary for enforcement of the Civil Code. For example, when drafting government ordinances such as those concerning "deposit in lieu of performance" (*bensai kyotaku*)[40] and "property registration,"[41] he first collected relevant information from Japan and then translated that into Vietnamese. He then submitted the information to the Vietnamese, who would use it create drafts of ordinances. Then he sent the completed drafts to the Ministry of Justice of Japan and Japanese legal scholars to seek advice from them, added his own comments while taking their advice into consideration, and submitted them to the Department of Economic-Civil Legislation of the Ministry of Justice of Vietnam.

Another important job for him was providing seminars on law to the staff of the Ministry of Justice of Vietnam in charge of the drafting of laws attached to the Civil Code. Each seminar theme was selected in the following way. First, Muto examined

40 This is when a creditor does not or cannot accept repayment, and the borrower repays the debt at a depository instead. This has the same effect as discharging the debt to the creditor: it releases the borrower from his or her obligation.

41 Such a registration is a record of real property and valuable items of personal property in the form of a register, either on paper or in electronic format, showing the details of the rights pertaining to each asset, including who owns it. Anyone may inspect this record to determine the rights pertaining to any asset.

A seminar in Hanoi, 1997

the lawmaking schedule of the National Assembly of Vietnam and picked out an area that needed Japan's cooperation. Then he had a talk with the head of the Department of Economic-Civil Legislation to decide on potential themes. The themes were presented in consultation between Japanese stakeholders and the Ministry of Justice of Vietnam to make the final decision. When the need arose, and depending on the theme, short-term experts[42] were invited from Japan to provide a four- to five-day seminar. Such seminars were held about six or seven times each year.

42 Experts stationed in the partner country for less than one year are called "short-term experts." In the field of legal and judicial development, short-term experts provide forms of support that go beyond what long-term experts can offer. For example, they conduct local seminars in highly specialized fields or on subjects requiring special expertise. See the Quick Guide to Japan's Cooperation for Legal and Judicial Development on page 12.

08 Encounters with "Another World in Another Dimension"

Ikufumi Niimi,[43] a professor at the School of Law of Meiji University, was involved in this aid project from the very beginning. He delivered a seminar on "registration systems" in Hanoi as a short-term expert, and described the exchanges of legal information between Vietnam and Japan in those days as "a series of encounters with another world in another dimension."

In particular, Niimi was perplexed by differences between the social systems of the two countries, and the way the meanings of words changed as a result of those differences. Vietnamese, like

43 Niimi is a jurist expert in civil law and professor at the School of Law of Meiji University. He has dedicated himself to promoting the rule of law since the program's first days two decades ago, working on projects in Vietnam, Cambodia, and elsewhere.

Japanese, belongs to the Chinese-character cultural sphere and is heavily influenced by Chinese characters, so it shares with Japanese many words in common with similar pronunciation.

> For example, the Japanese term *toki* refers to the act of recording in a register certain items concerning one's right to real estate or other things, to make this known to third parties. In a nutshell, it means "registration for claiming one's right" through making the right public. Vietnamese also has a word, *dang-ky*, that originates from the same pair of Chinese characters. In socialist Vietnam, however, there was no need to make public the ownership of individual rights, since the country's land was "in the ownership of the entire people" and the state managed all land and acted as the representative of the owners. In other words, when Vietnamese people say *dang-ky*, they mean "registration for the state's management." From our viewpoint, this is closer to the idea of, say, registering one's gun with the state for legitimate possession. In this way, the same words can mean different things to people in different countries when the economic structures behind them are different. So we can't really discuss even a single article of law unless we carefully examine the different conditions of the partner country beforehand. This was the most startling revelation to me.

Niimi was surprised to see the huge differences between Japanese and Vietnamese societies. He also became anxious about the future of the cooperation for legal and judicial development, which had just begun and would soon go into full-fledged operation.

Besides this, one thing that further exercised Japanese members was bureaucracy. The aim of the JICA project was to support the development of laws and systems required for the Civil Code, the basic source of law for promoting Vietnam's transition to a market economy. To accomplish this objective, close coordination was essential not only with the direct counterpart Ministry of Justice but also with the Ministry of Commerce, government agencies that had jurisdiction over registration, court and prosecution authorities, and other involved parties. In Vietnam, however, there was so much territoriality between different administrative authorities that it was extremely difficult to establish good cooperative relationships with other government agencies.[44]

44 Source: Ikufumi Niimi, "ODA=Hoseibi shien no ippan (2): Betonamu to Kanbojia de no keiken (2)" [Aspects of ODA = cooperation for legal and judicial development (2): Experiences in Vietnam and Cambodia (2)], *Toki no horei* 1731 (February 2005), 45–48.

On the other side of the coin, however, it was not only the Japanese but also the Vietnamese that were perplexed by these "encounters with another world in another dimension." Amid the anxiety and bewilderment between both parties, however, lines had been cast off and the ship destined for better legal and judicial systems in Vietnam was slowly setting sail.

09 Revision of the Vietnamese Civil Code

With respect to JICA's cooperation for legal and judicial development in Vietnam, the Civil Code, where it all started, can be said to be its symbol. Since the launch of the first project in 1996, JICA has been providing constant assistance to the revision of the Vietnamese Civil Code, including support for the revisions in 2005 and 2015, although the scale has varied considerably depending on the conditions of the Vietnamese.

Ikufumi Niimi lecturing on the civil code

The first Civil Code of Vietnam, which had been drafted with advice from Morishima, was established in October 1995 and put into effect in July 1996. However, this Civil Code was modeled after the Civil Code of Russia, which contained heavy undertones of the socialist planned economy, so people began to point out the necessity for its revision immediately after it began being enforced.

At the same time, the Vietnamese government was aiming to

become a member of the World Trade Organization (WTO) as soon as possible, as well as to sign a trade treaty with the United States. For this reason, by the end of the 1990s Vietnam had requested JICA's advice on a revision of the Civil Code, which the government was planning to make in order to further promote the country's transition into a market economy.

This was also when JICA's first legal and judicial development project was entering its final stage. Before revising the Civil Code of 1995, the drafting team from the Ministry of Justice of Vietnam had reached the conclusion that they would independently draft a revision to the Civil Code based on their own judgment, while taking into account their knowledge of civil codes and civil law studies of Japan and other countries which they had obtained through JICA's cooperation. As such, the Vietnamese requested that the Japanese "add their comments after the Vietnamese had finished the draft revision."

Niimi's view of this policy is as follows:

> Vietnamese people had already created their own draft civil codes for the 1995 Civil Code, albeit with advice from another country. They were also highly vigilant against foreign countries invading their realm of sovereignty, especially to conduct "legal system development." This is why it never occurred to them that they could ask Japan to create a draft for them. The problem, however, was whether they really had the ability at that point in time to independently create a draft revision that could enable the Civil Code to effectively back up a market economy.[45]

45 Source: Ikufumi Niimi, "ODA = Hoseibi shien no ippan (11): Betonamu to Kanbojia de no keiken (11)" [Aspects of ODA = cooperation for legal and judicial development (11): Experiences in Vietnam and Cambodia (11)], *Toki no horei* 1766 (July 2006), 68–72.

When Japanese members talked to bureaucrats in the Ministry of Justice of Vietnam, they were astonished at the differences in how they viewed the law. In a market economy, laws such as regulations concerning contracts lay down ground rules governing the effectiveness of the actions of a party, but they also require the judgment necessary to make exceptions to those ground rules for irregular situations by taking into account different interests that need to be respected in that market economy.

Vietnam, on the other hand, had yet to fully break out of its planned economy; laws were regarded as rules showing "how things should be" that all members of society always had to observe without exception. Because laws were developed under this presumption, no anomalous situations were assumed in the first place, and people did not even imagine that they should examine different interests through comparison of such situations or deal with exceptions when necessary.

One typical example of this way of thinking is the way Vietnamese people viewed protection of third parties without knowledge. Shiro Muto, the lawyer, states:

> For example, imagine that someone had been caught in a scam and sold a product unwittingly, and another person had purchased this product. In Japan, where importance is placed upon security of transaction, the commonly held view is that the right of a third party without knowledge, who has purchased the product without knowing that the seller had been caught in a scam, should be protected [i.e., the person should be able to obtain the product].
>
> In Vietnam, by contrast, people believed that once a deal was invalidated as being fraudulent, it would be absolutely invalid, and anything invalid could not be regarded as valid, even in relationship to a third party without knowledge. The commonly held view there was that granting the third party the right to demand compensation from the fraudster would be enough to protect the individual.
>
> When the product is transferred from one person to another, we should protect the third party unwittingly caught in the scam by regarding the action that would normally be judged to be invalid as valid as far as the third party is concerned. The aim is to protect the third party, who has unknowingly received the product as the result of the scam and thus can be seen as not having made any mistake himself or herself, above the original owner who is at least responsible for falling victim to the scam. This is because the former can be considered to be more innocent than the latter when balancing the interests of the two. Nevertheless, the Vietnamese people did not see things that way.

As part of an effort to bring about changes in the legal consciousness of Vietnamese people to be more compatible with a market economy, the Joint Research Team for Revision of the Vietnamese Civil Code[46] was formed by members from both countries to carry out joint research for successor projects.

46 The Joint Research Team was made up of Vietnamese and Japanese members, including personnel from the Vietnamese Ministry of Justice, tasked with drafting revisions to the Civil Code. It was set up as a forum where the two sides could work together on completing the draft bill while comparing notes.

10 | Formation of a "Team of Civil Code Professionals"

The Record of Discussions (R/D) for the Japanese Technical Cooperation in the Legal and Judicial Field (Phase II) was signed between Morishima, who acted as the leader of the ex-ante evaluation mission of JICA,[47] and Minister Loc in November 1999, and the three-year project began in December. The three pillars of this support project were: (1) provision of advice on the drafting of civil and commercial laws and related regulations, (2) provision of advice on legal system development (creation of a big picture of ongoing laws in Vietnam and implementation of joint research for revision of the Civil Code) and (3) development of legal professionals (judicial officials, judges and prosecutors).

Local seminar on the civil code

The first thing to do was to establish a system to offer opinions on draft revisions to the Civil Code prepared by the Vietnamese. Morishima and Niimi immediately sought participation from Japanese civil law scholars. Appropriate people were recruited by taking into account the balance of areas of specialty, and a task force[48] was formed. Morishima recalls,

> As even the term "cooperation for legal and judicial development" was not in common use at that time, we had no alternative but to ask scholars whom we knew personally, one by one. Fortunately, most of them were unusually curious

47 An ex-ante evaluation mission is a team sent to the partner country prior to project implementation to assess conditions and needs on the ground, consult with the counterpart and other relevant agencies, and verify the details and benefits of the project. A Record of Discussions (R/D) is drawn up with the counterpart based on the mission's findings. See the Quick Guide to Japan's Cooperation for Legal and Judicial Development on page 12.

48 (1) The Japanese contingent of the Joint Research Team for Revision of the Vietnamese Civil Code was referred to as a "task force," a term also used during drafting of the Cambodian Civil Code and Civil Procedure Code. In subsequent legal and judicial development projects, the term "advisory group" was used instead, because Japanese support primarily took the form of advice to the counterpart. See the Quick Guide to Japan's Cooperation for Legal and Judicial Development on page 12.

(2) Original members of the Vietnam Task Force included Akio Morishima, professor, Sophia University; Ikufumi Niimi, professor, Meiji University; Toyohiro Nomura, professor, Gakushuin University; Katsuichi Uchida, professor, Waseda University; Tsuneo Matsumoto, professor, Hitotsubashi University; Kiyoe Kado, professor, Rikkyo University; Keita Sato, professor, Chuo University; Yasuhiro Akiyama, assistant professor, Waseda University; Japanese Ministry of Justice personnel (titles current at time of writing).

> people; they were willing to join us when we asked them and actually worked with lots of enthusiasm at their own expense. When I approached Professor Matsumoto of Hitotsubashi University, I said, "Vietnam has an udon-like noodle soup called *pho*, which is extremely delicious. If you accept my offer, I'll treat you to it." Professor Matsumoto agreed readily, saying, "That sounds fun. I'll join you."

When Morishima, who acted as the leader of the task force, looks back on those days, his face takes on a mischievous expression, like that of a little boy who has just pulled off some trick. According to Niimi, who helped in this one-on-one recruiting, people were attracted to Morishima's special passion.

Around the same time, the current Japanese Civil Code, which had been enforced in 1898, marked its 100th anniversary. Under such circumstances, there were heated debates in Japan as to the processes through which Japan had learned from foreign countries and established its own civil code during the Meiji era. Niimi, who scrambled to find members for the centenary's task force, said,

> The dominant atmosphere within the academic circle of civil-law scholars in Japan at that time was their readiness to celebrate the centenary of the Japanese Civil Code by emphasizing the influence of French law, saying "French law is the mother of the Japanese Civil Code." At the same time, there were many Japanese scholars who thought the Japanese Civil Code should be seen from other perspectives, giving proper credit to German and Anglo-American law as well. Professor Morishima and I were among them.

Many of the members of the task force had been born in the 1940s. They had experienced the era of Japan's dramatic economic growth as students and were the first generation able to read overseas legal documents freely. In fact, the task force was a well-balanced group of researchers specializing in French, German and Anglo-American laws. Niimi continues,

This, too, was because Professor Morishima organized it that way. The Civil Code of Japan was based on the legal systems of Western countries. What social needs had given birth to each of these Western law systems? Were there the same social needs also in Vietnam now, or would Vietnamese society have them in future? Professor Morishima wished to discuss such questions with legal professionals in Vietnam, so the composition of the group reflected his concern to have such matters considered.

Since the Meiji era, Japan had introduced legal systems from Western countries with different historical, cultural and social backgrounds and established its own "hybrid" legal system. This could not be found anywhere else, as it had adapted these foreign systems to suit the actual needs of the country. Morishima wanted to put Japan's precious experience to use, this time in the nation-building processes of Southeast Asian countries. His passion was so great that it gradually rubbed off on those around him.

11 Workshops

In Phase II, lawyers replacing Muto, and public prosecutors from the Research and Training Institute of the Ministry of Justice, (in which the International Cooperation Department[49] was founded in 2001 in order to be engaged in the rule of law cooperation) were posted to Vietnam, so that there were now several long-term experts stationed in Hanoi. Discussions revolved around fundamental questions such as what problems the ongoing Civil Code had, what the basic philosophy behind it was in the first place, and if a revision were made, what its purpose should be.

In particular, discussions about core concepts started in March 2001, in which the Vietnamese side presented a report titled "Concerning the Implementation of the Present Civil Code in the Past Four Years" at a workshop[50] held in Hanoi. After this, one workshop after another took place: "General

49 See inset, page 79.

50 A small meeting for exchanging views is called a "workshop." Workshops typically involve more in-depth discussion on a specific issue than do local seminars, which are primarily intended to share information with a larger audience.

Provisions of the Civil Code, Ownership and Security Systems" in the same month, "Position of the Civil Code, Protection of Third Parties without Knowledge and Agency" in May, and "Ownership Rights" in June.

Another goal in creating the joint research team was to provide Vietnamese members with the opportunity to develop the knowledge and skills required to conduct coherent drafting work as they carried out their joint research with Japanese members, while at the same time allowing the Japanese to gradually build up their implementation system through continued discussions with the Vietnamese. Consequently, their support style was established as a package of local seminars provided by short-term experts, workshops, training programs in Japan, legal advice offered by long-term experts, and other services used in combination.

At the same time, JICA's attitude as a donor agency, which paid great respect to Vietnam's ownership,[51] affected the attitude of the Vietnamese, who had been extremely wary of intervention by other countries, and little by little won them over. The former Minister of Justice Ha Hung Cuong,[52] who served as the head of the ministry from 2007 to 2016, looks back:

Ha Hung Cuong

> The Vietnamese are a very proud people. We have fought to protect our independence and autonomy at the risk of our own lives through fierce combat. This history is what has made the Vietnamese such a valiant people. Professor Morishima and other Japanese people understood this very well, paid utmost respect to us and provided us with ongoing support. It was around this time that our relationship of mutual trust rapidly deepened.

In November 2001, the first draft revision to the Civil Code was created. At the beginning of the workshop held to review this draft, Japanese task force members pointed out problems

51 "Ownership" refers to the idea that the recipient country is in charge of its own development.

52 Cuong was minister of justice from 2007 to 2016, having previously served as director-general of the International Cooperation Department of the Ministry of Justice and Vice-Minister of Justice. He was also a deputy in the 12th and 13th National Assemblies.

found in individual articles. Consequently, Vietnamese draft committee members and Japanese members had discussions based on these points. A particular issue would be discussed through the following sort of procedure.[53] First, Vietnamese members asked questions regarding one of the problems, like "What does Japanese law say about this?" and "What is the rationale behind that?" Japanese task force members would answer these questions. Then Vietnamese members asked questions such as, "How is this point treated in civil law and common law?" and "What about German and French laws?" Japanese task force members would answer these questions, too. Vietnamese members also asked questions such as, "What effect will this regulation have on the market economy?" and "Will this regulation stimulate economic activity?"

The goal of the Vietnamese was to collect information from as many countries as possible and accordingly select what would be best for Vietnam. This was consistent from the beginning to the end of the process.

The message the Japanese wished to communicate through the training programs in Japan and seminars in Vietnam was understood well by the Vietnamese. By the time of ex-post evaluation (October 2002), conducted to summarize the outcomes of phase II of the Japanese Technical Cooperation in the Legal and Judicial Field, the work of drafting a revised Civil Code had reached the completion of its third draft. However, when it came time to create the fourth draft (the final stage of phase II), the Ministry of Justice of Vietnam, which had originally only planned a partial revision to the 1995 Civil Code, suddenly decided to extend the drafting period and make a complete revision, reflecting advice from the Japanese task force. Consequently, it was decided that support for Civil Code drafting would be carried over to the successor project, the next step in cooperation, as the most important item.

53 See Katsuichi Uchida, "Vetonamu minpo kaisei kyodo kenkyu no genjo to kadai" [The state of joint research on revision of the Vietnamese Civil Code and outstanding challenges], in *Hikakuho kenkyu no shin-dankai: Ho no keiju to ishoku no riron* [A new stage in comparative law research: Theories on the reception and transplantation of law], ed. Institute of Comparative Law, Waseda University (Tokyo: Seibundoh, 2003).

12 The Introduction of a Teleconferencing System

Once the Civil Code drafting work reached the final stage of phase III of the Japanese Technical Cooperation in the Legal and Judicial Field, which commenced in July 2003, the drafting team of the Ministry of Justice of Vietnam began to have difficulty finding time to come to Japan to receive training. Instead, support work had to be implemented through written comments and on-site seminars in Vietnam, provided by Japanese task force members and other supporters. A teleconferencing system called "JICA Net" was particularly effective at the final stage. This system connected the JICA Vietnam Office to the JICA Headquarters in Japan through a dedicated line to allow the task force and Department of Economic-Civil Legislation of the Ministry of Justice, which was in charge of drafting the revised Civil Code, to hold online workshops. Morishima recalls those days:[54]

54 See Akio Morishima, "Dainanakai hoseibi shien renrakukai. Kicho koen: Betonamu minpoten no kaisei to Nihon no hoseibi shien" [The 7th Conference on Technical Assistance in the Legal Field, Keynote speech: The revision of the Vietnamese Civil Code and Japanese Cooperation for Legal and Judicial Development], *ICD News* 27 (June 2006), 16–21.

> The local time in Vietnam is two hours behind that of Japan. As such, our meetings started around half past six in the evening and ended past ten o'clock Japan time. There were even times when we carried on talking and ended up leaving

A teleconference

> the JICA Headquarters around eleven. These meetings were where the Vietnamese gave us an almost endless series of questions, and we made many proposals in response....
>
> One thing I would like to emphasize is that unlike other donors, we never said things like, "You're wrong. Do this." We told them that there were many different ways of thinking, and explained what the premise for each of them was; we were careful to respect the diversity of ideas. While Vietnam was aiming to establish the laws required in the age of globalization, Vietnamese society could face some friction in the course of accepting them as the socialist country went through its transition to a market economy. We were always thinking what solutions the Civil Code could provide to this problem. We were consistent from beginning to end in our belief that it was Vietnam, not Japan, that should choose the means of problem-solving.

As the result of continued exchanges of opinions and provision of advice through these teleconference-based workshops, the final bill was completed in 2005. It was adopted by the National Assembly on May 19 of the same year and was put into effect on January 1, 2006.

The 2005 Civil Code was treated as a new civil code rather than a revision to the 1995 Civil Code. In fact, it was a major change not only in form, but also content: it was completely different from the largely socialist 1995 Civil Code, and had finally become compatible with a market economy.

By this point in time, the Japanese members had been able to make their thoughts well understood by the Vietnamese side, at least among the drafting staff of the Ministry of Justice. This is also attested to by the fact that Japanese advice was incorporated into many parts of their draft. Nevertheless, the draft would have to pass the National Assembly to become established as law. In fact, quite a few ideas did not make their way into the 2005 Civil Code due to inability to gain the understanding of National Assembly members.

13 Further Revisions to the Civil Code: The 2015 Civil Code as Proof of Self-sustained Growth

Even after the overall revision in 2005, the Vietnamese Civil Code was still struggling to balance state control and private autonomy, as it had to govern the market economy under a socialist system.

More than ten years had passed since its first civil code was established in 1995, and Vietnam was already part of the global economy. Furthermore, Vietnamese society itself was rapidly becoming more of a market economy, resulting in the growing importance of the Civil Code, the legal basis supporting the market economy, as it played an increasingly essential role in the lives of citizens. This was why the Vietnamese government decided to launch a large-scale project to revise the 2005 Civil Code to make it more compatible with a market economy and more internationally acceptable, aiming to obtain approval from the National Assembly by the end of 2015. For this revision work, Vietnam examined the systems employed by several foreign countries to see which ones would meet international standards. In particular, Vietnam had great expectations for assistance from Japan, which had offered proactive support for the 2005 revision to the Civil Code.

After the 2005 revision to the Civil Code, JICA continued to provide support through phase III of the Japanese Technical Cooperation in the Legal and Judicial Field and other projects, and then moved on to the Project for Harmonized, Practical Legislation and Uniform Application of Law Targeting Year 2020, which was launched in April 2015. Meanwhile, the Japanese also continued to provide support for Vietnam's Civil Code revision efforts through training programs in Japan and workshops in Vietnam.

Through all of these efforts, the revised Civil Code was finally established in Vietnam in 2015. More than twenty years had passed since Minister Loc had first approached Morishima. Niimi, who had been involved in this Civil Code revision support since the very beginning of the project in 1996, found the establishment of the 2015 Civil Code particularly moving and meaningful. The provision regarding the protection of third parties without knowledge, which had been a cause for concern since the beginning, had finally made its way into the Civil Code. Niimi recounts,

> When the Vietnamese person in charge told me that protection of third parties would be incorporated in this revised Civil Code, I thought, 'At last.' At the same time, I was moved to realize that Vietnam was now one of the world's full-fledged market economies. Laws and legal systems change when society demands it. In my opinion, it was proof that Vietnam had begun to grow independently.

Dinh Trung Tung

There was also a person on the Vietnamese side who felt a special attachment to the establishment of the 2015 Civil Code. This was Dinh Trung Tung,[55] who currently serves as an advisor to the Ministry of Justice of Vietnam. He was the section chief who, seemingly on the verge of tears, had handed Morishima "homework" and made an emotional plea for him to come back soon at the end of Morishima's visit to Vietnam to assist in establishing the 1995 Civil Code.

55 See page 55, note 20.

Tung, who was born in 1956, is now 61 years old. At the time, he was the head of the department in charge of civil code drafting and was still in his thirties. After serving as director of the Department of Economic-Civil Legislation of the Ministry of Justice, he acted as vice minister of the Ministry of Justice of Vietnam until 2016. He had witnessed the birth and growth of the Vietnamese Civil Code throughout his professional career.

When he visited Japan in January 2017, he looked back on the history of the Vietnamese Civil Code, which Vietnam had nurtured in cooperation with Japan, and made the following comment:

> Those Japanese scholars and experts discussed with us each

article of the draft prepared by the Vietnamese. They showed great persistence, and gave us a wide range of useful comments. Although we had a poor understanding of what they were saying at first, we gradually developed a better understanding as days went by, thanks to those patient teachers. The Vietnamese Civil Code has been established and revised three times to date. Professor Morishima says that our Civil Code has improved with each revision. He also speaks positively of our laws, saying that Vietnamese laws have been steadily approaching something that is compatible with the market economy and international standards.[56]

56 Source: "Koeki zaidan hojin Kokusai Minshojiho Senta setsuritsu nijisshunen kinen shikiten, koenkai kinen koen" [Commemorative speech at the ceremony and symposium in honor of the 20th anniversary of the International Civil and Commercial Law Centre Foundation], in *ICCLC News* 43 (March 2017), 17. http://www.icclc.or.jp/pdf/info170306.pdf.

There was a hint of affection and pride in his eyes as he spoke, like the look in the eyes of a father boasting that his son has grown to be a strong man.

14 Gains by Those Providing Support

After more than twenty years of effort, Vietnam has finally achieved a civil code suitable for a globalized market economy. Needless to say, however, this 2015 Civil Code is not perfect. As long as a civil code is a legal basis supporting people's lives, exploring "an even better civil code" is an ongoing process. In this regard, it can be said that Vietnam has just embarked on the journey of creating the laws it requires for itself, implementing them and identifying and correcting problems in them.

Terutoshi Yamashita

This is also true for Japan. Do the current laws of Japan really suit today's social lifestyle? In fact, throughout the time that Japan was working with the Vietnamese people to develop and improve their Civil Code, it had a considerable impact also on the consciousness of the Japanese legal scholars and judicial practitioners involved in the work.

One of them, Terutoshi Yamashita,[57] who worked to launch the International Cooperation Department (ICD) and assumed several important positions, including that of ICD director, reminisces:

What I always say is, we don't teach. We provide information, but we learn, too—through interaction. Cooperation for legal and judicial development provides us with the opportunity to take a fresh look at the conventional wisdom of the Japanese system that Japanese legal specialists take for granted, and it encourages us to go back to the basics and consider why Japan has such systems. Thinking about the fundamentals is a good

57 Yamashita is a notary and former prosecutor with a strong commitment to the Japanese Ministry of Justice's legal and judicial development programs. He played a key role in getting the ICD up and running while on the staff of the Ministry's Research and Training Institute. He has served as director of both the ICD and UNAFEI (see inset, page 261).

OTHER ORGANIZATIONS INVOLVED IN PROMOTING THE RULE OF LAW

International Cooperation Department (ICD), Research and Training Institute, Japanese Ministry of Justice

Overview

The Japanese Ministry of Justice has cooperated with Asian countries in legal and judicial development since 1994. To offer more systematic support, it established the International Cooperation Department (ICD), a unit dedicated to cooperation in this area, within the Ministry's Research and Training Institute in 2001. The ICD is staffed by professors who have legal, prosecutorial or judicial experience and international cooperation experts who support organization of training programs and other tasks.

Main Activities

- Supporting JICA projects by sending long- and short-term experts abroad as a major Japanese partner in JICA's efforts in legal and judicial development; helping plan and implement local seminars; and helping plan and implement training programs in Japan.
- Pursuing joint research with South Korea and other partners and conducting studies in the fields of civil and commercial law.
- Organizing the Conference on Technical Assistance in the Legal Field and other events.
- Publishing the magazine *ICD News*.

Timeline

1994	Initiates assistance to Vietnam.
1996	Initiates assistance to Cambodia.
1998	Initiates assistance to Laos and Indonesia.
2000	1st Annual Conference on Technical Assistance in the Legal Field.
2001	The ICD is established (relocating to the Osaka Nakanoshima National Government Building); begins assistance to Uzbekistan.
2002	Starts publishing the magazine *ICD News*.
2004	Initiates assistance to Mongolia.
2007	Initiates assistance to China.
2008	Initiates assistance to East Timor.
2009	Initiates assistance to Nepal.
2013	Initiates assistance to Myanmar.
2017	Relocates to the International Justice Center in Akishima, Tokyo.

mental exercise for legal professionals. What's more, you can't communicate well unless you put aside your own values. You need to have the communication skills to persuade people by understanding and fitting in with the standards of others, not those of the Japanese. In fact, this can help us a lot when we are back in Japan, in many legal work situations.

The support work gives Japanese legal professionals invaluable opportunities for cultural exchange. When you look into the laws of another country, you also need to do research on its society, listen to people living there to find out what they think, and work to develop a better understanding of that country in many other ways. This is actually a lot of fun. Once you are into it, it's hard to break away.

The twenty years during which Japanese and Vietnamese researchers and law practitioners have come together in discussion have resulted in the development of a great bond between the parties involved in both countries, with many revelations. The Civil Code of the Socialist Republic of Vietnam, which comprises 27 chapters and 689 articles, will undoubtedly continue growing through cooperation between the two countries and evolve further in the future.

15 Development of Personnel to Implement Laws and Manage Systems

In addition to the civil code, JICA's cooperation for legal and judicial development has assisted in the drafting of many other laws, including the Code of Civil Procedure (2004),[58] the revised Law on Bankruptcy (2004),[59] the Law on Enforcement of Civil Judgments (2008),[60] the Law on State Compensation Liability (2009),[61] and the Administrative Litigation Law (2010).[62] However, establishing laws is only the first step in achieving the greater goal of building a good legal infrastructure for the market economy and civil society. Even when a country has laws, they cannot fulfill their roles completely unless judicial organizations and administrative authorities can apply them

58 The Code of Civil Procedure is the Vietnamese law that sets out procedures for settlement of disputes (contentious civil cases) and filing of applications and petitions (non-contentious civil cases) pertaining to civil matters, marriage and family matters, business, commerce, and labor relations. The division between contentious and non-contentious cases differs from that in Japan.

59 The revised Law on Bankruptcy completely overhauled the corporate bankruptcy law enacted in 1993. This legislation, which applies only to corporations, establishes two types of bankruptcy proceedings: reorganization and liquidation. JICA assisted with the 2014 revision as well.

60 The Law on Enforcement of Civil Judgments established procedures for enforcing civil judgments and decisions. It also set out confiscation and disposal procedures for criminal judgments and decisions. JICA assisted with the 2013 revision as well.

61 The Law on State Compensation Liability governs the state's liability to individuals and organizations suffering losses as the result of the actions of anyone officially engaged in state administrative management activities, litigation or enforcement of a court judgment.

62 The Administrative Litigation Law sets out the basic principles of administrative litigation, defines the rights and responsibilities of the parties concerned, establishes steps and procedures for

appropriately to bring benefit to the people. This inevitably requires the development of personnel who can apply those laws appropriately and properly manage the judicial system. In other words, judges, administrative officials, lawyers, and other legal professionals must acquire the necessary level of specialist knowledge and skills to carry out their duties in a fair manner, so that citizens can trust them.

Workshop on the Law on State Compensation Liability

instituting legal proceedings, and governs appeals against administrative decisions, appeals in administrative cases and resolution of complaints.

From the very early stages of its cooperation, JICA has been striving to promote the development of local human resources in the legal and judicial sectors by conducting workshops in Vietnam and training programs in Japan. What kind of attitude did Japanese experts adopt toward the development of human resources? Taro Morinaga,[63] who joined phase III of the Japanese Technical Cooperation in the Legal and Judicial Field as a long-term expert in May 2004 and acted as chief advisor, shares his answer:

> The most important thing is that you should always be respectful to the target country. As local people express their opinions from their own standpoints, it is difficult for you to persuade them to accept your opinions as an expert if you talk to them in a patronizing manner. Respect is the key. This is always true, whether at individual, project or inter-country level. I believe that the best policy is always to give top priority to the interests of the target country when providing support toward efforts to improve the legal system.

This is the stance JICA has taken to promote the development of human resources in Vietnam. Quite a few Vietnamese people involved evaluate JICA's achievements in this area as "the most far-reaching effect of Japan's aid activities." Dang Hoang Oanh,[64] director-general of the International Cooperation Department of the Ministry of Justice (currently Vice-Minister), is one of these people. She says,

63 Morinaga is a prosecutor who supported efforts in legal and judicial development in Vietnam as an ICD professor in Japan. Later stationed in Vietnam as a long-term expert (2004–2007), he subsequently served as deputy director of The United Nations Asia and Far East Institute for the Prevention of Crime and the Treatment of Offenders (UNAFEI). He is currently director of the ICD, in which capacity he plays a leading role in Japan's cooperation for legal and judicial development.

64 Oanh served as deputy director-general of the International Cooperation Department of the Ministry of Justice before becoming director-general in 2013. She also studied at Nagoya University.

Dinh Thi Bich Ngoc

Dang Hoang Oanh

> By 2016, hundreds of Vietnamese legal professionals will have participated in training programs in Japan. I've also experienced learning in Japan myself. Actually, the majority of the staff members in the Ministry of Justice today have benefited from JICA's project in some way or another. Hanoi has the Nhat Tan Bridge [Vietnam-Japan Friendship Bridge]. Human resource development aid, provided as part of the cooperation for legal and judicial development, can be said to be a "bridge of knowledge." It may be intangible, but it can produce a significant effect across the entirety of Vietnamese society. I'm hoping that JICA will continue to cooperate with us in our legal specialist development efforts in the future.

Dinh Thi Bich Ngoc,[65] who was in charge of the Asia-Pacific region in the International Cooperation Department of the Ministry of Justice at the time, also speaks highly of the devoted work of Japanese long-term experts, which she believes has contributed substantially to the development of human resources in Vietnam.

65 Ngoc was involved in Japanese cooperation for legal and judicial development efforts as a specialist with the International Cooperation Department of the Vietnamese Ministry of Justice for many years. She retired in 2016.

Working together with Japanese experts has brought about visible changes in the motivation, attitude toward work, and behavior of our staff members. For example, when a meeting with Japanese experts is scheduled for the following week, the idea that it's necessary to do lots of preparation beforehand has become the norm among staff members, as Japanese experts are hard workers and have a good understanding of Vietnamese laws. It's been hugely beneficial for us to be able to learn from the good qualities of Japanese people, like diligence and discipline, in addition to their knowledge.

16 Improving the Quality of Judges and Prosecutors

In the early days of cooperation by JICA, there were serious disparities in ability between the judges and prosecutors in the capital city and those in other parts of Vietnam. In order to put laws into operation in a consistent manner across the entire country, it was essential to first resolve these disparities.

This is why the Technical Assistance Project for Legal and Judicial System Reform was launched in 2007, starting full-on efforts to improve the capacity of judicial professionals, such as judges, prosecutors, and lawyers, as well as law-related government employees, in order to realize "fair, convincing, and transparent" trials in cooperation with the Ministry of Justice of Vietnam, the Supreme People's Court, the Supreme People's Procuracy, and the Vietnam Bar Federation. In particular, a special base was set up in Bac Ninh province, the eastern neighbor of Hanoi, to build the capacity of rural judges and prosecutors. In this way, JICA worked to develop human resources and improve practical work performance.

Seminars were provided in the provincial court of Bac Ninh province to enable judges to handle legal proceedings more appropriately, and a collection of questions and answers about practical court practices was compiled. In addition, project members worked with Vietnamese judges to create reference materials on court proceedings, such as practical work manuals, and put them into common use across the country.

Takeshi Matsumoto[66] describes the organization of seminars concerning the improvement of practical work performance related to civil suits:

> First, we observed several court proceedings to identify what improvements needed to be made before planning a seminar. For example, we learned that in Vietnam they didn't conduct what we call "proceedings to sort out the points at issue" [*soten seiri*] in Japan. This term refers to the process in which the court, plaintiff, and defendant discuss the points at issue of the case in advance, in order to expedite the efficiency and

66 Matsumoto, a prosecutor who supported efforts to promote the rule of law in Vietnam as an ICD professor in Japan, was later stationed in Vietnam as a long-term expert and chief advisor (2013–2016).

> productivity of the trial. Vietnamese courts, however, did not conduct such a process. Therefore, we explained the significance of the proceedings to sort out the points at issue to judges and trained them through seminars.

The capacity building of judges and prosecutors continued into phase II of the Technical Assistance Project for Legal and Judicial System Reform (April 2011–March 2015). A unique endeavor called the "Prosecutor Contest" was also implemented in the city of Hai Phong, where a new base was set up for the new phase. Matsumoto recalls:

> When I was in charge of training in Japan, many prosecutors from the procuracy of Hai Phong City participated. I gave them a seminar in the form of a trial using a moot court. As they were able to learn in a more practical fashion than from lectures, they liked this mock trial so much that they decided to use this style to measure their own abilities as prosecutors. I've heard that the Prosecutor Contest has been held each year since then.

When we visited Vietnam to gather material for this book, Nguyen Tuan Khanh,[67] chief of the office of the Hai Phong People's Procuracy, also told us about the Prosecutor Contest. He was one of the participants who visited Japan in 2012 to receive training. He said the training programs that had been traditionally provided in Vietnam had been mostly lectures, making it difficult for participants to maintain their motivation to learn, but JICA's work was different. "For the Prosecutor Contest, we prepared a scenario modeled after an incident that actually occurred in the city of Hai Phong, and mock trials were held in cooperation with lawyers," Khanh recalled. "Each contestant's judicial proceedings, the way he or she questioned the defendant, and so on, were evaluated and ranked by the contest's judging panel." The contest ended with the panel commenting on each participating prosecutor. "Through the Prosecutor Contest, the quality of prosecutors in the city of Hai Phong has improved a lot. This initiative has been received so

67 Before becoming chief of the office of the Hai Phong People's Procuracy, Khanh served as head of the Procuracy's prosecutor's office, where he worked on resolving administrative, financial, and labor relations cases.

Matsumoto at a seminar

The Prosecutor Contest

well that a nationwide contest is also being held," Khanh says with pride.

17 Linking the "Neurons" between the Central and Local Administrations

Phase I and phase II of the Technical Assistance Project for Legal and Judicial System Reform also addressed another challenge, in addition to the improvement of quality of judges and prosecutors. Matsumoto recalls:

> In Vietnam at the time, the "neurons" between the central and local administrations did not seem connected. The central government seemed to adopt rules without paying due attention to how the laws were being implemented and how actual on-site work was being done in each region of the country. On the other hand, local administrative authorities did not seem to observe instructions from the Supreme People's Court when they did not match the local situation. We were worried that we would not be able to make any difference to this situation if we stuck to conventional methods and continued to provide support for drafting work and efforts to improve work performance through separate programs. A new direction arose out of this fear—more specifically an initiative toward the development of a system allowing the central government agencies to effectively communicate their

ideas across all parts of the country by reinforcing "vertical coordination" between the central and local administrative authorities.

This coincided with Vietnam's push for delegation of greater authority from provincial courts and procuracies to their rural district counterparts, which was causing an urgent need to improve the abilities of rural district judges and prosecutors working more closely with the general public. As such, the central judicial authorities were compelled to adopt some efficient measures to achieve this goal.

Phase II of the Technical Assistance Project for Legal and Judicial System Reform was carried out with the goal of making effective use of the knowledge and skills which the Supreme People's Court, Supreme People's Procuracy, and other central judicial agencies had accumulated through past projects. It identified nationwide issues and discussed possible solutions, while at the same time working to establish a series of activities as the standard workflow of the central judicial agencies. Matsumoto explains,

> When we conducted activities in other parts of Vietnam, officials from central judicial authorities such as the Supreme People's Court and Supreme People's Procuracy also had to participate in them. This naturally enabled them to take information about what was actually going on in each region back to Hanoi with them. This resulted in the knowledge and experience acquired in the respective regions becoming reflected in the development of new laws. Our aim was to put this kind of cycle of feedback in play. We thought it would inevitably bring together the "neurons" that seemed to have been disconnected.

In Phase II, activities took place across all parts of Vietnam, including the province in which the base for the phase was located, to promote better understanding of the contents of laws and how to implement them.

We were requested by the Vietnamese to cover the entire country, rather than focusing on specific areas. This was the reason that Phase II saw a dramatic increase in the number of target regions for the project. Vietnam has sixty-three rural districts. I worked in about thirty of them, and my predecessor, Prosecutor Takeshi Nishioka,[68] worked in as many as fifty different rural districts.

68 Nishioka, a prosecutor who supported efforts to promote the rule of law in Vietnam as an ICD professor in Japan, was later stationed in Vietnam as a long-term expert and chief advisor (2010–2013).

The method was as follows: officials from central judicial authorities first conducted fact-finding on the situation of a particular rural area, and then fed what they learned back into the central administration to develop new rules that would better suit the actual needs of each region. This method has been adopted by central law-related organizations, resulting in remarkable changes. Matsumoto says, smiling, "I likened the situation between the central and local administrations to disconnected neurons, but that improved enormously by the end of the project. Actually, when I visited the Supreme People's Court and Supreme People's Procuracy and talked to people in charge there, it was almost as if they had always been reflecting what was happening in each province in their reports."

Official signing of a project agreement between Japan and Vietnam

JICA's activities have helped connect the "neurons" between the central and local administrations, and have been highly praised by donor countries and aid organizations from Western countries.

When I began working in the post, the JICA style had become something of a fad among other donor countries and aid organizations. Following JICA's lead, they had begun to work by setting up centers for their activities in rural areas, implementing activities there, and relaying what they learned there back to the central administration. I'm hoping that best practices like this will spread even more widely in the future.

18 Efforts to Boost the Status of Lawyers

The Vietnam Bar Federation (VBF) joined the Technical Assistance Project for Legal and Judicial System Reform as a new counterpart. VBF is a relatively new organization, having only been established in May 2009. It is a national federation consisting of lawyers across Vietnam and regional bar associations in different parts of the country.

In Vietnam, the work of lawyers is not widely understood, and their social status is lower than that of judges and prosecutors. It is difficult to gain access to highly trained and ethical lawyers in rural districts, where the number of lawyers itself is very small. Even when appropriate laws and legal systems are in place, they cannot be properly applied or executed unless there is an adequate number of lawyers who can give citizens legal advice and speak for them in court.

In addressing these problems, JICA provided assistance for the foundation of the VBF, with the proactive and ongoing cooperation of the Japan Federation of Bar Associations (JFBA).[69] JICA has continued its support even after the foundation of the VBF by inviting Vietnamese lawyers to Japan and providing them with training, in addition to assisting the organization and management of Vietnamese bar associations.

Over the seven years since the project's inception, what changes have been observed in Vietnamese lawyers? Lawyer Luu Tien Dzung,[70] director of the International Cooperation Department of the VBF, has long been involved in JICA's project activities. He remarks,

> First, people's recognition of the social status of lawyers has changed. Second, courts, procuracies and investigative organizations of the police have begun to pay more respect to lawyers involved in lawsuits. Third, lawyers have improved their

69 See inset, page 105.

70 Dzung has been director of the International Cooperation Department since the VBF's inception. He works on building relationships and promoting exchanges with bar associations in other countries.

abilities and have gained greater self-awareness as professionals. The launch of the VBF has contributed substantially to these changes. Of course, behind this was the hard work of Japanese experts.

Masanori Tsukahara,[71] who was sent to work in Vietnam, speaks about reinforcing the VBF and the significance of boosting the social status of lawyers:

> The VBF is interested in the Japanese "duty lawyer" system.[72] However, this type of system cannot be introduced to Vietnam unless Vietnamese lawyers and associations of lawyers improve their abilities and social status, and also increase their influence over courts, procuracies, and the police. Once they achieve this, a Vietnamese version of the system can be discussed, just as the duty lawyer system was launched in Japan following a proposal by the JFBA. It's essential for lawyers and lawyers' associations to improve their social status and skills in order to protect people's rights—including guaranteeing every arrested individual the right to the assistance of a lawyer—and to establish the rule of law.

Luu Tien Dzung is not satisfied with the status quo himself, needless to say. He, too, emphasizes that it is important for individual lawyers to develop more advanced skills and higher moral standards to boost the overall social status of lawyers. "The goal is a society in which everyone will respect you when you introduce yourself as a lawyer. I'm not sure whether this will come about in five years, or even in ten. However, if every lawyer works hard to make a difference, our society is bound to appreciate us eventually. That's what I believe."

When the young people who will inherit Vietnam's future start to show a greater interest in, and care more about, the activities of lawyers and regard them with admiration, that will be a huge driving force for establishing "the rule of law" in the country.

71 A lawyer registered with the Aichi Bar Association. Stationed in Vietnam as a long-term expert since 2014, having previously practiced law in Japan.

72 The "duty lawyer" system is one that provides anyone who has been arrested with free access to a duty lawyer. This ensures that people who are arrested can obtain professional legal advice.

19 The Introduction of a Case Law System That Suits the Legal System of Vietnam

A "precedent" is a judicial decision made by a court in a past trial. If a court's decision makes it likely that similar cases in the future will refer back to this and be decided in the same way, the decision can provide important information that will help the interested parties and their lawyers predict the outcomes of their trials. In many countries, past judicial decisions are compiled into casebooks and databases that legal practitioners and scholars consult.

Ensuring the consistency of legal decisions by accumulating and publishing precedents is not only important for "legal stability" but also matches the civil demand for "equality under the law," as well as the needs of citizens and companies that require trials be predictable. In Vietnam, however, the importance of accumulating precedents and making them public was not understood.

According to Shiro Muto, the lawyer, "Predictable trials form the basis for a market economy. Imagine that a conflict has occurred and you want to take legal action. If precedents have not been established or made public, there is no telling as to what the verdict will be."

The Vietnamese also recognized the significance of precedents. In 2005, the Politburo of the Central Executive Committee of the Communist Party of Vietnam announced Resolution No. 48, "Strategy for the Development and Improvement of Vietnam's Legal System to the Year 2010 and Direction for the Period up to 2020 (LSDS),"[73] and Resolution No. 49, "Judicial Reform Strategy to 2020 (JRS),"[74] to begin specific reform activities to establish the rule of law. In this reform initiative, the Supreme People's Court was defined as having the role of "developing precedents."

In 2014, the new Law on the Organization of People's Courts was established with the support of JICA. In Article 27 of that law, "summarizing, developing, and publishing precedents" was added as a new duty of the Supreme People's Court. In response to this, the Supreme People's Court established the Resolution

73, 74 In 2002, the Vietnamese government performed a comprehensive assessment of the development needs of the Vietnamese legal system up to the year 2010, known as the Legal Needs Assessment (LNA). Meanwhile, the Politburo of the Central Executive Committee of the Communist Party announced Resolution No. 8 of 2002, the Politburo resolution on key judicial tasks for the future. It was in the context of these moves to evaluate the issues facing the country's legal and judicial systems and take steps to reform them that the two strategies focused on establishing the rule of law were announced. Together they set the direction of efforts to develop Vietnam's legal system and reform its judiciary through the year 2020.

Concerning Procedures for the Selection, Publishing, and Application of Precedents in October 2015, launching Vietnam's very own case law system.

The chief justice of the Supreme People's Court published six precedents on April 6, 2016. They were to be applicable to trials across Vietnam beginning June 1 of the same year. This shows that the judicial system of Vietnam has made steady progress toward a more transparent and predictable system. Naoki Sakai,[75] who was stationed in Hanoi for two years starting in 2015, evaluates the introduction of the case law system:

Naoki Sakai

75 Sakai is a judge who, after serving on the bench in Japan, was stationed in Vietnam as a long-term expert (2015–2017).

> There will be a growing number of civil conflicts in the future as Vietnam accelerates its transition to a market economy. Of course, these conflicts will need to be resolved through application of the relevant laws. However, it's impossible to clearly stipulate everything concerning all kinds of situations in laws. When a sufficient number of precedents have been accumulated to allow courts to make stable judicial judgments, people's confidence in them will increase, leading to greater stability for the country's judicial system.

Matsumoto, also, places high expectations on the introduction of the case law system, which he believes will help stimulate legal studies in Vietnam.

> Currently, legal education in Vietnamese universities mainly involves students' rote learning of the wording of laws, such as, "This is how it is stipulated in law. The definition of this term is found in Article X." The introduction of the case law system is sure to lead to an improvement in the overall level of legal studies in the country if legal scholars are given opportunities to freely express their views to each other regarding the purposes of the legal system and the definitions of wording. To enable Vietnam to carry out

"independent and continued legal system development," in the most precise and genuine sense of the phrase, I think it is essential for the country to establish an effective system that will allow it to maintain and improve the level of its legal studies and education independently and continue to produce human resources with sufficient legal expertise for society. I feel that the Vietnamese people's determination for reform is strong enough, and the international community, including Japan, is willing to back them up.[76]

76 See Takeshi Matsumoto, "Betonamu hoseibi dayori" (Legislative news from Vietnam), *ICD News* no. 64 (September 2015): 38–49.

20 "We Would Like to Seek Your Support for Amending the Constitution of Vietnam."

JICA's cooperation for legal and judicial development in Vietnam entered its 16th year in 2012. In this year, an event occurred that marked a huge milestone in the relationship of cooperation between the two countries.

When Hideo Hiraoka, minister of justice of Japan, visited Vietnam in January of the same year, Deputy Prime Minister Nguyen Xuan Phuc, Chief Judge of the Supreme People's Court Truong Hoa Binh, and Minister of Justice Ha Hung Cuong informed him that "Vietnam would like Japan to provide assistance to Vietnam's constitution amendment process,

The Judicial Survey Mission in Japan

considering Japan's experience and knowledge," in addition to expressing their gratitude for Japan's involvement in their legal and judicial system improvement efforts.

The fact that Vietnam sought support from Japan to amend its own constitution, "the supreme law of the country," revealed how much Vietnam appreciated and trusted the legal system development support activities that Japan had implemented over the years.

In July 2012, JICA invited the Judicial Survey Mission of the Vietnamese Government to Japan, supported by leading Japanese constitutional scholars, as well as the Ministry of Justice and the Supreme Court of Japan, the Legislative Bureau of the House of Representatives, and other stakeholders in Japan. The mission consisted of about twenty members, including six cabinet ministers and their equivalents from the Supreme People's Court, such as Justice Minister Cuong and Chief Judge Binh, in addition to Deputy Prime Minister Phuc, who acted as the leader of the mission.

During their stay of about one week in Japan, they not only listened to Japanese constitutional law scholars and other experts speak about the principles of the Constitution of Japan, including local autonomy and the separation of powers into the three branches of government, but they also conducted research on referendum systems, which were not found in Vietnam, and the power granted to the court to determine the constitutionality of laws.

The Vietnamese government published a draft amendment to the Constitution at the beginning of 2013 and solicited public comments on it. Consequently, several million Vietnamese citizens submitted their comments on a website run by the National Assembly, where bold debates took place.

In this way, the wheels of autonomous legal and judicial reform in Vietnam were set into motion.

21 "I Want Japanese People to Look Forward to the Future of Vietnam."

In April 2015, the Project for Harmonized, Practical Legislation and Uniform Application of Law Targeting Year 2020 was launched. The target year for the legal and judicial system reform, 2020, was just around the corner. This new project was designed as a summary of the past twenty years of Japanese cooperation, but before it came into being, it was confirmed with the Vietnamese that the goal of the project was for Japan and Vietnam to establish a stronger and more equal relationship, based on mutual understanding, from 2021 onwards.

Hajime Kawanishi,[77] chief advisor for the project, emphasizes that there must always be personal connections between Vietnam and Japan, no matter what kind of cooperative relationship the two countries will have after 2021.

> Many staff in Vietnamese judicial organizations who have been involved in the project have later become top officials of their respective organizations, retaining strong relationships of trust with Japan. This is an intangible but hugely important outcome. For example, Justice Minister Le Thanh Long,[78] who took office in April 2016, was a staff member of the International Cooperation Department of the Ministry of Justice when lawyer Shiro Muto was sent to Hanoi. Over the past twenty years, there have always been long-term experts from Japan stationed in Vietnam, concerning themselves with local problems and thinking about them together with the Vietnamese people. This experience, I suppose, is the reason that Vietnamese people treat us as old friends now. I think that the relationship with our counterparts is really precious, something that has been built over the past twenty years. In fact, I feel on a daily basis that I actually owe it to the accumulation of many years of trust built up by those who came before me that I'm not only allowed to work in Vietnam as a long-term expert, but I'm also invited to dinner by Vietnamese people and share jokes with them. We can't continue to provide assistance of the kind we're providing now forever.

77 Kawanishi is a prosecutor who supported efforts to promote the rule of law in Vietnam as an ICD professor in Japan. He was later stationed in Vietnam as a long-term expert (2015–2017).

78 Long served as deputy director-general of the International Cooperation Department of the Ministry of Justice and then vice minister of Justice before becoming minister in 2016. He has a doctorate in law from Nagoya University and is a member of the Central Executive Committee of the Communist Party of Vietnam (12th Communist Party Congress).

Kawanishi and Oanh conferring on a project

Le Thanh Long

> At the same time, the laws that have been established with Japanese support are going to be changed by Vietnamese people themselves in the future, but the 'personal relationships between individuals' which have been built up over such a long time are sure to remain unchanged and stay in our hearts forever. In this regard, we can't begin to imagine that these connections will be severed anytime in the future.[79]

Looking back on his own experience as an international student in Japan, Justice Minister Long also talks about the bonds between Japan and Vietnam:

> I received my Doctor's Degree in Law from the Nagoya University Graduate School of Law. Even today, each time I see my supervisor or fellow students from back then, I feel close to them, as if they were my family members. Over the past twenty years, many Vietnamese people studied in Japan just as I did. In fact, many of them now play important roles in the legal and judicial areas in Vietnam; and as fellow professionals, what they have in common is the knowledge and experience they gained in Japan. The more people who personally interact with those from the other country like this, the deeper, I believe, the relationship of trust and mutual understanding between the two countries will become. Of course, it is possible to quantitatively evaluate the outcomes of Japan's aid work, like 'how many laws have been passed by the National

79 See Hajime Kawanishi, "Hoseido seibi shien no genba kara: Hito to hito o tsunagu hoseido seibi shien" (From the front lines of legal technical assistance: Legal technical assistance as a bridge between people), *Homusho dayori akarenga* 54, (October 2016), http://www.moj.go.jp/KANBOU/KOHOSHI/no54/7.html#report07.

> Assembly with, in one degree or another, Japanese technical assistance.' The most important outcome for me, however, is that we've been able to establish an invaluable relationship of trust that will certainly stay with us in the future.

Ngo Cuong

We have interviewed more than ten Vietnamese people involved in the project to create this book. What they have told us varies significantly depending on when they were connected with the project and in what position, but there are words that virtually all of them used: "family-/friend-like relationship of trust" and "persistent support."

When we asked Ngo Cuong,[80] director of the International Cooperation Department of the Supreme People's Court, what he believes characterizes Japanese aid activities, he looked out the window and said quietly,

80 Cuong became director of the International Cooperation Department of the Supreme People's Court of Vietnam in 2008 after serving as deputy director of the Court's Institute for Judicial Science. He retired in October 2017.

> Support from Japan can be compared to a long spell of light rain. It evenly penetrates every corner of a wide area. Heavy downpours instantly run off. By contrast, light rains penetrate deep into the ground to nourish plants. Trees that are still small right now are certain to grow into huge trees and bear plenty of fruit in the future. I'd like Japanese people to look forward to seeing the fruits of their labor.

How did you get involved in the JICA legal and judicial development project?

I worked for a Japanese firm on a short-term contract after graduating from university, and that's when I first learned about JICA. Around the time the contract ended, I heard that JICA was recruiting people for its legal and judicial development project, so I applied. I've been involved in the project since October 1997. Back then the office was a small room in the Ministry of Justice, and there were only three people including me. Looking back, it was certainly a small team. Now we have more staff than we did then, and I'm struck by how impressive the project has become.

What kind of workplace is the project office?

It's a friendly place that's efficient to work in. The Japanese experts are all nice people, so we're able to exchange views frankly and honestly. Sometimes when we're not busy with work, all of us will have lunch together. On our days off we sometimes go out together with our families in tow. The other day we all went to the mountains up north—what's known as the Vietnamese Shangri-La. And when an expert finishes their stint and heads back to Japan, we stay in contact by email or snail mail.

How have JICA's efforts to promote the rule of law changed Vietnamese society?

When JICA started its cooperation, Vietnam had only the Civil Code of 1995; now we have a wide range of laws and guidelines in the civil law area. As a result, in the past, if people bought a house, they just exchanged a written paper between the buyer and the seller to certify that transaction. Now, we all know that in order to secure our transaction, we have to make a contract to be notarized at the notary office. The laws have gradually entered into the ordinary life of every citizen.

Nguyen Thi Thu Ha

Vietnam project office staffer

PROFILE:
Graduated with a degree in foreign languages from Vietnam National University, Hanoi, in 1994. Has worked for the JICA legal and judicial development project in Vietnam since 1997.

Chapter 2

Laying the Foundations for Peace —Cambodia

The mass killings by the Pol Pot regime eradicated Cambodia's legal community and laws. So Japanese experts had to start completely from scratch when they arrived to help draft a new civil code and civil procedure code and train people to administer them. Through those efforts, they lent a hand in building a society where people could live in peace and security.

The Cambodian capital, Phnom Penh.
The Independence Monument with a tuk-tuk and motorbike whizzing by.

PROJECT FACT SHEET Cambodia

Legal and Judicial Development Project

March 5, 1999–March 4, 2003

COUNTERPART: Ministry of Justice

This project helped Cambodia write a new civil code and civil procedure code as part of efforts to rebuild the country and reconstitute the legal system abolished under the Pol Pot regime. A Cambodian working group and a Japanese task force took turns drafting the text.

Legal and Judicial Development Project (Phase II)

April 9, 2004–April 8, 2008

COUNTERPART: Ministry of Justice

After they were drafted, the new codes needed to clear all the legislative hurdles and be enacted into Cambodian law. The ministry responsible, the Ministry of Justice, briefed the legislature on the bills and made adjustments with other ministries to ensure consistency across laws, while JICA experts provided support from the sidelines. They also helped draft related legislation. The Civil Procedure Code was enacted in 2006; the Civil Code in 2007.

Legal and Judicial Development Project (Phase III)

April 9, 2008–March 31, 2012

COUNTERPART: Ministry of Justice

JICA assisted with compiling commentaries designed to foster awareness of what was stated in the recently enacted Civil Code and Civil Procedure Code. It also helped draft related legislation and harmonize the two codes with legislation overseen by other ministries. A law on applying the Civil Code was enacted, and the new code started being enforced at the end of 2011.

Legal and Judicial Cooperation for the Bar Association of the Kingdom of Cambodia

July 1, 2001–July 31, 2002
September 1, 2002–August 31, 2005
June 11, 2007–June 10, 2010

COUNTERPART:
Bar Association of the Kingdom of Cambodia

This project supporting the Bar Association of the Kingdom of Cambodia was carried out on contract by the Japan Federation of Bar Associations (JFBA). First it provided assistance with establishing and running the Center for Lawyers' Training and Professional Improvement (LTC); then, with the JFBA's cooperation, it helped develop teaching materials for the center and upskill its instructors.

Project for Improvement of Training on Civil Matters at the Royal School for Judges and Prosecutors

November 10, 2005–March 31, 2008

COUNTERPART:
Royal Academy for Judicial Professions

After the Royal School for Judges and Prosecutors was founded in 2005, JICA helped put together a curriculum, produce teaching materials, and educate future instructors in readiness for the enactment of the Civil Code and Civil Procedure Code. Educating future instructors involved selecting the best graduates and training them as instructor candidates by involving them in developing teaching materials and enlisting their participation in moot-court sessions for students.

Project for Improvement of Training on Civil Matters at the Royal School for Judges and Prosecutors (Phase II)

April 1, 2008–March 31, 2012

COUNTERPART:
Royal Academy for Judicial Professions

JICA helped the Royal School for Judges and Prosecutors establish the educational infrastructure necessary to teach administration of the Civil Code, the Civil Procedure Code and other civil legislation. Training of instructor candidates continued, 40 of whom completed the program.

Legal and Judicial Development Project (Phase IV)

April 1, 2012–March 31, 2017

COUNTERPARTS: Ministry of Justice
Royal Academy for Judicial Professions
Bar Association of the Kingdom of Cambodia
Royal University of Law and Economics

For this project, JICA partnered with three bodies it had worked with before—the Ministry of Justice, the Royal School for Judges and Prosecutors, and the Bar Association—plus a fourth, the Royal University of Law and Economics. By assisting each of these in developing core personnel, it helped train the people who would one day be responsible for administering the Civil Code and the Civil Procedure Code, embedding them in Cambodian society and educating the next generation about them.

Legal and Judicial Development Project (Phase V)

April 1, 2017–March 31, 2022

COUNTERPARTS: **Ministry of Justice** **Royal Academy for Judicial Professions** **Bar Association of the Kingdom of Cambodia** **Royal University of Law and Economics**

Tapping the human resources developed at partner organizations to date, this project provides support in several key areas, including developing legislation on real estate registration, producing litigation forms, and making civil judgments public. It thus seeks to promote better administration of the Civil Code and the Civil Procedure Code.

In the wake of the 1979 oil crisis, Japan was steadily becoming a major economic force. Sony had just released the Walkman, and Space Invaders was all the rage. In the meantime, in Cambodia the regime of Pol Pot, which had been in power since 1975,[1] was toppled in January of 1979. Pol Pot left a stain on world history for the genocide he ordered against his own people while he was still in power, a recent atrocity that had taken place all too close to Japan.

After a military coup in 1970, the Kingdom of Cambodia[2] plunged into civil war. In 1975, the victorious Khmer Rouge[3] established the state of Democratic Kampuchea, headed by Pol Pot. The regime destroyed most of the existing social systems, including the modern judicial system that had been introduced under French colonial rule. Urbanites were driven out into rural Cambodia. Teachers, doctors, engineers, capitalists, public servants, and other intellectuals were sent to concentration camps, where many of them were tortured and killed. While there are no accurate figures, out of the total population of 5 to 6 million back then, around 1 to 2 million Cambodians are believed to have lost their lives as a result of the genocide, disease and starvation. Many of the intellectuals murdered by the Pol Pot regime were legal professionals.

"Only a few judges and court clerks were left in Cambodia by 1979," recalls You Bunleng,[4] who played a core role in JICA's cooperation for legal and judicial development. Currently, he doubles as a co-investigating judge (of the Office of Co-Investigating Judges) of the Khmer Rouge Tribunal[5] and as the president of the Appeal Court. Supreme Court Judge Sathavy Kim,[6] who also participated in the JICA project, had survived the

1 The regime was headed by Prime Minister Pol Pot, a founding member of the Communist Party of Kampuchea. It abandoned cities, abolished the currency and banned education during its brutal reign of terror, which was rooted in an extreme form of communism.

2 The kingdom was established in 1953 when Cambodia achieved independence from France, which had ruled the country since the end of the nineteenth century. The first king was Norodom Sihanouk, leader of the independence movement.

3 The Khmer Rouge, or the "Red Khmers," was the Kampuchean Communist Party movement led by Pol Pot. It was also known as the Pol Pot faction.

4 Bunleng joined the bench immediately after the overthrow of the Pol Pot regime, becoming president of the Appeal Court in 2007. He has been a judge in the pretrial chamber of the Khmer Rouge Tribunal since the tribunal's establishment.

5 Established in 2006 under an agreement between the Cambodian government and the United Nations to try senior members of the Khmer Rouge

regime, the tribunal is composed of both Cambodian and international judges.

Kim Sathavy

You Bunleng

mayhem of Pol Pot by hiding her high educational background, a story detailed in a memoir she published in French[7] to share her experience. This iron-willed, quietly-spoken intellectual also recalls that there were only six judges left in the country at the time—hard to believe, but that was the brutal reality. In Cambodia, where you hardly needed the fingers of both hands to count the number of trained lawyers, the rule of law had to be reestablished from almost absolute zero.

Civil war dragged on for more than ten years after the collapse of the Pol Pot regime. In 1980, before he graduated from high school, You Bunleng applied to the Cambodian Ministry of Justice (MOJ) and was recruited. That same year, Courts of First Instance were set up, which were followed by the Courts of Appeal in 1986 and the Supreme Court in 1987. But there were no judges to fill them. Pressured by necessity, the ministry staff searched for primary school teachers above a certain level of literacy and students with any training in law and appointed them as judges and prosecutors after a brief training. You Bunleng took charge of recruitment and searched for individuals with experience working in judicial organs, but many of these people were already employed in other jobs. One former court clerk he finally found was earning a living by repairing bicycles. These hastily trained judges and prosecutors had no choice but to learn trial proceedings on the job. Later, the number of legal professionals gradually increased as students returning from Vietnam and the former Soviet Union filled the gap. Even so, around 1997, there were only around 170 judges and prosecutors in total in Cambodia.

The Paris Peace Agreements[8] were signed in 1991, ending the

6 Kim remained in Cambodia during Pol Pot's rule and survived to become a judge. She has been on the Supreme Court since 2006.

7 *Jeunesse brisée* (Actes Sud), published in English under the title *Shattered Youth* (Maverick House).

8 The treaty, which was signed in Paris, France, by Cambodia's warring factions, provided for the establishment of the Supreme National Council of Cambodia.

The Supreme Court of the Kingdom of Cambodia

Miha Isoi

civil war. In the following year, the United Nations Transitional Authority in Cambodia (UNTAC)[9] provisionally took over the country's administration. The year 1993 marked the revival of the Kingdom of Cambodia, with a new constitution following a general election sponsored by UNTAC.

In those years, Cambodia had no civil code that systematically compiled rules for the conduct of civil life. Instead, the country only had Decree-Law No. 38 on Contracts and Other Liabilities,[10] the Law on Marriage and Family,[11] and the Land Law.[12] Sathavy Kim, a newly appointed judge in 1983, recalls that "there were so few laws I didn't know what I should base my rulings on."

The generation lost under the rule of Pol Pot has left a huge and long-standing void in Cambodian society. Miha Isoi,[13] a Japanese attorney, began focusing on getting involved in the cooperation for legal and judicial development in Cambodia in 2009, exactly thirty years after the fall of the Pol Pot regime. Isoi could not fail to notice this "absence" of an entire generation in Cambodia. "Most of the people I met were either junior professionals around the age of 30 or veteran professionals in their late 50s. The mid-career professionals who should have been the drivers of society were missing. Then I realized the long-lasting impact of genocide, and that this would continue for decades to come." To make matters worse, many people from the generation following the lost generation did not have access to basic

9 UNTAC was a United Nations body established under the Paris Peace Accord, headed by Special Representative of the Secretary-General Yasushi Akashi. It monitored the cease-fire, disarmed combatants, supervised elections, and repatriated refugees.

10 Decree no. 38 was issued by the Council of State in 1988, before the peace accord. It governs such matters as validity of contracts and tort liability.

11 The Law on Marriage and Family, enacted in 1989, governs conditions of marriage and divorce, the validity of marriages and divorces, parent-child relationships and adoption.

12 The Land Law was drafted in 1992 with support from the Asia Development Bank (ADB). It was then in the jurisdiction of the Ministry of Agriculture. The Ministry of Land, which was established afterwards, oversaw the enactment of a revised version of the law in 2001 with the support of the World Bank and the ADB.

education during the civil war that followed the fall of Pol Pot. The complete lack of human resources would come back to haunt them in many stages of the project.

13 Isoi, an attorney registered with Dai-Ichi Tokyo Bar Association, has been involved in JICA's efforts to promote the rule of law abroad for over a decade, both as a long-term expert in Mongolia (2006–2008) and Cambodia (2013–2014) and as a senior advisor to JICA (2009–present).

01 A Country Driven by the Aid Industry

Kimitoshi Yabuki

Attorney Kimitoshi Yabuki[14] visited Cambodia's capital, Phnom Penh, for the first time in 1996. This would begin his long engagement in JICA's cooperation for legal and judicial development, along with other assistance for international justice through the Japan Federation of Bar Associations (JFBA). He remembers, "The capital city appeared dark and somewhat intimidating. I sensed a lack of self-confidence among the people as they tried to read each other, because politics were still conducted through violence. This overall social instability was also visible through domestic violence and human trafficking, which should have been addressed legally."

Yabuki describes Cambodia in those years as a country driven by the "aid industry." Countries and regions affected by conflict have difficulty earning the necessary foreign currency through industry and tourism, so international aid tends to be their largest source of revenue. Cambodia was no exception, and accepted aid from many countries and international agencies. The salaries from the international agencies raised the level of wages in Cambodia, and even attracted migrant workers from neighboring countries. But as this high income was sustained by aid brought in from other countries, domestic industries remained underdeveloped.

Likewise, in its endeavor to develop legal systems, Cambodia promulgated a barrage of new bills drafted by foreign donors, even when they were not appropriate for the local situation. Unfortunately, many of the donors ended their assistance once

14 Since the 1990s, Yabuki, an attorney registered with the Tokyo Bar Association, has devoted himself to promoting the rule of law in developing countries like Cambodia through the JFBA's international legal assistance program. He is the moving spirit behind that program, having served in such key posts as chairman of the JFBA's International Exchange Committee.

these bills were drafted, and did not provide any follow-up on how the resulting laws were to be applied. Naturally, this meant that Cambodia remained short of professionals who could understand and apply these laws, and many laws drafted by donors ended up gathering dust on a shelf.

Nagoya University professor emeritus Akio Morishima[15] paved the way for Japan's cooperation for legal and judicial

15 See page 45, note 2.

OTHER ORGANIZATIONS INVOLVED IN PROMOTING THE RULE OF LAW

Japan Federation of Bar Associations (JFBA) (International Exchange Committee)

Overview

The Japan Federation of Bar Associations (JFBA) was established in 1949 during postwar reforms to the Japanese justice system. All practicing lawyers in Japan must register with one of the country's 52 bar associations and the JFBA. The JFBA's International Exchange Committee was established in 1978 as the Japanese legal profession became more engaged with the international community. The committee's lawyers inform international audiences about the Japanese judicial system, study other countries' judicial systems, and interact and share information with their peers overseas. Promoting the rule of law by providing international legal assistance is an important aspect of the JFBA's activities.

Main Activities in the Field of International Legal Assistance

- Taking part in JICA legal and judicial development projects as a major Japanese partner (sending long- and short-term experts abroad; helping plan and implement local seminars; and helping plan and implement training programs in Japan).
- Assisting bar associations in developing countries by tapping the JFBA's international cooperation fund and private sector support.
- Organizing a conference on access to justice in Asia.
- Providing information and training to lawyers in Japan.
- Organizing seminars on international legal assistance.

Timeline

1949	The Japan Federation of Bar Associations is established.
1978	The International Exchange Study Committee is established.
1986	The International Exchange Study Committee is renamed the International Exchange Committee.
1994	A Subcommittee on International Cooperation is established within the International Exchange Committee.
1999	A registration program is set up for lawyers providing international legal assistance.
2000	The JFBA signs a friendship agreement with the Bar Association of the Kingdom of Cambodia.
2006	The JFBA signs a friendship agreement with the All China Lawyers Association.
2007	The International Exchange Committee's Subcommittee on International Cooperation is reorganized into the International Legal Cooperation Center (ILCC).
2008	The JFBA signs a partnership agreement with JICA.
2013	The JFBA signs a friendship agreement with the Vietnam Bar Federation.
2017	The JFBA signs a three-way friendship agreement with the Association of Mongolian Advocates and the Mongolian Bar Association.

Note: Including the above, the JFBA has signed friendship agreements with a total of 14 foreign and international bar associations.

development. In the summer of 1997, during a conference in Phnom Penh, Nguyen Dinh Loc,[16] then Vietnamese Minister of Justice, introduced Morishima to Chem Snguon,[17] who happened to be the Minister of Justice in Cambodia. Snguon invited Morishima to his home and appealed for Japanese assistance in drafting a civil code for Cambodia. This was about half a year after a similar project had begun in Vietnam.

16 See page 47, note 4.

17 Chem Snguon was the government in exile's ambassador to Beijing during the Cambodian civil war. After the Paris Peace Accord was signed, he was deputy chairman of the Constitution Drafting Committee, and then served as minister of justice until 1999.

Morishima remembers the conversation as follows:

> The drafting of a new civil code that underpins a country is a major undertaking. It's not comparable to the revision of the Vietnamese Civil Code, which only required our feedback on a draft presented by our Vietnamese counterparts. But Minister Snguon earnestly asked me to help Cambodia to draft a civil code one way or another, as the country desperately needed one. I responded that I couldn't give him an immediate answer, but I would do my best. Hearing that, the minister was on the verge of tears. I was deeply touched by such enthusiasm, which probably was related to the nation's unimaginable suffering under Pol Pot's rule. I was driven by a sense of duty to do something about it.[18]

18 See Akio Morishima, "Wagakuni ni yoru kaihatsu tojokoku no hoseibi shien" (Japanese cooperation for legal and judicial development in developing countries), *Gakushikai kaiho* 892, no. 1 (January 2012): 30–36.

Prior to this, in 1996, JICA had begun to provide training for the judicial and legislative branches in Cambodia in cooperation with the Japanese Ministry of Justice, the Supreme Court, and the JFBA. Morishima's return to Japan after the impassioned request from Minister Snguon was followed by a conference on providing cooperation for legal and judicial development in Cambodia. Cooperation was sought within the framework of the Japanese Cooperation to Support the Formulation of Key Government Policies[19] to assist formerly socialist countries in their democratization and transition to a market economy.

19 The Japanese Cooperation to Support the Formulation of Key Government Policies was a Japanese program to support countries making the transition to a market economy in the aftermath of the fall of the Soviet Union in the early 1990s; it assisted them in developing legislation and implementing economic reforms. Under the program, which commenced in 1995, projects were carried out in Indochina, Eastern Europe, Central Asia and elsewhere.

Initially, the Cambodian Ministry of Justice sought to draft civil and criminal codes and codes of civil and criminal procedures with assistance from France, their former colonial ruler. But these four laws would lay the groundwork for the country; every one of them would consist of a huge number of provisions, each containing numerous articles. For this reason, it was difficult to draft everything all at once. The drafting of the civil code and civil procedure code was stalled, as France focused its efforts on drafting the criminal code and criminal procedure code. In 1998, only a preliminary draft of the civil procedure code had been prepared—and it was written in French. Drafting of the civil code was almost neglected. Substantial work remained to be carried out on both drafts.

As requested by the government of Cambodia, JICA dispatched a preliminary survey team led by Morishima in February 1998. During a discussion with the team, the Cambodians requested assistance from the Japanese in the initial drafting of the civil code and in finalizing the draft of the civil procedure code—the latter being based on the preliminary draft in French.

In March 1999, the Legal and Judicial Development Project was initiated to assist Cambodia in the drafting of its Civil Code and Civil Procedure Code, and to cultivate the necessary human resources in the legal and judicial sector through that process. According to the Record of Discussions (R/D)[20] signed by the two countries, the strategy to draft a civil procedure code was modified to begin from scratch with Japanese assistance, instead of using the French preliminary draft. There were two major reasons for this change. First, there was criticism within the Cambodian Ministry of Justice that the French preliminary draft was not geared to local realities. Second, the Cambodians understood and supported Morishima's policy to draft these codes in Khmer and in line with local realities, based on discussion between Cambodian and Japanese stakeholders.

The drafting process was facilitated with the creation of a working group[21] in Cambodia and a task force in Japan. The task force[22] was divided into teams in charge of the Civil Code and the Civil Procedure Code. The former was headed by Morishima, whereas the latter was headed by Morio Takeshita,[23] a leading scholar on the Japanese Civil Procedure Code.

The drafting of these two laws alternated between the Cambodian working group and the Japanese task force. First, the working group provided the relevant local information for the task force in Japan to prepare the first draft in Japanese as a springboard for discussion. A rough Khmer translation was shared with

20 See page 59, note 33.

21 The Civil Code and Civil Procedure Code Enactment Committee, consisting of a dozen or so senior Ministry of Justice officials, judges and others.

22 (1) See page 69, note 48, (1).

(2) Original members of the Civil Code Task Force included the following: Akio Morishima, professor, Sophia University; Ikufumi Niimi, professor, Meiji University; Michitaro Urakawa, professor, Waseda University; Kaoru Kamata, professor, Waseda University; Yutaka Yamamoto, professor, Sophia University; Tsuneo Matsumoto, professor, Hitotsubashi University; Yoshihisa Nomi, professor, University of Tokyo; Toyohiro Nomura, professor, Gakushuin University; Masayuki Tanamura, professor, Waseda University; Keita Sato, professor, Chuo University; Atsushi Motoyama, associate professor, Aichi University; Toshifumi Minami, judge, Yokohama District Court; Japanese Ministry of Justice coordinator (titles current at time of writing).

(3) Original members of the Civil Procedure Code Task Force included Morio Takeshita, president and professor, Surugadai University; Toshio Uehara, professor, Hitotsubashi University; Kazuhiko Yamamoto, professor, Hitotsubashi University; Junichi Matsushita, professor, Gakushuin University; Koichi Miki, professor, Keio University; Tatsuo Ikeda, professor, Osaka University; Masahiko Omura, professor, Faculty of Law, Chuo University; Ichiro Kasuga, professor, University of Tsukuba; Masahiro Takada, professor, Waseda

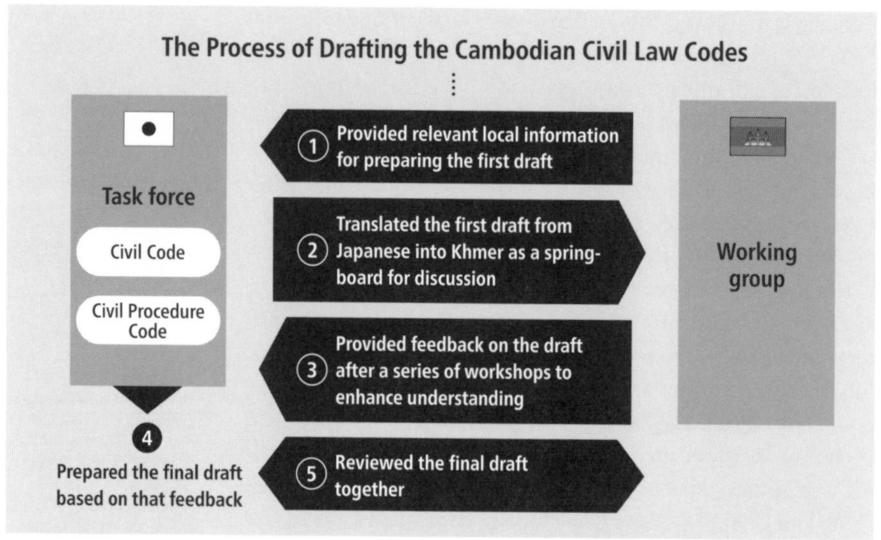

University; Kozo Yanagida, judge, Tokyo District Court; Japanese Ministry of Justice coordinator (titles current at time of writing).

23 Takeshita, an expert in civil procedure law, is a professor emeritus of Hitotsubashi University. He has served as chairman of the Legislative Council of the Japanese Ministry of Justice and president of the Japan Association of the Law of Civil Procedure. As head of the Cambodian Civil Procedure Code Task Force, he played the leading role in drafting the code.

the working group so they could provide feedback, but only after gaining a deep understanding of the document with necessary advice from long-term experts and workshops led by task force members. In addition, the rough translation was scrutinized to decide which legal terms in Khmer should be applied in the letter of the law to express what was intended by the Japanese. Based on the feedback from the working group, the task force then prepared the final draft for a joint review with the Cambodians.

Morio Takeshita

In a clear departure from the approach taken by Japan in other countries, the initial drafts of the legal documents were prepared by the Japanese. This was due to the distinctive circumstances in Cambodia, where there was an utter lack of the necessary professionals needed for drafting laws.

02 A Task Force Made Up of Leading Researchers from Japan

The task force on the Civil Procedure Code held its first meeting in January 1999. In the beginning, they discussed their basic course of action for the project. Takeshita reflects on this discussion:

> There were two possible courses of action that could have been taken. The first approach was to study how litigation is practiced in Cambodia and draft laws that can legally back them up—basically in keeping with the status quo. The second approach was to adequately conform laws to international standards, providing the legal infrastructure for Cambodia to attract foreign investors and develop as a market economy. Our task force leaned toward the latter approach to deliver a civil procedure code that deserves international recognition.

Two months after the first task force meeting, a workshop was organized in Cambodia to coincide with the start of the project. Takeshita, who was present at the time, still clearly remembers what then Undersecretary of State Soth Sothonn[24] remarked on behalf of the Ministry of Justice.

> Undersecretary of State Sothonn clearly told us that they wanted to draft a civil procedure code that would deserve international recognition in the future. By no means did they want to go with the status quo in Cambodia. This was a wish we shared with them, and it made us think that this project was worth doing. Two accompanying members of the task force also shared the same pleasure that we had the same understanding as our Cambodian counterparts. All of us got fired up in this partnership to draft the law.

Two task-force meetings were each held once a month. The civil procedure code meeting usually met in the afternoon of the last Saturday of each month and discussed about twenty to thirty articles per meeting. The drafting assignments were

24 Soth Sothonn was undersecretary of the Ministry of Justice when the Japanese program began, and later, from 2003 to 2008, served as a member of the National Assembly.

divided among the nine members. They brought together their drafts to discuss at the meeting at the end of the month. In addition, they visited Cambodia every quarter to have face-to-face discussions with their local counterparts.

As a member of the working group in Cambodia, You Bunleng explains what the draft presented by the task force was like.

> In their draft, our Japanese colleagues indicated for us why and how they came up with their proposals, including how they reached their decisions and how they compared with the laws of other countries. This allowed us to understand why a particular idea was proposed. Any opposition to an idea required us to closely study the realities in Cambodia, explain our reasoning, discuss it with the Japanese team, and get them to understand. It was quite demanding, but neither side dominated the drafting process. We discussed options and adopted what was more reasonable. Teams from both countries could proceed on the basis of mutual agreement. This was quite sound cooperation.

Some of the task force members were deeply involved in drafting Japanese laws. Members of the civil code task force would later play cardinal roles in the revision of the law of obligations, a part of the Japanese Civil Code.[25] Members of the task force on the Civil Procedure Code included many members of the Legislative Council[26] involved in the 1996 revision of the Japanese Civil Procedure Code.[27] Takeshita, the leader of the task force, served as the chairperson of the council in 2001 during the ongoing project with Cambodia.

Naturally, the task force members were quite busy. Yet, from the beginning until the drafting was complete, almost nobody missed the monthly meetings of the task force on the Civil Procedure Code. Takeshita explains,

> The Japanese team drafted the law based on discussion among all members. As everyone had a shared understanding regarding the draft, one task force member could visit Cambodia and adequately discuss with their Cambodian

25 See page 51, note 15.

26 The Legislative Council, an advisory council of experts within the Japanese Ministry of Justice, studies and discusses civil and criminal law matters and other legal questions and advises the Minister of Justice. Subcommittees are set up as necessary; e.g., the Subcommittee on the Civil Procedure Code.

27 Japan's first Civil Procedure Code, enacted in 1890, remained in effect, with amendments, until undergoing a major revision in 1996.

counterparts, even for the parts not drafted by that member. Of course, one representative alone may make mistakes. Just to be sure, at least two members represented our team during discussions held in Cambodia.

With such sincere efforts by these part-volunteers, the task force kept on working for almost three years. It was genuine dedication by leading law scholars from Japan.

"Truly a team of leading Japanese law scholars," is how Yabuki remembers the task forces on the Civil Code and the Civil Procedure Code. "People in such important positions dedicated their energy to draft laws for another country. This would have been inconceivable by other donors." Yabuki points out that their dedication transformed the mindsets of Japanese lawyers and law students.

People who witnessed the way renowned specialists engaged in heated discussion and put effort into drafting Cambodian laws took interest in cooperation to promote rule of law. Universities began to offer courses in these subjects, which attracted many eager students. The subject became an all-time favorite in law schools. This had been unimaginable in the 1990s. This change was probably owing to the extended engagement of many leading scholars.

The Ministry of Justice

The Japanese Ministry of Justice bound the Civil Procedure Code of Cambodia, along with related laws, into a volume in 2007. With a gentle smile, Takeshita holds up a 1.5-cm-thick A4-sized copy. "When our efforts took shape like this, my heart was filled with joy. We had worked together and overcome many difficulties. I was so glad to see the tangible result. Whenever I open this volume, memories of our discussions fill my mind."

The introduction to the Code of Civil Procedure of Cambodia states that civil procedures are intended for protecting people's rights and that everyone has the right of access to the court. Takeshita explains,

> Normally, civil procedure codes do not mention such facts. It's the civil procedure code that protects the rights of citizens, and it's the civil procedure system that allows them to seek redress from the court when their rights cannot be exercised. As we cooperated in promoting the rule of law, we upheld our purpose to safeguard the human rights of the citizens of our partner country and promote their welfare. That letter of the law is the manifestation of our intent to people in Cambodia. Our Cambodian colleagues also understood this.

The unique introduction in the Cambodian Code of Civil Procedure, not found in its Japanese equivalent, is the message from the Japanese task force members that they cooperated in legal and judicial development for the benefit of citizens of the partner country.

03 Difficulties Involved in Drafting Laws in Khmer

Due to various delays in the drafting process, the Legal and Judicial Development Project, initially intended to end in March 2002, was postponed another year to March 2003. One of the reasons for the initial delay was that the system for getting it set up was not yet in place in Cambodia at the start of the project, what with political factors and a lack of human resources at the Ministry of Justice—the project counterpart. Joint drafting is difficult without a proper implementation system in place in the partner country. Not until the third year of the project could work be carried out smoothly, partly owing to facilitation from Japan to set up an implementation system.

JICA and Japanese stakeholders had never before assisted in drafting a civil code or a civil procedure code from scratch. They did not anticipate some of the problems that emerged in the planning phase, which hampered progress. In particular, a vast amount of time and effort, much greater than initially estimated, proved necessary to translate the Japanese draft and settle upon the correct terms in Khmer.

Issei Sakano

There had been no organized civil code or civil procedure code in Cambodia. The introduction of modern laws to protect the rights of citizens and pursue a sound transition to a market economy would entail the introduction of many new and unfamiliar legal terms and concepts into the country. Issei Sakano[28] was involved in the translation of these documents as a long-term expert. In 1992, he visited Cambodia as a UN volunteer and taught himself Khmer. During the drafting process, Sakano visited the National Archives for three weeks to collect legal terms in Khmer.

> Legal terms are rigidly defined. First of all, I found it extremely difficult to find out whether there are Cambodian terms that carry the same meaning as Japanese legal terms. Many documents were destroyed under Pol Pot's rule, and laws were mostly scattered about or lost. I had to closely examine laws made under French colonial rule and after independence, as well as the ways they were revised. I even collected tattered scraps of paper and documents written in pencil. When I couldn't find the necessary documents, I often directly asked people who used to be judges or had worked at courts. Thanks to the kindness of many people, I managed to gather legal terminology, bit by bit.

28 Sakano spent over a decade working as a long-term expert in Cambodia beginning in 1998. With his excellent knowledge of Khmer, he has contributed greatly to legal and judicial development efforts in Cambodia.

The newly drafted laws employed concepts that could not be expressed with those archaic terms collected from old documents. As a solution, new terms were created in Pali, said to be the root language of Khmer. If that was impossible, a descriptive explanation was employed by combining words. Some everyday words were used to express special meanings. The draft was examined word by word to decide which solution should be used for each term.

Application of the right word is only possible provided the contents of the laws are properly understood. The discussion involved in confirming terminology boosted the competence of the Cambodian counterparts.

In Cambodia, some criticize these new terms in the Civil Code and Civil Procedure Code, saying that they are not sufficiently clear. Chan Sotheavy,[29] the current project manager[30] involved in the drafting process and the only female secretary of state at the Ministry of Justice, analyzes the situation. "New terms are applied to accurately explain the background behind each article of law. Critics of this probably don't yet understand why new terms are necessary." She also recognizes the establishment of new terms as an ongoing task for the future: "The only solution is to familiarize people with new terms. To do so, we need to explain the definition of these terms in detail in addition to explaining the articles of a law. This involves a huge amount of time and effort."

Chan Sotheavy

29 Sotheavy served as vice chair of the Cambodian National Council for Women, on the bench and as an undersecretary of the Ministry of Justice before becoming secretary of state at the Ministry in 2007.

30 When executing a project, JICA usually designates a project director to oversee the project on behalf of the partner government and a project manager to oversee administrative matters.

04 A Civil Code That Incorporates Culture and Tradition

"Citizens reach adulthood at age twenty." "Renting an apartment." "A couple divorces." "A child inherits property after the death of his/her parent." These situations are typical in Japan, but they are possible only thanks to the civil code. A civil code needs to be deeply rooted in a country and underpin the lives of people there. This code is organically intertwined with various factors of local customs and culture such as family, property, and contract. If one country aspires to assist in the drafting of another country's civil code, the first country must deeply understand the country they are offering assistance to.

Under the Civil Code of Japan, a couple is supposed to choose either the husband's or the wife's surname when they marry. This provision is premised on the culture of Japan, where people carry both a surname that represents their familial affiliation and an individual given name. In contrast, there is no unified rule regarding surnames and given names among Cambodians. In some families, married couples use the same surname, but others do not. Some use surnames that incorporate part of the given names of their parents or ancestors. At the final stage of drafting the Civil Code, attorney Yoshiko Homma[31] found it quite difficult to design a family law that would be relevant to this kind of family structure. "I couldn't learn of any consistent rule on surnames or given names, not even from local judges. I conducted many more interviews, but the rules were still not clear. It took great effort for our team to draft the relevant provisions."

Whether local tradition and customs should be codified was also a sensitive issue, she found.

> For instance, Cambodian men observe a matrilocal custom and live with their fiancées at their parents' homes, but this was never codified. If it were made into a law, it would be enforceable, and we agonized over the extent to which such customs should be codified. The family law part of the civil code must respect local customs. The experience brought home to me how difficult it is for us foreigners to understand and codify Cambodian customs.

More than 1,300 articles of the Civil Code were repeatedly worked over to make the Code appropriate to the lives of the Cambodian people. In the process, each clause was carefully discussed with an eye to respecting the local culture. For instance,

31 Homma, an attorney registered with the Tokyo Bar Association, is a professor of international law studies and civil jurisprudence at Soka University Law School. She served as a long-term expert in Cambodia from 2002 to 2004. On her return to Japan, she remained involved in legal and judicial development efforts as a member of the Cambodian Civil Procedure Code Task Force.

unlike the Japanese Civil Code, the Cambodian Civil Code adopted a shared property principle to respect the indigenous system governing the property of married couples. Likewise, it adopted the indigenous system for divorce property settlement after some modifications, instead of introducing the Japanese model. Conversely, mortgages[32] and other concepts and systems that had been alien in Cambodia were introduced to support their market economy. As You Bunleng points out, "These provisions and systems made it possible for our people's property to be utilized effectively in the market economy, without leaving it to stand idle."

32 A mortgage is a security interest in real property held as security for a debt. If not repaid, the creditor can sell the property and recover the amount owed from the proceeds. Mortgages are recorded in the real estate registry.

The final drafts of the Civil Code and the Civil Procedure Code were completed and handed over to the Ministry of Justice in March 2003. These were the products of joint efforts by the Cambodians and the Japanese that had overcome countless difficulties. The Civil Procedure Code was applied on July 6, 2007. The Civil Code would be applied after the promulgation on December 8, 2007, and the other related laws were enacted on December 20, 2011.

05 A Feud among Aid Agencies

The Legal and Judicial Development Project was completed once the final drafts of the Civil Code and Civil Procedure Code were handed over. Enactment of these laws required their passage at the National Assembly[33] after due review by the Council of Ministers[34] and the National Assembly. After the drafts were submitted, the Ministry of Justice required assistance in providing explanations as they were reviewed, and in making necessary modifications afterward. In addition, various laws and regulations to supplement the Civil Code and the Civil Procedure Code had to be drafted before these codes could start to be implemented. To address this, Phase II of the Legal and Judicial Development Project began in April 2004, immediately after the completion of Phase I.

33 The National Assembly is the lower house of the Kingdom of Cambodia's bicameral legislature.

34 The Council of Ministers is the equivalent of the cabinet.

Most provisions did not require any major revisions throughout the legislative process. But the Land Law[35] and Secured Transactions Law[36] had been drafted with assistance from other aid agencies, and therefore adopted different systems from that in the Civil Code drafted with Japanese cooperation. It took a vast amount of effort and time to coordinate and make the necessary adjustments.

Japan is just one of many countries and international agencies that are involved in the cooperation for legal and judicial development in Cambodia. An initial draft of the Land Law was drawn up by the Ministry of Agriculture in 1992 upon the receipt of financial assistance from the Asia Development Bank (ADB).[37] The drafting was later taken over by the Ministry of Land Management, Urban Planning and Construction (hereafter Ministry of Land[38]) before the revision in 2001. Because the revised Land Law preceded the Civil Code, it contained provisions governing land transactions and land registration procedures which really should have already been stipulated in the Civil Code or other related laws. They included the systems pertaining to the provisions for real estate transaction agreements and transfer of ownership, which differed from the principles of those being drafted for the Civil Code at the time. More specifically, while the draft Civil Code stipulated that real estate ownership transfer must be done by mutual agreement,[39] the Land Law relied on registration.[40] However, a cadastral survey had not been conducted throughout Cambodia, and as yet there was no comprehensive registration system. Registration as a precondition for real estate ownership transfer therefore should have posed a huge impediment for the country, which was why the draft Civil Code relied on mutual agreement to effect land transactions. Notwithstanding this, Akio Morishima says, as a condition of their provision of finance, international financial institutions (such as the ADB) demanded the introduction of security, registration, and other systems for ensuring the recovery of loans they offered. They did not seem to care how the systems underpinning private law should be organized, but offered ad hoc systems that served the interest of financial institutions.[41] They had a piecemeal land registration system introduced into a part of Phnom Penh, and stipulated in the Land Law the requirement for registration for

35 The Land Law set out procedures for reestablishing land ownership after it had been disrupted by the civil war, and regulating the purchase, sale, lease and mortgage of land. See page 103, note 12.

36 The Secured Transactions Law governed the creation of security interests over assets other than real property and established the necessary procedures to do so. It was enacted by the Ministry of Commerce with the assistance of the Asia Development Bank (ADB).

37 See page 47, note 9.

38 Officially the Ministry of Land Management, Urban Planning and Construction. Established in 1999.

39 Mutual agreement refers to the principle that, in a real estate transaction, title is transferred without the need for further paperwork as long as agreement exists between the parties. This is the principle followed in Japan. Real estate is a valuable asset, however, and the registered title must be transferred in order to assert the transfer of title against a third party. This is called the perfection requirement.

40 Registration refers to the principle that the registered title must be transferred in order for the transfer of title to be valid, the agreement of the parties being insufficient on its own. This is called the validity requirement.

41 Source: Akio Morishima, "Kanbojia minpo soan no kiso shien jigyo ni tazusawatte" [Taking part in the project to assist in drafting of the Cambodian Civil Code], *ICD News* no. 11 (September 2003): 4–131.

real estate transactions in Cambodia, which did not have any national land registry.

As the draft of the Civil Code was almost ready, the Japanese team requested the deletion of provisions on registration in the Land Law, relying on the Ministry of Justice to act as a liaison; but the Ministry of Land complied with the wishes of the ADB, and did not agree to the modification. To resolve this problem, Morishima, the leader of the civil code task force, visited Washington, DC, at the end of 2002 to discuss and coordinate with ADB and the World Bank, which had been helping to introduce the land registration system into Cambodia. The World Bank readily understood that land transaction would be virtually impossible if registration were required in a country with an underdeveloped registration system. Ultimately, however, agreement had to be reached with regard to the existing provisions in the Land Law to include a clause in the draft of the Civil Code. This would require registration for transactions of land which *had* already been registered.

On the other hand, the rift over the Secured Transactions Law could not be bridged despite all the effort put in. The Secured Transactions Law was drafted by the Ministry of Commerce with assistance from the ADB. They were about to introduce a system that would undermine the efficacy of some provisions in the draft Civil Code related to security. Although this became known, coordination failed between the Ministry of Justice and Ministry of Commerce, and the secured transaction bill ended up with the Council of Ministers. Later, the Japanese also encouraged the government of Cambodia to modify this bill. Unfortunately, the law was promulgated without resolving its contradiction with the Civil Code. Though the Law on the Implementation of the Civil Code addressed the contradiction afterward, the risk remains that problems will arise in its application in the future due to the complexity of these provisions.

One of the reasons behind these problems involving the Civil Code, Land Law, and Secured Transactions Law was the inadequate capacity of the government of Cambodia of the day in bridging the differences among the Ministry of Justice, the Ministry of Land, and the Ministry of Commerce. Because the ADB and other donors provide loans to developing countries in exchange for the enactment of specific laws, the government of Cambodia, as their loan recipient, could not address certain contradictions even if they wanted to. This kind of problem always haunts countries assisted by multiple aid agencies. The issue left a huge impact on the project, highlighting the difficulty of the coordination among aid agencies and contradictory laws.

Another problem that should be pointed out with Japan's cooperation for legal and judicial development is its modest international appeal. Yoshiko Homma, mentioned earlier, participated in a conference of aid agencies in Cambodia, where she was asked what kind of assistance Japan could provide. "Later," she said, "I was asked the same question by my host when I paid a courtesy call to the World Bank." Homma explained that Japan provided assistance in drafting of the Civil Code and the Civil Procedure Code. Then she was asked whether there was an English version available. No English version was then available as the codes were being drafted in Japanese and Khmer. "Upon hearing my explanation, my host called the drafts meaningless, as they were not in English. I was shocked and mortified. I still can't forget that exchange."

At a seminar

Later, Homma began periodically to issue English reports about the Japanese teams' current project activities to other aid agencies. Immediately after she started doing so, they expressed surprise: "We didn't know that your team was doing these wonderful things!" Homma continues, "That left a strong impression on me. I found that publications in English alone boosted our international appeal. But it also made me realize how Japanese contributions are not fairly appreciated."

Issei Sakano (see page 113), recalls that when arguments occurred, Japan did not have the clout to hold serious discussions with other aid agencies and win. He goes on to point out a challenge that still remains today: "Japan was always a step behind in dealing with issues relating to the Land Law and Secured Transactions Law, and it allowed the complications to grow worse. Japanese tend to think that quiet, diligent work is rewarded. But it is high time for us to take the initiative in fixing problems and to effectively explain to other aid agencies how we provide assistance." The chaos involving the Land Law and Secured Transactions Law in Cambodia highlights the need for Japan to enhance its international presence in countries where it provides cooperation for legal and judicial development.

06 I Can't Draw a Giraffe If I've Never Seen One

Phase II of the Legal and Judicial Development Project was completed in April 2008. During the project, the Civil Procedure Code was enforced. Preparation for the enforcement of the Civil Code was in steady progress. Training programs and seminars were organized mainly for drafting other related laws, along with clause-by-clause commentary on both codes and compilation of textbooks. During this period, however, the project members from Cambodia became extremely busy. Many of the members who had been involved in the drafting process up to Phase II assumed such important positions as minister of justice, Secretary of State for the Ministry of Justice, and judge of the Supreme Court. On top of this, the country had a small

The Ministry of Land

supply of human resources to begin with, so the project members built up their know-how through the drafting and legislation process. As a result, much of the higher administrative work fell to them, making it increasingly difficult for them to participate in the project activities. Moreover, You Bunleng and some others had to retire from the project after being appointed as judges of the Khmer Rouge Tribunal. Such problems arose as a result of the enhanced capacity of the members who had propelled this project so far.

Phase III of the Legal and Judicial Development Project, starting in April 2008, was mainly conducted in Cambodia, and was based on the output from the project up to Phase II. Younger members joined the drafting process of other related laws to relieve former members, who were now too busy, of their burdens.

The work procedure also changed. Hitherto, the Japanese team had provided outlines of laws as a basis for initiating discussion. In this new phase, the drafting team from the Cambodian Ministry of Justice independently drafted laws with assistance from the Japanese long-term experts and the task forces in Japan. More than ten laws were drafted in this project. Notably, two joint ministerial ordinances on the registration of real estate, one concerning the Civil Procedure Code[42] and another concerning the Civil Code,[43] were drafted in an unprecedented

42 These were called joint ministerial ordinances because they were issued jointly by the Ministry of Justice and the Ministry of Land. The ordinance concerning the Civil Procedure Code sets out procedures for registering action taken by a court with respect to real property based on the Code, such as compulsory execution measures (attachment and compulsory auctions) and provisional remedies (provisional attachment and provisional disposition).

43 This ordinance set out procedures for registering transfers of rights executed under the provisions of the Civil Code, such as the purchase, sale, and inheritance of real estate; the granting of usufruct rights; and the creation of security interests.

effort by the joint committee formed by the Ministry of Justice and the Ministry of Land with jurisdiction over registration. The committee fostered cooperation among personnel involved in registration in one way or another. Their participation in the committee enabled Ministry of Justice personnel to understand the unfamiliar on-site registration procedure. Similarly, Ministry of Land personnel were able to deepen their understanding of the Civil Code and Civil Procedure Code, providing a legal basis for their registration practice.

During her long-term assignment, Emiko Kanetake,[44] a Japanese judicial scrivener, assisted in the drafting of the two joint ministerial ordinances on real estate registration, a ministerial ordinance on registration of juridical persons/corporations/legal entities,[45] and a ministerial ordinance on marital property agreement registration.[46] When she joined the project halfway through Phase III in April 2010, meetings for these four ordinances had been scheduled to take place once or twice a week. But the poor attendance by team members hampered the drafting process. With only two years left, the project could not afford to lose any more time. So Kanetake began to visit the members at their offices in turn. "I knocked on each door and asked them in person to attend an upcoming meeting. I also spoke with Secretary of State Chan Sotheavy at the Ministry of Justice, who was the project manager, to help speed up the work being done by the drafting team."

Emiko Kanetake

Finally, the members began to attend meetings properly. Most of them were junior professionals whose knowledge of the Civil Code or Civil Procedure Code was not sufficient for them to take the initiative in drafting ministerial ordinances. As the core principle of Phase III was to get the drafting team to take the initiative in the drafting process, Kanetake felt that this principle was being jeopardized. She began to lecture them on the Civil Code and Civil Procedure Code. After each lecture, focusing on parts that were relevant to the drafting of ministerial

44 Kanetake, a judicial scrivener, was stationed in Cambodia as a long-term expert from 2010 to 2013. She subsequently became a legal advisor to the Cambodian Ministry of Land.

45 This ordinance, issued by the Ministry of Justice, sets out procedures for registering and disclosing the necessary information when establishing a company.

46 Another Ministry of Justice ordinance. The assets of married couples are regulated by the Civil Code, but married couples are free to conclude their own agreement on different terms. This ordinance sets out procedures for registering a special agreement of this nature and disclosing it to business partners and others.

ordinances, she would assign the team the "homework" of coming up with proposed provisions in the meeting in the following week. Kanetake worked with Masayoshi Harada,[47] another long-term expert, to support the drafting team and draw up their own version. Every week, they compared the provisions proposed by the drafting team with their version to fine-tune their draft proposal. Kanetake recalls the challenges that the team faced.

> They lacked knowledge—but it is understandable that they wouldn't know about laws and institutions that they never had. I remember one time when we were drafting provisions on revolving mortgages.[48] The team members had only just started learning about mortgages, so revolving mortgages were even newer to them. Regardless, we had to draft provisions on revolving mortgages right then and there. That's when one of the team members said, "I can't draw a giraffe if I've never seen one!"
>
> I probably can't understand medical terminology because I just don't have knowledge in that field. The issue was the same here. The fact that people don't have knowledge of something doesn't mean that they cannot understand it. Even if they don't know what a giraffe is, they can draw it once they are taught what that animal looks like. From then on, I began to empathize with them by remembering the days when I first started studying law. It was hardly surprising if they did not know a specific legal term.

Kanetake took every opportunity to visit the members of the drafting team and communicate her feelings in words, making efforts to deepen her relationships with them through daily conversations. "I didn't particularly distinguish my daily communications from the meetings with the drafting team. I tried to build trust by explaining both my feelings and the law equally, in every way I could." Kanetake's approach gradually won her the confidence of the drafting team. Team members began to regularly attend meetings, but they initially hesitated to ask questions. They were simply embarrassed by their lack of knowledge.

Kanetake told them that she also did not know anything in

47 Harada, a lawyer registered with the Aichi Bar Association, was stationed in Cambodia as a long-term expert from 2010 to 2012. He is currently deputy director of the International Trade and Investment Dispute Settlement Division, Economic Affairs Bureau, Japanese Ministry of Foreign Affairs.

48 Whereas a regular mortgage (see page 116, note 32) is used to secure a single debt, with a revolving mortgage the same collateral can be used to secure multiple debts up to a set limit when a line of credit is tapped repeatedly, such as for business purposes.

the beginning. "For me, it was a given to have this knowledge. Unlike the Cambodians, who had hardly any books on laws, I could access tens of thousands of books in Japan to study whenever I wanted." But she repeatedly reminded the team that she did not have this knowledge from the beginning. Hearing this from her, the members began to change their attitudes. "They began to feel that it was totally fine to ask questions. Then I asked them to discuss and come up with their own answers to a given question before I told them the answer. Once that habit of thinking is established, their capacity can be built up."

Kanetake motivated the members by giving them positive feedback on the draft provisions they brought every week while making necessary corrections. Initially, members would not attend meetings unless she knocked on their doors. But half a year later, they began taking the initiative, and even requested ad hoc meetings. "Almost 80 percent of my weekly schedule was filled up with various meetings with the drafting team, half of which was ad hoc meetings. With their newly acquired knowledge, they found it interesting to engage in discussion."

Kanetake also recalls a moment when she almost cried with joy to see how much the members had grown. It happened during a seminar on real estate registration in March of the year after she arrived in Cambodia.

Attachment,[49] provisional attachment,[50] and provisional disposition[51] are three different types of procedures involved in real estate and debts. They carry almost the same meaning as "prohibition of disposition," but they must be distinguished according to the different stages at which they are used. The members of the drafting team regarded these three types as the same. Kanetake explained to them, "At the introductory level, these procedures can be regarded as similar, but they need to be treated differently to properly draft laws. Let's understand these three procedures one by one." She then conducted lectures on these procedures for three to four months. In due course, the members could easily explain the differences between these three procedures during a seminar on real estate registration. "I noticed a radical change in them. I guess their growth became a source of motivation for me."

49 A court prohibition on the disposal of property by the borrower before compulsory execution measures are initiated.

50 If, say, a creditor files a suit to collect money owed, it takes time for a final decision to be reached. Provisional attachment is a means of preventing the borrower from concealing or spending his or her assets in the meantime, by placing temporary restrictions on their disposition.

51 Whereas provisional attachment (note 50) involves seizing the borrower's assets to ensure that money owed can be recovered, provisional disposition is an order issued to ensure enforcement of the court's decision in cases of nonmonetary claims (e.g., the transfer of a specific item of property, or temporary maintenance of an employee's position during a wrongful dismissal suit).

In addition to their deeper knowledge and greater skills, the change in their mindsets was also remarkable. "They began to treat their laws as their own children. The sense of ownership translated into expectation that people would respect them, which made them think hard how to make sure that people would abide by the laws. They paid close attention to the wording of each provision and took the initiative, saying, for example, 'Oh, this term is unclear, so let's add a description.'"

Kanetake recalls, "The drafting process was so intense that I didn't have time to gain a sense of achievement. That changed gradually as we saw our Cambodian colleagues gaining knowledge, their mindset changing and their motivation increasing." She sought heartfelt communication with her Cambodian counterparts using every possible means to make progress together, step by step. Through this approach, Kanetake truly embodied the spirit behind Japan's cooperation for legal and judicial development.

07 Cultivating Talent among the Younger Generations

The final drafts of the Civil Code and Civil Procedure Code were completed in 2003. While the assistance in their legislation and preparation of other related laws was underway, a new challenge emerged in anticipation of their enactment and enforcement—development of staff who could properly apply these new codes. In November 2005, the Project for Improvement of Training on Civil Matters at the Royal School for Judges and Prosecutors was launched to support the fledgling Royal School for Judges and Prosecutors (RSJP).[52]

The government of Cambodia gave top priority to legal and judicial reform. In November 2003, it opened the RSJP in order to address the critical shortage of workers in the legal and judicial sector. The school initially faced various obstacles, including an inadequate curriculum, short supply of learning aids, and instructors with a poor understanding of the Civil Code and Civil Procedure Code. Worse still, all the instructors were employed

52 A school that trains future judges and prosecutors en bloc. Enrollees must have studied law at university and passed the entrance exam. Their career path is decided upon graduation. The RSJP became one of the four schools under the Royal Academy for Judicial Professions (RAJP) in 2005.

on a part-time basis. If something came up at their main job, classes would not be held as scheduled or would be poorly prepared, and the quality of instruction could not be maintained.

The project was carried out to develop a curriculum for civil affairs training and to prepare lecture materials. The Procedure Manual for First Trials of Civil Affairs was created as a training aid for the Civil Procedure Code by first translating the training aid that had been used at the Legal Training and Research Institute in Japan into Khmer, and subsequently adjusting it to the Cambodian Civil Procedure Code. The project started before the Civil Code and Civil Procedure Code passed the National Assembly. But Supreme Court Judge Kim Sathavy, who served as the first president of RSJP, explains that they had already conducted training during the drafting process of these codes in anticipation for their future application.

Initially, this project was led by a working group set up with instructors and managers of RSJP to develop training aids and syllabuses. However, all of these instructors were part-timers who had main jobs as judges and the like. They overlapped with the members of the ongoing Phase II of the Legal and Judicial Development Project in partnership with Japan. The additional activities from the new project put them under extreme pressure. The Japanese counterparts changed their approach once they realized that the planned activities had stalled.

Noriko Shibata,[53] the first long-term expert in the Project for Improvement of Training on Civil Matters at the Royal School for Judges and Prosecutors, describes the situation back then:

53 Shibata, a prosecutor stationed in Cambodia as a long-term expert 2006–2008, became deputy director of the ICD on returning to Japan. She has been Crime Prevention and Criminal Justice Officer at the Regional Office for Southeast Asia and the Pacific of the United Nations Office on Drugs and Crime (UNODC) since December 2015.

> The original working group was formed by judges of the Supreme Court and Secretaries of State at the Ministry of Justice. They were quite busy playing many roles. So as a last resort, we formed a team of fresh graduates from RSJP. We called them instructor candidates, though they were not expected to be of immediate use. Nonetheless, we

Noriko Shibata

formed a working group with these junior professionals to jointly develop training aids and a curriculum in the hope that they would lead the judiciary branch of Cambodia and become instructors in twenty years' time.

The members of the new working group, including the instructor candidates, quickly acquired professional skills as they created simulated records and procedure manuals as learning aids for civil trial procedures.

"Eight years after the start of my assignment in Cambodia, as of 2014, these members are leading local judicial practices with the skills they have developed."[54]

Some of these members became lecturers at academies for court secretaries[55] or associate professors of the Center for Lawyers Training and Professional Improvement (LTC).[56] More of them are now ready to train the younger generation.

The initial project was completed in April 2008 after two years and five months of cooperation. This was followed by Phase II of the project, which further assisted the capacity building of RSJP. Focusing as it did on developing the skills of instructor candidates, by its end, Phase II had succeeded in enabling forty of them to conduct lectures just like instructors. These instructor candidates drafted training aids based on lectures by Japanese experts, and incorporated comments from these experts. They

54 See Noriko Shibata, "Kanbojia hoseibi shien no kako, genzai, mirai" [The past, present and future of Cooperation for Legal and Judicial Development in Cambodia], *ICCLC News* no. 33 (October 2014): 17–36.

55 Court secretaries are officers who keep trial records, manage court proceedings, and assist the judge. The exact range of their duties differs from country to country.

56 The LTC is a law school that trains future lawyers. It was established under the auspices of the Bar Association of the Kingdom of Cambodia. Enrollees must have studied law at university and passed the entrance exam.

The Royal Academy for Judicial Professions (RAJP)

took initiatives to compile Q&As on civil cases, civil execution, and civil preservation. They also revised the Procedure Manual for First Trials of Civil Affairs.

President Chhorn Proloeung[57] of the Royal Academy for Judicial Professions (RAJP),[58] the superior institution of RSJP, expects much from the instructor candidates "who should no longer be called 'candidates,' as they are capable of training their juniors. They're able to update their materials by themselves from now on."

These instructor candidates are already playing active roles as instructors for enforcement officers[59] and notaries[60] at the RAJP. The benefits proved more extensive than expected as the project also helped train judicial staff who were not directly targeted. Training was effectively conducted in tandem with other projects being conducted by JICA. For example, instructor candidates attended seminars organized by the Ministry of Justice as a part of the Legal and Judicial Development Project.

08 Training of Lawyers Resumes

Cooperation for legal and judicial development in Cambodia was also conducted in the form of assistance from the Japan Federation of Bar Associations (JFBA) to the Bar Association of the Kingdom of Cambodia (BAKC). The partnership between the two bar associations dates back to 1996, when the JFBA provided a lecturer for the training of Cambodian lawyers who were invited to Japan. The trainees included people who would later play important roles in the Cambodian legal community and a range of JICA projects. Examples include the current Minister of Justice Ang Vong Vathana,[61] Y Dan,[62] and You Bunleng. In 2000, the JFBA applied and was chosen by JICA to conduct seminars in Cambodia in a Small Partnership Project[63] to assist the local bar association,[64] commencing in 2001. For an additional three years starting in 2002, the JFBA conducted another project to assist the local bar association in a Development Partner Project[65] with JICA (Legal and Judicial Cooperation for the Bar Association of

57 Proloeung completed a doctorate at Peoples' Friendship University of Russia and taught there as an assistant professor before returning to Cambodia. After serving on the Council of Jurists of the Council of Ministers, he became president of the RAJP in 2011.

58 Set up in 2005, the RAJP consists of the Royal School for Judges and Prosecutors and three other schools: one for court clerks, one for enforcement officers, and one for notaries.

59 Court officers responsible for compulsory execution procedures.

60 Individuals authorized to validate legal acts (such as contracts) and attest to certain facts. Depending on the country they may be either public officials or private practitioners licensed or certified by the government.

61 Vathana was studying in France when the Khmer Rouge came to power. After returning to Cambodia, he served successively as an UNTAC election officer, advisor to the deputy prime minister, and secretary of state at the Ministry of Justice. He became minister of justice in 2004.

62 Dan was undersecretary of state of the Ministry of Justice when the Japanese legal and judicial development program began. He later became secretary of state at the Ministry of Justice, in which position he continued to develop cooperative links with Japan. He passed away in June 2007.

the Kingdom of Cambodia). This project was mainly aimed at resuming the operation of the Center for Lawyers Training and Professional Improvement (LTC).

The LTC was established with American sponsorship following the enactment of the Law on the Bar[66] in 1995. They trained up to the class of the third year, but the center could not operate after the discontinuation of American sponsorship following the armed conflict in 1997. As there were no other institutes offering special training in laws for attorneys, no training of attorneys took place for almost five years in Cambodia. The original shortage of legal professionals was exacerbated by the paralysis of the academy of lawyers, which naturally invited social criticism. Seeking a breakthrough, the BAKC requested assistance from the JFBA. In 2002, the LTC made a new start as an academy sponsored by Japan to develop curricula and textbooks on the Civil Code and the Civil Procedure Code, as well as continued professional training for practicing attorneys.

In June 2007, or one and a half years after the commencement of the Project for Improvement of Training on Civil Matters at the Royal School for Judges and Prosecutors, the Project for the Legal and Judicial Cooperation for the Bar Association of the Kingdom of Cambodia began to train attorneys who would serve the legal community along with judges and public prosecutors. This new project was conducted to further the two earlier activities by the JFBA. The main thrust of this project was the improvement of the operation of the LTC and the quality of training. Seminars and training were conducted to ensure continued education of students at the LTC and of practicing lawyers.

To align courses and continued education offered at the LTC, training aids developed in other JICA projects, such as a textbook on the Civil Procedure Code and a DVD of a simulated trial for learning the proceeding of first trials of civil affairs, were utilized. For continued education, a working group formed by active lawyers developed a handbook of requisite facts.[67] Moreover, Japanese experts conducted several lectures a year that proved popular, each attracting about a hundred lawyers.

Since its establishment, the LTC has produced fifty to seventy graduates every year. As of August 2016, 723 out of 1,134

63 Small Partnership Projects are conducted by JICA under a program to support NGOs, universities, and other organizations in their efforts to assist developing countries. Small-scale undertakings of one year's duration are eligible for the program.

64 During this project the JFBA, which applied for the JICA small partnership program as a nongovernmental organization, assisted the Bar Association of the Kingdom of Cambodia by conducting seminars on civil law.

65 Development Partner Projects, like Small Partnership Projects (note 63), are a way for JICA to support NGOs and other organizations in their efforts to assist developing countries. They currently take the form of Grassroots Technical Cooperation Projects.

66 The Law of the Bar regulates lawyer licensing requirements, the disciplining of lawyers, and the establishment and operation of bar associations.

67 Requisite facts are the constituent elements into which an act or an event involving different parties can be broken down from a legal standpoint to give it legal effect. For example, before you can bill someone a million yen for the purchase of a car, three specific elements must be in place: you must have (1) concluded a contract (2) to sell that car (3) for a million yen. The working group put together a handbook explaining that principle and giving typical cases of its application in a Cambodian context.

lawyers in Cambodia are LTC graduates. In only thirteen years since its opening, the LTC has trained more than half of Cambodia's lawyers.

09 The LTC and Activities by the JFBA Resume

Kimitoshi Yabuki, as the leader of the JFBA's international judicial assistance, wryly reflects on the resumed operation of the LTC: "We had to do everything laboriously from scratch. We were worried whether we could really make it. But at the same time, we were excited that we could try out our ideas."

To start with, classroom space is necessary to set up an academy, but that space could not easily be secured. Yabuki sought help from Yuok Ngoy,[68] who participated in the first training in Japan in 1996. "Mr. Ngoy was the president of the academy of laws, which later became the Royal University of Law and Economics (RULE).[69] He helped us to rent two rooms for conducting classes." Teachers were contacted by Yabuki himself at a party of the Cambodian Ministry of Justice. "I approached Ngoy's fellow trainees starting in 1996, like You Bunleng, and asked each of them to become an instructor for the LTC."

Students of the Royal University of Law and Economics (RULE)

68 After working at the Ministry of Education, became deputy director of RULE's predecessor, the National Institute of Law, Politics and Economics, in 1989. Was rector of RULE from 2004 to 2010.

69 Originally founded in 1949 as the National Institute of Law, Politics and Economics, becoming the Royal University of Law and Economics (RULE) in 2003. The University has trained more legal professionals than any other institution in Cambodia. The Nagoya University CALE Research and Education Center for Japanese Law is located on campus.

The questions for the entrance exams had to be written out by hand. "Our team met in a hotel room with the president of the bar association, Secretary of State of the Ministry of Justice, and judges, and spent the night making cheat-proof questions. They were one-sentence questions, but we had to manually write a copy for each examinee, as we didn't have a photocopying machine. The next morning, we put them in an envelope and took them to the test site." The information was thoroughly controlled to prevent leaks and cheating. Examinees' mobile phones were even collected to disable communication beyond the test site.

"Once I accomplish one thing, I already begin to think of the next step. So I rarely feel a sense of achievement," Yabuki explains. But gazing at a photo from the first graduation ceremony after the reopening of the LTC, he admits, smiling, "There was a sense of accomplishment when students graduated from the academy we painstakingly created together."

The direct assistance to the LTC from the JFBA was discontinued following the completion of the Legal and Judicial Cooperation for the Bar Association of the Kingdom of Cambodia by JICA. Even so, the collaboration between the bar associations continues to this day. During the project, the LTC offered education free of charge: but afterwards they began to charge an annual tuition fee of $2,000.

> They say that they will have to charge tuition once funding from JICA is discontinued. I initially thought it was unacceptable to charge tuition fees, but those funds will allow the LTC to sustain its operations and continue to produce new graduates every year without assistance from JICA.
>
> Collection of tuition fees demonstrates the sense of ownership by our Cambodian partner. A project is not a genuine success unless the product can be reshaped to fit the needs of local partners. In fifty years' time, no one at the academy will remember that the JFBA was involved. Only when that happens may we have a genuine sense of accomplishment.

This is how Yabuki feels after his long engagement with the cooperation for legal and judicial development in Cambodia.

10 Breathing New Life into the Project

Three projects were concurrently conducted starting in the mid-2000s in the field of legal and judicial development: the Legal and Judicial Development Project, the Project for Improvement of Training on Civil Matters at the Royal School for Judges and Prosecutors, and the Legal and Judicial Cooperation for the Bar Association of the Kingdom of Cambodia. In the first project, the Civil Code was put into force in December 2011 following the completion of other related laws for the Civil Code and the Civil Procedure Code. The next two projects targeted law practitioners trained by the RSJP[70] and the LTC. As the Civil Code and the Civil Procedure Code finally entered the application phase after earnest discussions and painstaking efforts, the emphasis of the project shifted from providing cooperation in making laws to cooperation in their application.

70 See page 125, note 52.

In 2012, a new project titled "Legal and Judicial Development Project (Phase IV)" integrated the earlier three projects into a single project while focusing on developing capable professionals who were expected to play a core role in the Cambodian legal community. They were to ensure that the Civil Code, the Civil Procedure Code, and other related laws would take root in the country. Intended targets included personnel of the Ministry of Justice, judges, prosecutors, lawyers, and teachers at the Royal University of Law and Economics (RULE). RULE was added to the existing counterparts (MOJ, RAJP/RSJP, and BAKC) jointly conducting this new project. Each of these four organizations formed their own working groups and engaged in discussions with their Japanese counterparts.

Japanese long-term experts exercised their ingenuity in their discussions with these working groups to build up their practical skills. Yasuhiko Tsuji[71] carefully crafted summaries for discussions with the RULE working group. Case studies reflected the lifestyles of Cambodians in order to stimulate interest among Cambodian members through realistic scenarios.

71 Tsuji, a prosecutor who supported efforts to promote the rule of law in Cambodia and elsewhere as an ICD professor in Japan, was later stationed in Cambodia as a long-term expert (2014–2017).

One case study on the marital property system defined in

the Civil Code was a story of a couple that detailed everything from the moment they met until when they divorced. Possible issues involving property were embedded in the story. A typical Cambodian couple was represented, in terms of their ages at marriage, as well as their occupations and incomes. In this manner, fellow members could realistically imagine the application of the Civil Code.

Yasuhiko Tsuji

In this project, the working groups of each organization were formed mainly of junior professionals in their twenties and thirties. Attorney Sadao Matsubara[72] looks back on his long-term assignment that ended in 2014: "Most of the junior professionals participated in the group with a hunger for pursuing their studies. I enjoyed my discussions with them in the weekly study sessions." Ayako Tamiya,[73] another attorney who supported the MOJ and BAKC working groups, comments on her long-term assignment that ended in 2013: "Among the group members, the lawyers demonstrated a particularly ardent desire to learn new laws, as they needed to address questions and consultations from their clients in their day-to-day work." These highly motivated junior professionals sought greater skills and deeper knowledge and breathed new life into the project, which had depended on a limited number of regular members due to the shortage of human resources.

Sadao Matsubara

Ayako Tamiya

72 Matsubara, an attorney registered with the Dai-Ichi Tokyo Bar Association and former prosecutor, supported efforts to promote the rule of law in Cambodia as an ICD professor in Japan. Later stationed in Cambodia as a long-term expert (2012–2014), he is currently an advisor at a Phnom Penh law firm.

73 Tamiya, an attorney registered with the Dai-Ichi Tokyo Bar Association, was stationed in Cambodia as a long-term expert 2011–2013. She is currently an advisor at a Phnom Penh law firm.

11 | A Civil Code That Can Last a Century—Too Futuristic and Incomprehensible?

In their reconstruction and nation-building efforts in war-torn Cambodia, local partners apparently sought to draft a civil code that would last a century. Respecting their wishes, leading Japanese law scholars formed task forces and prepared an initial draft after rounds of discussions. The new Civil Code and Civil Procedure Code, drafted by devoted lawyers from both countries, included many systems that were alien to Cambodia. Some provisions were based on legal precedents that are not even codified in Japan yet.

However, despite the best efforts of all project members, the Civil Code and Civil Procedure Code are criticized by some Cambodians for their "complicated and unwieldy provisions." It is naturally difficult to understand and apply precise laws. Some point out clumsy expressions originating from the literal translations of Japanese into Khmer, which were included to accurately express the intent of the laws.

One of the major obstacles for Cambodian lawyers in understanding new laws is the underdeveloped state of legal studies in the country. Even when practitioners can already conduct trials and engage in practical discussions, they rarely engage in scholarly discussions to interpret laws and refine desirable legal

The Civil Code and Civil Procedure Code

systems. In Japan, law students can consult textbooks to check whether their understanding of a law is correct. There are no such in-depth textbooks on the Cambodian Civil Code or Civil Procedure Code. Detailed clause-by-clause commentaries are available, but they alone cannot explain the underlying legal theories behind the provisions. "In Japan, laws can be studied alone, as there is an abundance of books. In contrast, self-education is almost impossible in Cambodia, where there are only provisions, commentaries, and a few books issued through JICA projects," Matsubara explains, adding that learning aids were in short supply for anyone seeking to gain a deeper understanding of new laws.

Sometimes misunderstandings among Cambodian colleagues due to this lack of learning aids on basic legal theories went unnoticed by the Japanese. Atsushi Kamiki,[74] for example, experienced one such misunderstanding about the double refund of earnest money[75] during his long-term assignment for the Legal and Judicial Cooperation for the Bar Association of the Kingdom of Cambodia and other projects, starting in 2005.

Atsushi Kamiki

In a transaction involving a sale of goods, the principle of double refund of a deposit requires the seller receiving a deposit to refund double the amount of that deposit for any cancellation of sales. But some Cambodian colleagues misunderstood to the effect that the seller must add twice the amount to the original deposit and therefore refund three times the amount of the deposit. Kamiki explains: "The wording of double refund can be misleading. It's no surprise that some interpret double refund of earnest money as a penalty charged to the seller who must pay double the deposit in addition to the original deposit." Such a simple misunderstanding can be avoided by simply reading a textbook. As such a misunderstanding is unimaginable in Japan, Kamiki failed to notice this for some time. In Cambodia, even small misunderstandings often go unnoticed, which is why local law practitioners cannot easily correct their mistakes.

74 Kamiki is an attorney registered with the Iwate Bar Association. Stationed in Cambodia as a long-term expert 2005–2010, he became an advisor at a Phnom Penh law firm after the project ended.

75 Money paid to confirm the conclusion of a contract of sale; e.g., when real property is sold.

Seminar on the joint ministerial ordinance on real estate registration

Emiko Kanetake, mentioned in section 06, continues to serve as a legal advisor to the Cambodian Ministry of Land. She admits that "the new Civil Code and Civil Procedure Code are quite difficult to understand, and the registration system employed is unprecedented in Cambodia. The confusion on site was only apparent once the codes were applied in practice." Tamiya, who also left the project in 2013, works in Phnom Penh as an advisor in a law firm and often provides consultation for her Cambodian colleagues. "For instance, mortgages are a new concept in Cambodia. Resistance is even greater with complex concepts like revolving mortgages. But I explain to my colleagues that these are mutually useful mechanisms for lenders and borrowers that are commonly used in Japan. I've encouraged them to help registration officers to understand these mechanisms too."

Let us see how Cambodian partners evaluate the current situation.

Bun Honn,[76] a former president of the BAKC and an Undersecretary of State of the Ministry of Justice, shares his satisfaction as an attorney to see the new Civil Code and Civil Procedure Code. He reasons,

> Before these codes were established, a defense lawyer in a trial might plead based on one particular law, but the judge

76 Honn has been an attorney since 1998. After serving in senior positions in the BAKC, he was an undersecretary of state at the Ministry of Justice between 2007 and 2012, becoming president of the BAKC 2012–2015. He has been a member of the Council of Jurists of the Council of Ministers since 2004.

might apply another one. As a result, it wasn't clear which laws the lawyer should use to advocate for the client, and no convincing explanation could be provided for the client. The two new codes put lawyers and judge on the same footing in trial proceedings.... We were lucky to partner with Japan in promoting the rule of law. No other countries or agencies followed up once the relevant laws were completed. In contrast, Japanese long-term experts are still with us to closely observe issues encountered in the application of new laws in Cambodia. They make sure they are compatible with our society and provide advice on possible solutions. They take responsibility even after bills are passed. Examples include the compilation of commentaries and textbooks, training of instructor candidates, and follow-up on the application of laws.

Bun Honn

Chan Sotheavy, the current project manager and Secretary of State at the Ministry of Justice, remarks as follows:

Pioneering laws are complex. Our country would be a mess if we failed to properly apply the Civil Code. To be honest, some provisions were adopted during the drafting process without our adequate understanding. These parts ended up complicating the application of the code. If we alone cannot resolve issues involved in the application of laws, we can consult Japanese long-term experts. If that doesn't help, we can always ask the task force in Japan. This is the advantage offered by Japan's long-term assistance. New laws are wasted without proper application, and Cambodia greatly appreciates the Japanese-style cooperation that extends from the drafting process to the application of the law. Throughout my career at the Ministry of Justice, I have been involved in various projects sponsored by many countries for more than twenty years, but no other countries have cooperated with us like Japan.

12 The Lack of Balance between Society and Legal and Judicial Development

Kimitoshi Yabuki senses a sharp contrast between Phnom Penh today and his impression of the city in 1996 as a "dark, intimidating and unconfident" place. "First of all, everything is bright. Neon signs are everywhere. There are lots of tall buildings in the capital, along with a shopping mall built with Japanese capital. Real estate continues to develop. Roads are congested with cars. In this respect, this place has totally changed." Yabuki found it symbolic to see young students studying at cafés, taking occasional sips of coffee.

> It's just like in Japan. When I got involved in the cooperation projects, judges would earn 150 to 200 dollars a month at most. It was beyond imagination that a student would be drinking coffee that costs at least 3 dollars while studying. The income of ordinary people has risen. Business investment from other countries is on the rise. Aid gradually phased out as an industry. In this respect, I suppose Cambodia is on a normal track of development.

Both the Civil Code and Civil Procedure Code crucially underpin economic development. Foreign companies can best

At the project office

operate in places with established laws and rights to a fair trial. A developed market economy is one ideal pursued through the cooperation for legal and judicial development.

During her stay in Cambodia as a long-term expert in the early 2000s, Yoshiko Homma (mentioned earlier) met a peddler family in a poor region who worked hard to send their children to university. A few years after the completion of her assignment, Homma met the family in Cambodia again. Their dream had come true and their two children had gone to university. "I heard that their daughter became a doctor. I noticed a significant rise in living standards among people in general."

Jun Uchiyama,[77] on a long-term assignment to Cambodia to assist in a new project starting in 2017, agrees: "I saw that everything was already there the first time I visited Phnom Penh. The avenue leading from the airport is crowded with cars. Restaurants and shopping malls have already been built with foreign capital. Inconvenience is hardly felt in daily life. I even wondered if such a place really needed assistance."

Jun Uchiyama

77 Uchiyama is a prosecutor who supported efforts to promote the rule of law in Cambodia and elsewhere as an ICD professor in Japan. He was later stationed in Cambodia as a long-term expert (2017–).

With regard to legal systems, however, the Civil Code and the Civil Procedure Code, which are basic laws, have yet to be widely applied. Yabuki sees a great contradiction: "The pace of development in legal systems is disproportionately slow compared to the pace of infrastructure development and the flow of money. I wonder why this country, with its remarkable economic growth, can barely afford to apply the Civil Code."

The imbalance between the society and its legal and judicial systems is also highlighted by the problem of serving of court documents under the Civil Procedure Code. In a trial, complaints and judgment documents must be served to ensure opportunities for a contending party to review and counter them. The Cambodian Civil Procedure Code stipulates that relevant documents be served by the court by postal mail. Unfortunately, the postal system is still underdeveloped in this country, even though people living in the provinces own smartphones, and Wi-Fi connectivity is increasingly available in many restaurants and cafés. "When asked what kind of practical problems they encountered, many people complained that civil procedure couldn't commence because the complaint cannot be served due to a failure in the postal service. Of course, in the drafting phase we were already aware of the poor postal system, but we never imagined that the problem would be so dire," confesses Homma.

As a judge, Kim Sathavy also faces the challenge posed by inadequate services for legal documents. She reflects, "I guess we assumed that the postal system would be more developed a decade from when we were drafting laws. Of course, nobody can predict the future, but in hindsight, we should have drafted laws by presupposing this difficulty with the postal services and later modifying the means of serving writs." Inadequate serving of writs remains a formidable challenge in properly applying the Civil Procedure Code.

13 Challenges That Come with Development

Judge Sumiko Sekine[78] was assigned as a short-term expert in the preparation phase of the Project for Improvement of Training on Civil Matters at the Royal School for Judges and Prosecutors (RSJP). In the course of cooperating with the RSJP to develop their curriculum, she witnessed the difficulty in supporting legal and judicial development in the world's developing countries.

78 Sekine is a judge who supported efforts to promote the rule of law in Cambodia and elsewhere as an ICD professor in Japan 2004–2007.

In those years, multiple aid agencies supported the RSJP. Coordination with these other agencies was necessary to develop a curriculum by assigning class hours for different laws. Sekine believed that the Civil Code and Civil Procedure Code were essential laws in any society, and warranted high priority and a substantial number of class hours. "The Civil Code and Civil Procedure Code form the basis of laws. I believed that no complex issues could be addressed without their proper understanding. But other aid agencies insisted that the laws they were assigned, including relatively minor ones like the Law on

Domestic Violence and Protection of Victims[79] or the Law on Environmental Protection and Natural Resource Management,[80] deserved similar priority when assigning class hours."

As the home countries of several donor agencies were contending with a flood of pirated products from Southeast Asia, great importance was placed on laws concerning intellectual property rights. The Cambodians themselves also hoped to develop their country into one with robust protection of intellectual property.

Sekine continues,

> We naturally believe that the Civil Code and Civil Procedure Code are crucial as fundamental laws. In practice, no time should be wasted in protecting intellectual property rights either. In its modernization effort after the Meiji Revolution, Japan took a long time to create its own Civil Code. In those years, the gap between developed and developing countries was smaller compared to today. The Japanese were able to catch up with Western nations because the slower dynamics of the world afforded a long time for Japan to develop its Civil Code. Today, in contrast, as developing countries reasonably believe, rapid technological advances and globalization do not afford them enough time to build up everything from the basics. The complexity in the development of legal systems in our time cannot be compared to that experienced in Meiji-era Japan.

As society and the economy have developed, new types of demands have emerged among ordinary people for the Civil Code and Civil Procedure Code, extending beyond legal circles. For instance, an increasing number of farmers lease tractors and large farm equipment, even in remote parts of Cambodia. Payments for leased equipment are made in installments, or by pledging other equipment or land. Such practices require a basic knowledge of contracts. Unfortunately, many people sign contracts with highly disadvantageous terms for interest rates and mortgages, as they lack such knowledge. Ayako Tamiya, mentioned earlier in section 10, deals with clients like these

79 This legislation to prevent domestic violence sets out procedures for obtaining a protection order that, for example, forbids the perpetrator from having any contact with the victim.

80 This is legislation that establishes policies for protecting the environment. The name is often used as a blanket term for any legislation that regulates pollution or mandates conservation measures.

every day at her law firm. "It's high time that leaders of farmers, or district representatives who often serve as coordinators for local farmers, acquire basic knowledge on typical contracts." So saying, she points out the need for common people to become familiar with the Civil Code to deal with the new challenges brought about by the development of the country.

Graft and corruption are unavoidable problems when we discuss Cambodian society today. An underlying problem is believed to be the chronically low pay of public servants. And with insufficient budget allocation from the national government, courts cannot even afford toner for printers or gasoline for motorbikes unless extra fees are collected in one way or another from parties involved in trials. Such anecdotes are not unusual, and they discourage brilliant law students from choosing careers as public servants out of disdain for these disreputable practices. Instead, they opt for legal positions in foreign companies.

JICA's cooperation for legal and judicial development produced the Civil Code and Civil Procedure Code for protecting people's rights. But is it possible to prevent the judiciary from intentionally abusing these codes? Homma faced such a question through her exchange with ordinary citizens who heard that she is assisting in the drafting of the Civil Code. "Once the Civil Code is complete, our society might finally be governed by law,

The Ministry of Justice building housing the JICA project office

as trials will be based on laws without any bribery." In response to such a hopeful comment, Homma had mixed feelings. "I wasn't sure how to react. I knew that such an ideal cannot be achieved immediately after the completion of the Civil Code. I could only thank them for welcoming our efforts and promise them that we would do our best." Of course, many conscious Cambodians are concerned about the current state of affairs. Still, graft and corruption cannot be eliminated overnight. The grim truth is that they are deeply seated throughout Cambodian society.

14 | Expectation for the Disclosure of Court Decisions

The completion of the Legal and Judicial Development Project (Phase IV) was followed by the new Legal and Judicial Development Project (Phase V) that began in April 2017. This new project had three pillars: enshrining the joint ministerial ordinance on real estate registration by the Ministry of Justice and Ministry of Land into law,[81] development of forms to be used in practices of civil affairs,[82] and disclosure of court decisions.

The publication of court decisions literally means that court decisions from trials are disclosed for public review. Some countries receiving Japan's cooperation do not publish their court decisions.

Publication of court decisions has enormous significance. Jun Uchiyama, who is on long-term assignment as the chief advisor for the new project, explains:

> Court decisions and precedents have a certain binding force. Any accessible court decisions provide "predictability" that similar cases will be resolved in a similar manner. People can expect fair handling of their cases. In contrast, if court decisions are not made public, parties may believe that different judges would make different court decisions, even when their cases would result in the same court decision by any judge. Such uncertainty compromises confidence in the judiciary.

81 A joint ministerial ordinance is an ordinance issued jointly by two or more ministries. Anything directly affecting the rights and responsibilities of the citizenry should in principle be governed by legislation enacted in parliament. Cambodia's regulations on real estate registration as contained in the ordinance therefore needed to be systematized and enshrined in law.

82 This involved creating a set of forms for implementing certain common legal procedures: litigation, compulsory execution, etc. These forms are designed to be completed and used by anyone following such procedures.

A Phnom Penh street

Kimitoshi Yabuki comments:

> Nobody can complain even if judges make court decisions solely based on their own experience. This is the biggest problem resulting from the court decisions not being published. I've also learned recently that any scrutiny of court decisions or criticism of precedents constitutes contempt of the judge in Cambodia. Unless this rule is changed, no critical comment could be made even if court decisions were published. Genuine studies and understanding of laws will be difficult unless court decisions can be published with the guaranteed freedom to scrutinize and comment on them.

The idea of publishing judgments still encounters a negative reaction in Cambodia. Yasuhiko Tsuji, mentioned earlier in section 10, explains that "people agree in principle, but disagree on the details." Their negative response may derive from the issue of capacity of judges. Normally, a ruling comprises a decision and a justification. The justification includes the statements by all parties, indisputable facts based on evidence, points at issue, and a decision by the court on the points at issue. Many Japanese long-term experts suspect that many judges are unable to write clear justifications. Uchiyama thinks that "some judges may be concerned that the publication of an unclear justification may jeopardize their position or lead to their punishment." Many people point out that judges may resist publication for fear of the unraveling of their corrupt or unethical practices. Many obstacles must be overcome to establish a sustainable system for publishing court decisions.

Certainly, not all are opposed to the move. Uchiyama is hopeful.

> The publication of court decisions is included in the project agenda because our counterpart demonstrated their determination to take up the challenge. There's no doubt that many Cambodians believe that court decisions must be published.... Building a framework for publication is possible, but it's meaningless unless Cambodians themselves are resolved to do so. Even the publication of one or two court decisions per year is a good start. I hope that legal professionals gradually move ahead, based on their own convictions regarding the significance of the publication of court decisions.

Cambodia has taken the first step toward a future where everyone can read court decisions, and studies of jurisprudence can advance based on precedent.

Many lives were claimed, and even laws were once lost in Cambodia, but the people rose up from that devastation to effect remarkable development of their economy and society. At the same time, that development gave rise to waves of new challenges that need to be addressed by the arm of the law. For instance, institutions remain inadequate to address graft, corruption, and other problems associated with rapid economic growth. The Civil Code and the Civil Procedure Code will continue to play important supporting roles in the lives of Cambodians, who keep moving forward after overcoming their harsh history. Cambodian lawyers exert themselves to use the arm of the law to protect and sustain people's lives.

Sidelights on Cooperation for Legal and Judicial Development

Cambodia

Svay Leng
JICA training coordinator and Khmer interpreter

PROFILE:
A native of Cambodia who came to Japan as a Japanese government scholarship student in 1973 and became a naturalized Japanese citizen in 1991. An accomplished interpreter and translator who has been invaluable to successive long-term experts in Cambodia.

What's the most difficult thing about interpreting in the field of legal and judicial development?

The terms used in legal and judicial development are highly specialized, and I have to distinguish among them correctly. Legal terms of similar meaning have different legal implications, and in many cases the meaning of the law will change if I use the wrong word. I have to understand both Japanese legal terminology and that of the recipient country, plus I also have to understand the concept each term denotes. That, I feel, really complicates the task of interpreting and translating. Before I got used to it, a small job that would have taken me a couple of hours if it had been a regular translation could take me a whole week once I'd investigated what everything meant.

What exactly do you mean when you say you need to distinguish among different legal terms correctly?

Take, for instance, the Japanese terms *shucho* [assertion] and *chinjutsu* [statement]. In ordinary Khmer they would both be rendered the same way. In the legal realm, though, there's a big difference between them: *chinjutsu* counts as evidence in court, but *shucho* doesn't. I've been working in the field of legal and judicial development for years, but even now I come across terms that leave me scratching my head wondering how to translate them. When I'm not sure about a word, it's essential to ask a Japanese long-term expert or a local project member what it means and how it's used, so I develop an accurate knowledge of the field.

As an interpreter and translator, have you encountered any problems peculiar to Khmer?

In the early 2000s a special data-processing software to input Khmer into a computer was needed. When I edited Khmer documents on a computer, the system was so unstable that all the text would become garbled, so it was a real struggle. I therefore worked with people in the Cambodian government on encoding Khmer vowels and consonants in Unicode, the international script encoding standard, so now Khmer could be used on any computer. The establishment of an international standard has made it much easier to create and edit text.

Chapter 3

An All-out Focus on Developing Human Capacity—Laos

Laos, which is among the least advanced of the Southeast Asian nations and lacks a well-developed body of legal theory, has been slowly but steadily modernizing its legal system. JICA is helping with an aid program that is, above all, process-oriented. That program is focused on developing human capacity in the course of making laws, even more than on making good laws per se.

The Laotian capital, Vientiane, where the pace of life seems slower

PROJECT FACT SHEET # Laos

May 26, 2003–March 31, 2008

Legal and Judicial Development Project

COUNTERPART: Ministry of Justice | People's Supreme Court | Office of the Supreme People's Prosecutor

The first full-scale legal and judicial development project in Laos, this was designed to upgrade the basic legal skills of Laotians working in the law and justice fields. It involved preparing civil and commercial law textbooks, compiling legal databases, and drawing up practical manuals alongside personnel at the three counterpart agencies: the Ministry of Justice, the People's Supreme Court (PSC) and the Office of the Supreme People's Prosecutor (OSPP).

July 11, 2010–July 10, 2014

Project for Human Resource Development in the Legal Sector

COUNTERPART: Ministry of Justice | People's Supreme Court | Office of the Supreme People's Prosecutor | National University of Laos

The National University of Laos joined the Ministry of Justice, the PSC and the OSPP as a fourth counterpart for this project, which aided efforts to foster a better understanding of Laotian law at both the theoretical and practical levels. A joint working group was formed spanning the four agencies, and their staff developed a common understanding of Laotian law across organizational boundaries while studying where it could be improved. JICA began providing support with drafting a civil code midway through the project.

July 11, 2014–July 10, 2018

Project for Human Resource Development in the Legal Sector (Phase II)

COUNTERPART: Ministry of Justice | People's Supreme Court | Office of the Supreme People's Prosecutor | National University of Laos

While conducted with the same four counterparts as its predecessor, this project further deepened and broadened understanding of Laotian law by involving the Lao Bar Association as well as the police. Besides following in the footsteps of the previous project by helping to draft a civil code, it assisted with compiling practical documentation on civil and economic law and criminal law. It also helped refine the curriculum of the nascent legal training program.

There is a saying in Laos to the effect that the older brother knows one more thing than the younger brother. In this context, Japan is the older brother to Laos. Japan is a developed country that has a wealth of knowledge on laws and other matters. This is why Laos wishes to learn from Japan, its older brother. We do not think of people from JICA merely as experts; we regard them as our family members. (Chomkham Bouphalivanh,[1] director of the National Institute of Justice [NIJ][2])

Chomkham Bouphalivanh has been a member of the Legal and Judicial Development Project since it began in Laos in 2003. He compares the relationship between Japan and Laos to that of two brothers. Known for the rustic charm of its people and scenery, Laos is lagging behind in economic development among the member countries of the Association of Southeast Asian Nations (ASEAN), and is classified as a Least Developed Country by the United Nations. Japan's cooperation is there, placing the utmost importance on human development.

Chomkham Bouphalivanh

"This has resulted in a program that is, I think, the most process-oriented of them all." This is how Hiroshi Matsuo,[3] professor of Keio University Law School, evaluates the series of projects in Laos. He has been deeply involved in the cooperation for legal and judicial development in Laos from the beginning, and is currently working in a Japan-based advisory group[4] to support the project.

Hiroshi Matsuo

From the outset, JICA's cooperation was not supposed to be the "work" of drafting a law and just delivering the "result" to the recipient country. Prior to this support project in Laos, JICA had already begun providing similar support to Vietnam and

1 Bouphlivanh became the first director of the NIJ after serving as director general of the Law Dissemination Department at the Ministry of Justice and director of the Ministry's Judicial and Legal Training Center Institute. He is currently director general of the Ministry's Justice System Promotion Department.

2 The NIJ is an educational institution subordinate to the Laotian Ministry of Justice, established in 2015 to train judges, prosecutors, and lawyers. Students all study the same curriculum. See page 168.

3 Matsuo, an expert in civil law and law and development, is a professor at Keio University Law School. He has been closely involved in JICA's cooperation for legal and judicial development since the early 2000s, playing a pivotal role in projects in Laos and Nepal.

4 See page 69, note 48, (1).

Cambodia, where emphasis was also placed on the "processes" of establishing laws. For these projects, JICA offered their opinions on laws drafted by the respective countries and assisted with the drafting of these laws.

The aim of the project in Laos, which has been described as the "most process-oriented of all," is to "increase the capacity of human resources in the legal and judicial sector through the process of developing tangible things such as textbooks." Greater importance is placed on increasing the Lao people's understanding of jurisprudence and improving their skills related to developing and applying laws through discussion, rather than on completing the textbooks and other tangible things created in the course of the project. In fact, this thorough emphasis on process forms the core of JICA's support of legal and judicial development, which has extended to Laos, following Vietnam and Cambodia.

01 | Feeling Our Way in an Unsophisticated Country

The Lao People's Democratic Republic is a small country with an area about the size of Honshu island in Japan. It has a population of approximately 6.5 million people and is located in the center of the Indochinese Peninsula. Around seventy percent of Laos comprises mountains, and the population contains many ethnic minority groups. Surrounded by China, Vietnam, Cambodia, Thailand and Myanmar, it is also the only ASEAN member country with no sea access. Although the economic growth rate of the country has been at a consistently high level of around 8 percent in recent years, its nominal GDP per capita was only US$1,947 in 2015, one of the lowest amongst the ASEAN countries.

Laos has remained under the one-party rule of the Lao People's Revolutionary Party ever since 1975. Inspired by the Doi Moi (renewal) policy of its neighbor Vietnam and other similar policies, it launched a round of reforms in 1986, including the introduction of a market economy. Then in 1991 the country became the first socialist state to establish a national constitution. This was also around the time when it began to develop the regulations required to shift to a market economy. This led to the Minister of Justice of Laos requesting that the Japanese government offer support to the Ministry of Justice, the People's Supreme Court[5] and the Office of the Supreme People's Prosecutor[6] when he visited Japan in 1996. Following on from this, JICA began to provide training in Japan and seminars in Laos in 1998.

5 This is the highest of the people's courts. It is overseen by the National Assembly.

6 Offices of the People's Prosecutor prosecute criminal cases and oversee legal enforcement. The Office of the Supreme People's Prosecutor is the highest prosecutor's office in the country. It is overseen by the National Assembly.

Providing assistance to Laos is similar to providing assistance to Vietnam in the sense that the aim is to help a socialist state to shift to a market economy through providing help with legal and judicial development. Unlike the project for Vietnam, though, which had already set the specific target of revising its Civil Code when it sought assistance from Japan, the assistance work for Laos had to begin by exploring what was required to allow the country to achieve legal and judicial development. "We felt that it was important to provide future human resources in the legal and judicial sector with basic knowledge on civil and commercial laws. This would need to be done at a more fundamental level than in Vietnam, and thus we should offer the support required to do so. This intensely process-oriented development of human resources was not centrally planned from the beginning; it was more that the plan was gradually put together as we felt our way in the dark," says Matsuo.

It was in 2002, before the full-fledged start of the project by JICA, that Matsuo visited Laos for the first time to deliver seminars on civil and commercial law. Looking back on his experience at that time, he says, "I was immensely moved by the pure and fundamental nature of their questions." Laotian seminar participants asked him questions about regulations that were just taken for granted in Japan, and he found these questions "unexpected but to the point." He recalls:

> To give them a thorough understanding, I felt the need to go back to the basic principles. It is always important to understand the reasons why something is the way it is. The cooperation for legal and judicial development in a given country inevitably involves the need to explain rules that are

> unfamiliar to that country. There's a huge difference between drafting a law by just following conventions, and drafting it after becoming fully aware of why the regulations in it are necessary. The key is to understand the reasons why and develop full understanding, or to have discussions when necessary. In fact, such discussions sometimes resulted in the discovery of new solutions.

The first project in Laos, the Legal and Judicial Development Project, was launched in May 2003. The project involved the Ministry of Justice, the People's Supreme Court, and the Office of the Supreme People's Prosecutor. The goal was to improve the overall basic legal knowledge and skills of human resources in the legal and judicial sector. There were only two long-term experts stationed in Laos at the time; this increased to three later in December 2004.

In order to accomplish these objectives, documents such as civil law and commercial law textbooks, business law commentaries, legal databases, legal glossaries, a manual for drafting judicial decisions, and a manual for prosecutors were created. The basic work flow was that Japanese experts provided information about each law through seminars and lectures; drafts were prepared mainly by the Laotian side; the Japanese experts added comments to the completed drafts; and the Laotian side had further discussions based on their comments before making revisions to their drafts.

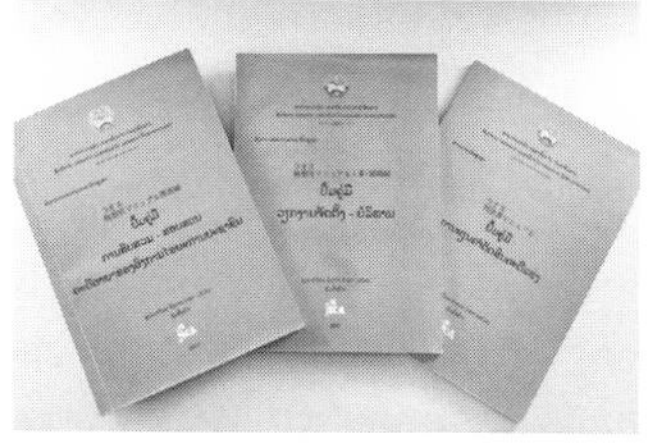

Prosecutors' manuals

The textbooks and manuals completed as the result of this project have been used in training programs for employees of the Ministry of Justice, judges, prosecutors, court clerks and other people already working as professionals, and have also been distributed to judges and prosecutors across different parts of Laos. They have also been made known to the general public through public lectures by members of the authoring teams.

Since there was a need to further disseminate the knowledge

At a workshop

contained in these project outcomes, it was decided that the project would be extended for one more year. Nevertheless, the long-term experts left Laos in 2006, as originally scheduled, because the work of producing textbooks and other materials that required advice from legal experts was already complete. During the extension period, JICA's Laos office did management work while their Lao counterparts implemented promotional activities in the form of seminars and workshops. In JICA it is rare for a project to continue to be carried out by a JICA office and their local counterparts without any involvement from long-term experts. Hideaki Matsumoto,[7] who was engaged in management work as a member of JICA's Laos office at that time, looks back on those days and says, "As far as I remember, I've never been involved in a project in which our counterparts prepared such a comprehensive set of informative materials to implement their project."

Seminars were held for law-related professionals such as judges, prosecutors, and police officers not only in the capital city of Vientiane but also in provincial cities. The seminars and workshops provided during this period saw a total of about 1,350 participants across Laos. Had the Lao people not regarded the promotional activities as their own responsibility, or had they been unable to fulfill them, they could not have continued with these activities without any support from Japanese experts.

7 Matsumoto, a JICA staff member, worked on projects in the governance field, including legal and judicial development, as a member of the Laos office staff 2006–2009. He is currently deputy resident representative of the JICA office in East Timor.

Matsumoto analyzes this: "I suppose that they thought highly of the manual for drafting judicial decisions and the manual for prosecutors, as they themselves had produced them through the project. This confidence energized them to proactively carry out promotional activities. I also think that the top management and central figures among the Lao counterparts believed that the work would be pointless unless the materials they'd created were understood by most judges and prosecutors."

02 A Turning Point toward Evolution

The extension period during which activities were carried out all across Laos to promote the textbooks and manuals ended in March 2008. As no plan had been established for a replacement project at this point in time, it marked a temporary end to cooperation in this area in Laos. However, soon after, movement toward the beginning of a new project began. The Ministry of Justice of Laos requested that Japan undertake a human resource development project targeted at a law school established under the ministry. An initial survey was conducted in January 2009 to evaluate the appropriateness of supporting this project.

The project was launched after thorough preparation involving four preliminary surveys. This allowed both Japan and Laos to share a good understanding of the project, as well as to clearly define its goals. "This is why the Laotian project is very stable today," says Katsunori Irie,[8] a lawyer involved in assistance activities in Laos and other countries as a senior advisor[9] from JICA's headquarters. He feels, from his own experience, that the framework and foundations built during that period are what makes the project so stable today. The preparation stage was a turning point that enabled the project to evolve toward cooperation that is more focused on human resource development.

The most fundamental problem facing the development of human resources in the legal and judicial sector in Laos at the time lay in jurisprudence, the basic knowledge required by all legal professionals. It remained underdeveloped due to a gap

8 Irie is a lawyer registered with the Tokyo Bar Association. A senior advisor to JICA since 2015, he was involved in efforts toward legal and judicial development in Laos and elsewhere before being stationed in Laos as a long-term expert in 2017.

9 Senior advisors are specialists directly affiliated with JICA who possess expertise in a particular field, such as education or health, coupled with experience in development assistance. In the field of legal and judicial development, experts in law and international cooperation who are qualified lawyers travel back and forth between Japan and other countries providing support as senior advisors.

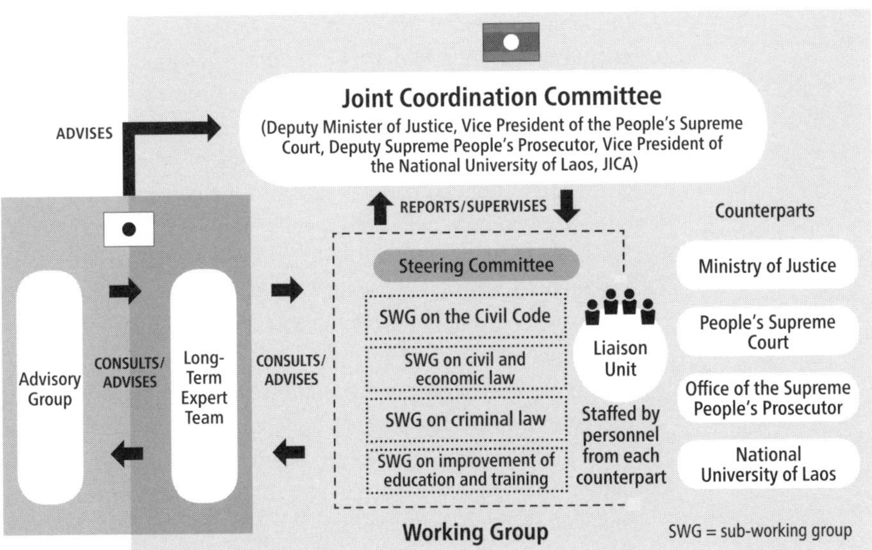

The structure of the Laotian legal and judicial development program (the diagram shows the organization of the Project for Human Resource Development in the Legal Sector, Phase II)

between theory and practice, rather than a lack of educators and teaching materials at the university level. This was why the survey results indicated that the next step should be to launch a human resource development project that would involve a greater number of related organizations, including universities that provided legal education. As with the previous project, it was also decided that the new project would adopt the policy of increasing the knowledge and skills of project members through the process of creating texts, such as model teaching materials.

Through workshops and other activities, JICA also endeavored to share their awareness of problems to be tackled with four counterpart organizations: the Ministry of Justice, the People's Supreme Court, and the Office of the Supreme People's Prosecutor, which had been involved in the previous project, and a new addition, the National University of Laos. After detailed consultations, all agreed that starting by laying solid foundations was the way to go, though that might initially seem roundabout, rather than dealing with specific problems individually when basic legal theory was not yet fully established. This way of thinking would later appear in many different situations, influencing cooperation for legal and judicial development in Laos.

As a result of the second preliminary survey conducted in September 2009, it was decided that the project would compile books that would be useful for all kinds of people, from students, practitioners, and educators to the general public. Discussions were also held as to specific implementation systems; for example, that a "liaison unit" should be set up to include a representative from each of the four organizations to undertake necessary coordination work, such as scheduling, with the working group.

A great deal of time, work, and careful planning was put into the new project. The Project for Human Resource Development in the Legal Sector was to be implemented over a period of four years, from July 2010 to July 2014. The four organizations involved in the consultations at the preparation stage became the project's counterparts. Taking the preliminary survey results into account, the project set the goal of allowing project members to develop an even better understanding of legal basics. Specifically, it was decided that three sub-working groups (SWGs) would be set up on Civil Code, Civil Procedure Law, and Criminal Procedure Law, to develop human resources through the process of creating handbooks and other documents on the respective laws.

Careful deliberations had taken place during the preparatory period preceding the start of the project to examine its aims and implementation systems. When the project began, however, no clear plans were in place as to what kind of books would be created and when. This was deliberate. "From the very beginning, this was a project in which we were to think together with our counterparts. As too many things remained undecided, however, we spent the first six months unable to draw up plans. I guess everyone was dismayed, since we hadn't even reached the stage of being able to discuss law," recalls Hitoshi Kawamura,[10] a long-term expert who has been supporting this project from the beginning as a project coordinator.[11] (There were originally three long-term experts working on the project, including Kawamura; there have been four since October 2014).

10 Kawamura is a long-term expert, stationed in Laos since 2010. He applies his excellent knowledge of Lao on the job as project coordinator. See the Sidelights section on page 186.

11 During implementation of a legal and judicial development project, someone needs to complete all the necessary procedures, keep track of income and expenditures, and liaise with the different people involved. That is the job of the project coordinator, a management expert who teams up with specialists in law to ensure that the project proceeds smoothly.

03 Two Laotian Methods

Joint activities between the four organizations and establishment of the liaison unit were unique initiatives, not adopted in other countries, that formed marked characteristics of the new project. In other countries where JICA is currently providing cooperation for legal and judicial development, each activity is carried out by members of a specific counterpart organization that best suits the purpose of the project activity: for example, the Ministry of Justice or other government agency when JICA assists with the drafting of a law, or a bar association when the activity is about professional development of lawyers. This does not apply to the project in Laos, where each SWG has members from all four counterpart organizations. What lies behind this unique style is the necessity for human resource development, which each of these organizations was already aware of before the start of the project. Irie says,

> It was a commonly held view among the organizations that it was necessary to start by doing all the groundwork from scratch, reviewing the process of developing legal professionals itself. Furthermore, there were only a small number of core human resources in the legal and judicial sector in this small country, so it was possible for them to get to know people from different organizations. I think that these factors, in addition to the friendly nature of the Lao people, have contributed to this cross-organizational environment. I don't think it would be possible, though, to regard this Laotian project as a model case and apply the same method wholesale to another country. The success in Laos is because the project has been designed to meet the specific requests of the Laotian side and their need for human resource development.

In Laos, not even judicial procedures and proceedings had been standardized before the start of the Project for Human Resource Development in the Legal Sector: judges, prosecutors, and lawyers used to have a different, inconsistent understanding of these things. Moreover, legal professionals in different positions did not have an adequate understanding of each other's work, resulting in little mutual confidence. Nyvanh Somsengsy,[12] a lawyer who has been involved in this project since Phase II,[13] smiles bitterly and says, "I know that judges and university professors used to believe that lawyers were always committing illegal and unjust acts." Even when thinking about the same law, university faculty members only thought from the point of view of jurisprudence, while lawyers had a practical perspective. It was this project and its discussions that enabled the two to see the difference in their points of view for the first time. Nyvanh says, "When we didn't properly understand each other's way of thinking, it wasn't unusual for us to discuss an issue all day long without reaching a single conclusion. By working very hard and having numerous discussions, we've come a long way from where we were in the beginning. Now we're able to understand each other's work and ways of thinking."

12 Nyvanh is a lawyer on the Executive Committee of the Lao Bar Association.

13 See page 167.

The liaison unit was composed of a total of four young members selected from each counterpart organization. This unit is in charge of the clerical work required for SWG management, such as coordinating and communicating the dates and times of SWG meetings, preparing information materials for the meetings, and circulating the minutes after the meetings. These tasks were conducted by JICA project staff in the previous project, in which many of the Laotian members forgot meeting dates and times or arrived late, making it difficult to implement meetings according to schedule. One reason that JICA decided to put the Laotian side in charge of scheduling meetings and related clerical work was that something needed to be done to improve the situation. The goal was to encourage greater independence among Laotian members and facilitate the development of basic work skills such as punctuality and good record-keeping habits.

It cannot be said that the first year of activities went as smoothly as expected, as it was often the case that Japanese members ended up having to do communication and coordination work for the Laotian members. Over time, however, the liaison unit gradually began to function properly. Currently, all operations related to the sharing of information, in addition to the scheduling of meetings, are taken care of by liaison unit members. They also frequently communicate with Japanese experts to act as a bridge between them and Laotian members. Kawamura says, "Given that they also have their own work to do, it must have been hard for them to do all these tasks. Their efforts mean that Laotian members are now basically able to get all of the work done independently."

04 The Product of Flowcharts

The project outputs include flowcharts that illustrate the progression of criminal and civil procedures. Take civil procedures for example: when a plaintiff submits a written complaint, it is examined by a court clerk and then numbered with the clerk's stamp, affirming receipt of the complaint providing it is judged to be appropriate. If it is judged to be inappropriate, the clerk will provide advice and instructions for revision. A flowchart was created to show these procedures, accompanied with information on applicable articles of law. These flowcharts, which have long been familiar to Japanese people, were unprecedented in Laos.

Converting procedures into charts, however, initially faced some resistance from the Laotian side. "Their customary way of thinking told them that laws should be read like a novel, in order from front to back, starting from Article 1. The order, however, can be reorganized on flowcharts. Some Laotian members questioned the appropriateness of this," recalls Osamu Ishioka,[14] a long-term expert who has been in charge of the creation of civil procedure flowcharts. Ishioka, whose quiet and unaffected tone suggests his serious attitude and determination toward his work, has been working for the project in Laos since 2010.

Osamu Ishioka

14 Ishioka is a lawyer registered with the Tokyo Bar Association. He spent seven years (2010–2017) in Laos as a long-term expert.

Despite the opposition that these charts, completed after many SWG discussions, met with at first, they are now commonly used, as they allow even those without any specialist legal knowledge to understand court proceedings simply by following the step-by-step instructions. In fact, when the National Assembly of Laos had deliberations on revision of the Civil Procedure Law in 2012, each National Assembly member had one of these flowcharts at hand.

The process of creating these charts was actually even more meaningful than their actual completion. The different organizations used to understand court procedures differently in the past, but through the concerted efforts of various professionals such as judges and prosecutors, they have developed a common understanding of them in the course of making the charts. This is a significant outcome of the initiative to form interorganizational SWGs consisting of members from the four organizations. Furthermore, the participatory-style workshop was new to the Lao people at that time; it was unprecedented for them to brainstorm together in front of a whiteboard to come up with and organize ideas, using cards and whiteboard markers, as well as having discussions. This activity has not only stimulated the professional development of young members, but has also changed the way of thinking among older members, leading them to realize that actively exchanging opinions can bring about results.

There was an unforgettable moment for Ishioka. Somsack

A sub-working group (SWG) at work

Taybounlack,[15] presiding justice of the People's Central High Court and an SWG leader, has been a project member ever since JICA first launched the cooperation for legal and judicial development in Laos. He is one of the leading judicial figures in the country.

Somsack Taybounlack

15 Somsack became presiding justice of the People's Central High Court in 2016 after serving as a judge on the court and then its deputy presiding justice.

Somsack and other Laotian members at the time regarded a "meeting" as an event where all participants were seated and spoke in a prescribed order. Members who were more senior in role or age had greater say, and the atmosphere did not allow other members to counter their arguments. Under such circumstances, the conclusion of a meeting was not the result of a discussion, but was a decision made by the leader. "When that is the norm, we can't develop people's abilities effectively. The aim of the project was to allow all members to contribute their own opinions and improve their abilities in the course of doing so, rather than the leader making all the decisions. Something needed to be done to change the group dynamics." Ishioka therefore proposed that on the first day of a three-day workshop, a participatory activity should be carried out in which all members would work together to compile court proceedings into a chart through manual tasks. However, this kind of activity was completely new to the Lao people, and his proposal was not received favorably. Not only Somsack, but all the other core members as well, insisted on having a regular seated meeting. The first day ended without much progress, as most members remained seated and refused to take part in the hands-on work.

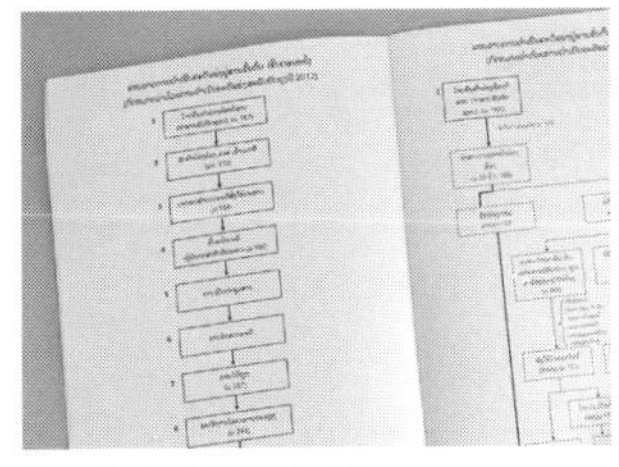
Flowchart of civil litigation

After this meeting, Ishioka made an appointment with Somsack to have a one-on-one talk, in which he told him that the goal of the project was to increase the abilities of all members, including inexperienced younger ones. He then explained how important it was to adopt a participatory approach to allow all individuals to express themselves and learn from each other's opinions so that the goal could be achieved. Somsack was somewhat persuaded by Ishioka's words, and supported the inclusion of a participatory activity on the following day.

The members in higher positions remained seated again throughout the following day. Younger members, however, stood up and took part in the creation of a chart. Until then, these young people had been listening to the other members and staying quiet, but now they began to express their own opinions as they worked on manual tasks and went through a process of trial and error.

Ishioka concluded the second day with the following words: "This participatory activity was devised by Somsack-san and me. I believe that it was very productive." Somsack also summed up the meeting by saying, "We tried something new this time. It has been really successful, since so many members expressed their opinions."

This was a turning point for Somsack. He began to proactively encourage younger members to take part in discussions, while taking care not to interfere in them himself. This change toward a more flexible attitude on the part of the leadership soon after the beginning of the project, as well as the resulting change in the SWGs, appears to have been the key to the success of this project.

Ishioka says, "In my opinion, none of those project outcomes could have been possible without this change. Its significance went beyond just the completion of the charts. I felt it was a step forward."

When they created another chart in response to the revision of the Civil Procedure Law in 2012, members were willing to propose one idea after another on their own initiative. The production of the chart went very smoothly. In fact, many ideas contributed by Laotian members were incorporated into this new chart and made it even easier to understand, such as the inclusion of the latest proceeding requirements, notes about frequently misunderstood points, and precedents.

These participatory SWG activities have helped younger,

less-experienced members and female members to proactively express their own opinions. Chomkham Bouphalivanh, another member mentioned earlier, like Somsack has been involved in the project since the very early days, and also feels the effectiveness of these activities. "Even the most junior members are now able to exchange opinions with Japanese experts in an open, relaxed manner. This is a great pleasure for top members like us."

Ishioka feels that a member is "fully fledged" when he sees them being able to express opposition to the opinions of more senior members.

> In the past, there were times when those with correct opinions failed to assert themselves in the face of objection from senior members, and the discussion would go off track. Recently members have gradually been finding the courage to offer differing opinions when necessary. This is because they now have greater confidence in their own views as the result of the many discussions from the project. It increased their knowledge and gave them access to information not only about their own country, but also about other countries. I think this is remarkable progress.

05 "Now Is the Time": Drafting Assistance for the Civil Code

The civil law system development that Laos implemented in the 1990s to enable a shift toward a market economy adopted an ad hoc approach. The country established the necessary laws in many small steps to meet the practical needs of the people at any given point. Further economic growth inevitably required the development of a systematic corpus of civil law. For this reason, the requests from the Laotians when the new project was planned in 2008 also included a request concerning the development of the Civil Code. At that point in time, however, there was no specific plan for its establishment, and it was ultimately not incorporated into the project.

The situation changed in 2012, when Laos decided that a draft Civil Code should be submitted to the National Assembly by June 2015. They then requested that Japan assist them in the drafting of the Civil Code as part of the project.

"I already knew that the Laotians had been seeking assistance in drafting their Civil Code for some time now, but Japan judged it premature at the time. After two years of project activities, however, I felt that now was the time." Ishioka went into action.

Hiroshi Matsuo, the professor mentioned earlier, immediately agreed with Ishioka, saying, "We definitely should do that now." The JICA headquarters also agreed. "Professor Matsuo had also been aware that Laos would soon require a civil code. He seemed to have been waiting for a long-term expert working in the country to propose that," says Ishioka. Naoshi Sato,[16] a lawyer who was in charge of the project in Laos as a senior advisor in JICA headquarters at that time, also says, "We had feared that the Japanese might end up creating the Civil Code for Laos by starting to assist them in the drafting process before the Laotian side was able to create drafts by themselves. Having seen them become quite able to do the drafting work on their own, however, we finally judged that the time had come."

Naoshi Sato

16 Sato, a lawyer registered with the Dai-Ni Tokyo Bar Association, was stationed as a long-term expert in Vietnam from 2004 to 2006. He has played a leading role in JICA's legal and judicial development programs as a senior advisor (2006–2015) and then legal advisor to JICA (since 2015). He is also the general editor of the original version of this book.

In this way, "assistance in drafting the Civil Code" became a new item added to the Project for Human Resource Development in the Legal Sector, which started in 2010. This assistance was not targeted at the drafting work itself; the goal was clearly defined as "developing human resources through the drafting process." This fact also attests to the coherent attitude governing the overall project in Laos.

Nevertheless, the drafting work, launched by the civil code SWG, stumbled at first. It was decided in advance that the draft would be prepared through the following workflow: the SWG would develop the initial draft; a Japanese advisory group would comment on it; and the SWG then revise the draft to reflect the

A spontaneous round of applause

comments. In reality, there were many occasions when the SWG changed the draft articles or undid changes without informing the advisory group as the above cycle was repeated. The drafting work kept progressing and regressing, and did not go as smoothly as Ishioka had hoped. "This was when I suddenly realized the weight of the burden which I'd taken up," he smiles wryly.

This confusion resulted from a lack of rules to govern the development of laws, and Matsuo thinks of it as an opportunity that has allowed "both the Laotians and the Japanese to understand the difficulty of establishing rules for making laws." He explains, "This is part of the reason why the legal system development policy adopted in Laos had to start by preparing the necessary rules for making laws through repeated trial and error. This is a singular kind of assistance, unlike that implemented in Vietnam and Cambodia."

There are two things that Matsuo pays particular attention to in cooperation for legal and judicial development. One is to speak to Laotian members face-to-face as frequently as possible. He has set up "innumerable" opportunities, not only by seeing them in person through visits to Laos and inviting Laotian members to come to Japan to receive training, but also by organizing many teleconferences. "Communication is always important, although it is difficult for both sides and quite time-consuming as well."

The other is to clarify the reasoning behind each argument when persuading others. The important thing is to make Laotian members understand and become convinced of the logic in discussions, rather than getting them to follow along without knowing why. According to Matsuo, doing this can trigger "a surge in motivation" among Laotian members.

> Things suddenly become far more interesting once you understand the reasoning behind them. In fact, Laotian members have begun to ask many questions and express opposing opinions. When presented with draft articles, Laotian members questioned what made them that way, proposed what could be done to improve them, and asked how they should be applied in some specific cases. In this way, discussions have gone from strength to strength.

These draft articles were often collectively discussed by grouping several related articles together, and in some cases completing all of the draft articles took years. It was one step forward, one step back. This cycle went on and on through repeated discussions. After all this, the moment came when the final draft would be completed, and this became a sort of cue for applause. "There were times when applause erupted spontaneously. Members just felt that they had reached an achievement, and

The opening ceremony of the National Institute of Justice (NIJ) in October 2015

had accomplished something by themselves, which gave them great pleasure. I suppose the real purpose of our assistance is to support them in finding such satisfaction."

The completed materials, such as the civil and criminal procedure charts and the civil code precedent workbook, have been distributed across Laos as teaching materials for legal education and as practical manuals. Workshops have also been implemented in provincial cities to promote these informative materials, resulting in their greater use in different parts of the country. In addition, members have been able to develop a more advanced understanding of jurisprudence and have further improved their practical skills in the course of creating these project outputs.

While the project produced remarkable results, one challenge that was identified was the need to improve the abilities of a wider range of practitioners, as only those in limited professions were able to benefit from the project outcomes. For this reason, the Project for Human Resource Development in the Legal Sector Phase II, launched in July 2014, opened up its SWG membership to the members of additional organizations, including the Lao Bar Association, the Ministry of Public Security (police), and the Ministry of Labour and Social Welfare. The project has since evolved into a forum where participants from an even wider number of organizations have discussions beyond their organizational boundaries, by involving many different organizations engaged in various areas of practical legal work. The implementation period was set to take four years, ending in July 2018. The project was designed to be carried out by four SWGs specializing in Civil Code, civil and economic law, criminal law, and improvement of education and training. The aim was to allow members of each SWG to improve their abilities by creating related documents; for example, research papers summarizing the assistance for drafting of the Civil Code, the purpose of individual articles, case examples, and so on (civil code SWG), handbooks on economic dispute settlement[17] and labor laws[18] (civil and economic law SWG), and investigation-related Q&As for practitioners (criminal law SWG).

The SWG for improving education and training was newly added to review the procedures at the National Institute of

17 A law setting out procedures for settling economic disputes out of court through mediation or arbitration.

18 The revised labor law was enacted in 2013. Consisting of 181 articles organized into seventeen chapters, it regulates, among other matters, employment contracts, wages, and occupational health and safety, and governs labor authorities.

Justice (NIJ) that Laos has established. When Laotian members visited the Legal Training and Research Institute[19] in Japan in 2012, they became hugely inspired by its integrated system for training all three elements of the judicial community: judges, prosecutors, and lawyers. This led to the establishment of the Laotian judicial educational institute, NIJ, in January 2015. The NIJ curriculum consists of two courses: "junior college" and "training" courses. The former provides basic legal education, while the latter gives practical training to those who have completed the basic education. This "training" course is where prospective judges, prosecutors, and lawyers are educated together.

19 The Legal Training and Research Institute is the training facility of the Supreme Court of Japan. It conducts research and education programs for practicing judges and judicial training programs for apprentice judges, prosecutors, and lawyers.

Chomkham Bouphalivanh, the first director of the NIJ, describes the reason why the NIJ was modeled after the Japanese judicial personnel training system: "This was because the three elements share the same mission as guardians of law for citizens, although at the same time, each of them has its own separate roles." A lack of consistent understanding of laws and court proceedings among judges, prosecutors, and lawyers has been pointed out by many Laotian members as an important problem concerning law in Laos. This seriously hampers smooth court proceedings, contributing to a lack of public confidence in judicial authorities. They have pointed out that this situation has come about because personnel in the three areas of the judicial community have traditionally been trained separately in Laos.

Currently, judicial education in Laos is provided in three stages. Basic legal education is conducted by a total of six institutions: two four-year universities, the NIJ junior college course, and branch campuses of the junior college course in the northern, central, and southern parts of the country. Graduates of these schools who wish to enter the legal profession then advance to the training course at the NIJ to develop more practical skills. After this, those who pass the recruitment examination, which is separately implemented for each of the three parts of the legal profession, receive specialist education in the training institutes of respective organizations. The SWG of the JICA project working on improving education and training has been reassessing the segregation of the curriculums between the three stages of education, at the four-year universities and the junior college course, the NIJ training course, and training institutes of respective organizations, and has been developing the necessary teaching materials, etc., to introduce more practical learning through case-study exercises and discussions.

One characteristic of the training course of the NIJ is that four months of the one-year education period are allocated to practical training, in which each student is given a legal assignment and experiences a whole series of trial proceedings about the assignment, from the beginning of the trial to a court decision. This kind of learning activity has not been provided in Laos before. The first group of graduates has already been engaged in frontline judicial services, and the People's Supreme Court has monitored and evaluated the work performance of these graduates. Khampha Sengdara,[20] vice president of the People's Supreme Court, is convinced of the effectiveness of this education by its results. He says,

> It's apparent that these new staff members graduating from the NIJ have significantly higher ability than those employed before them.... It used to be the norm that new staff members, fresh from university, joined the court with virtually no knowledge of how court operations were conducted. The first intake of NIJ graduates required less time to become competent at their jobs compared to staff members who had joined us in previous years. For example, whereas before the foundation of the NIJ, newly employed judges were able to create decision documents only after working for nearly two years, NIJ graduates were able to do the same in just three months. What made this possible was the practical training they had experienced.

NIJ has a unique system in its junior college course as well: its curriculum includes a program in which students visit provincial areas to conduct promotional activities concerning the Civil Code and Civil Procedure Law before graduation.

"Laos aims to become 'a country governed by law.' It is a national policy that laws under development should be widely understood not only by members of the legal community, but

20 Sengdara became vice president of the People's Supreme Court in 2007 after serving in such positions as director general of the Criminal Investigation Department of the Ministry of Interior.

also by the general public. This is the reason that over a thousand students go around different parts of the country to take part in educational and promotional activities concerning the basics of law there before graduating from the junior college course," explains Chomkham.

For these promotional activities, the NIJ has compiled various teaching materials that provide basic legal information in an easily understood style, printed using the budget of the Ministry of Justice. The completed publication is distributed to students and participants of promotional activities. What specific promotional activities do students carry out using the material? Chomkham explains,

> These promotional activities are conducted with the cooperation of the Ministry of Justice, the NIJ, and justice bureaus of respective provinces and districts. The type of venue used and the teaching method adopted vary considerably depending on the circumstances in each region. Sessions can take place in the village mayor's office, a school classroom, or a public square. Time is also scheduled very flexibly. For example, if it's difficult for local people to attend during the day, when they're busy with farm work, the activity is scheduled for the evenings.

Imparting legal knowledge is not the only role that students are supposed to fulfill in these promotional activities; they are also meant to offer advice on solutions to problems that have actually occurred in a given region. In other words, they provide a "free legal consultation service." Says Chomkham, on a humorous note:

> Students can often have difficulty giving the correct answers to questions from citizens, since they don't have much in-depth knowledge yet. This is why we teach them that they should consult more experienced people, like myself and other faculty members, or former NIJ students who are now working as professionals, before giving answers to participants for questions they find difficult to answer on the spot.

Despite the fact that this program is held during the coldest season of the year, students always sweat due to the stress.

The NIJ has more roles to play than just developing human resources in the legal and judicial sector. Chomkham says he hopes that NIJ graduates will contribute to society in many different ways in the future.

It's a commonly held view in Laos that those who have studied law should work as legal professionals. My hope, however, is that NIJ graduates will be able to contribute to society as "good human resources" in a broader sense, not only by working for a prosecutor's office or a court or as a lawyer, but also by making effective use of their legal knowledge in private-sector companies. By the term "good human resources," I mean individuals who have equipped themselves with knowledge through learning, are able to put that knowledge into practice, and are compliant with judicial ethics. We hope that graduates who have internalized these three criteria will play important roles in many different areas in Laos.

06 Creation of Words and Concepts

Language-related problems associated with the establishment of laws are always a difficult challenge for people engaged in the cooperation for legal and judicial development in any country.

Imagine that the following problem has occurred: "Person A wants to sell his land for 3 million yen, and has entrusted Person B, who is well versed in land transactions, to enter into negotiations on his behalf with people interested in buying his land. Person B, however, sells the land for 2 million yen without consulting Person A beforehand." Most Japanese people would understand what has happened even if the above situation is translated into a simple, abstract description like, "The agent sold the principal's land for an unacceptable price."

In Laos, however, this was not true until 2010. The Lao

people did not have the concept of "principal"; there was not even a Laotian word for "principal." They just understood Person A as "Person A," or some specific person like "me" or "my father," and had no way of developing an abstract understanding such as "the principal from a third-party point of view."

Nevertheless, there was no other word to replace "principal" to represent this concept, not only in the Civil Code that was being drafted at that time, but also in other law articles. This was the reason that Ishioka, the long-term expert mentioned earlier, and the civil code SWG, decided to borrow a word from Thai, which is similar to Lao, and use the Thai word "*jao-kan*" to refer to the concept of "principal." Besides this, many other new Lao words and concepts were coined during the Civil Code drafting support activities.

For example, the Thai word "*cam-nam*" was adopted to refer to the concept of "mortgage,"[21] which was another word that could not be translated directly into Lao. The Laotian language already had an expression for "land collateral" and a word for "pledge,"[22] meaning a movable collateral. However, in many other countries pledges are divided into "pledges of movables" and "pledges of immovable property," and mortgages into "mortgages of movables" and "mortgages of immovable property." These four phrases, of course, represent four different concepts. In Lao, however, they were all "land collateral." This meant that it was not possible to discuss them unless each of them were given a different name and regarded as four separate concepts. There were also cases in which a new concept was added to an existing Lao word. For example, the verb for "violate," "*kan-la-merd*," was adopted as the new noun for "illegal act."[23]

In law articles, the same words must be used to refer to the same concepts. Even this fundamental rule has not been fully established yet.

For "bail," the Lao word "*phoy-tua-pharng*" is used, which refers to the act of releasing a person temporarily. In-depth examination of articles of the Criminal Procedure Law and other Laotian laws, however, reveals that the word "*pa-kan-tua*," which means "paying money for a guarantee," is sometimes

21 A form of security that gives the creditor priority in receiving payment from the proceeds of the collateral (whether personal or real property) (see page 116, note 32). It differs from a pledge in that the borrower has possession and use of the collateral as long as he or she does not default.

22 A form of security that gives the creditor priority in receiving payment from the proceeds of the collateral (whether personal or real property). It differs from a mortgage in that the borrower does not retain possession and use of the collateral; rather, that is transferred to the creditor.

23 An illegal act is one that violate another's rights or interests, whether intentionally or through negligence. The violator is liable for the damages suffered as a result. Lao had words for liability arising from one's own actions and for liability arising from something under one's control, but it lacked the concept of tort, which subsumes both.

Hiroshi Suda (left) with a local project office staffer

Ketsana Phommachane

added to form the expression "*pa-kan-tua phoy-tua-pharng*" and other times only "*pa-kan-tua*" is used. When Hiroshi Suda,[24] a long-term expert in charge of the criminal procedure law SWG, asked Laotian members whether the above three phrases referred to the same thing, some answered yes, while others said no. This indicates that views are divided even among the Lao people.

24 Suda, a prosecutor who supported efforts in legal and judicial development in Laos as an ICD professor in Japan, was later stationed in Laos as a long-term expert (2015–).

Ketsana Phommachane,[25] an employee of the Ministry of Justice and a member of the civil code SWG, also recalls the language-related difficulties experienced during the drafting of the Civil Code:

25 Phommachane became director general of the Department of International Cooperation at the Laotian Ministry of Justice in 2017 after serving as deputy director of the Ministry's Law Research Institute and director general of the Department of Legal Affairs.

> When the work was separated into sections and assigned to around thirty members, different members prepared their drafts using their own knowledge and ways of writing, resulting in a lack of consistency in the language used. For example, while "the current day" was used in some places, "today" was used in others. It was an extremely painstaking task to standardize these varying expressions. There were also occasions when we asked Japanese experts for advice and they told us that we had to deal with some wording and grammar issues, even though our drafts were fine content-wise.

Ishioka says, "From an extreme point of view, it can be said that the ambiguity of the Lao language is reducing the effectiveness of laws in Laos." Different individuals use the same words to refer to slightly different things. Also when working out draft law articles, different individuals insist on using different words and expressions that they think are appropriate. Given the ambiguity of the Lao language, however, there is no telling which phrase is more appropriate than another from an objective point of view. The result is often a negative conclusion, like "Stop using this word" or "Remove this article," causing a holdup in the work of establishing a new law. This can happen not only with vocabulary, but also grammar.

Ishioka explains, "Laws are tools for cross-cultural communication. Not only Lao people but other entities, like foreign companies, will use Laotian laws. This makes the problem more difficult. When Laotian laws are only understandable from a Laotian way of thinking, such laws are no longer laws in the genuine sense of the term. This makes law both interesting and difficult."

The above example of "*pa-kan-tua phoy-tua-pharng*" also suggests another problem facing the law of Laos. Whether the three expressions are judged to mean the same thing depends on the individual, and Suda points out that this should indicate that legal theory, which provides a basis for making the judgment, is inadequate.

Most problems that arise in judicial practice cannot be resolved simply by applying laws as they are. When it is necessary to apply a specific law to a problem that may slightly deviate from its stipulations, one is required to clarify what the law was originally established for.

Suda explains this with the example of "*in flagrante delicto* [caught in the act] arrests" stipulated in the Criminal Procedure Law. Taking someone into custody is a serious violation of human rights unless under exceptional circumstances, and is only allowed when all of the requirements are met, such as implementation of a judicial review (by a judge if in Japan), clear evidence of the crime, fear of the culprit escaping, and so on. In the case of an *in flagrante delicto* arrest, however, it is permissible to arrest a culprit caught red-handed providing all these requirements are clearly satisfied, and it is thus permitted to hold the person without judicial review by a judge and without a warrant.

> You can judge against this standard of whether you can arrest culprits without warrants under many different circumstances. Many Laotian laws, however, do not provide such standards or theories on which these judgments can be based. Unless you understand the basic reasoning why someone who has been caught in the act of committing a crime can sometimes be arrested without a warrant, you cannot make an accurate judgment of whether this is allowed in the given situation. This can result in subjective decisions about arrests.

One major factor contributing to this lack of legal theory is that Laos has many "borrowed laws" due to having imported laws from neighboring Vietnam and Thailand, as well as retaining some French laws left over from the colonial era. When their laws are borrowed, Lao people have no grounds on which to identify the reasons why different expressions are used. In fact, the discussion concerning "*pa-kan-tua phoy-tua-pharng*" is found in a project record from as early as around 2010. To date, no conclusion has been reached. Suda says,

> In my opinion, this is because Lao people don't have enough information to judge whether the three expressions mean the same.... By now, Laotian members have realized that they need to go back to the fundamentals of law to resolve this situation, but they still don't have the capacity to do so, and are feeling frustrated. In the past, they failed to notice this. In other words, they've graduated from the stage where all they could do was passively accept what laws said, and have advanced to the next stage, where they sense that there should be reasoning behind each law and are anxious to know what this reason is.

Suda thinks that the key to breaking out of this situation lies in the Civil Code, which Lao people have been creating for themselves. The Civil Code of Laos is a collection of laws which the Lao people have been developing from scratch. This project has also produced a research paper to clarify the purpose of the Civil Code. Through reading this research paper, one can develop a clear understanding of why specific articles and words have been adopted. The Civil Code is the first law that has ever been developed by the Lao people themselves and thus has theoretical grounds which the Lao people can really understand. "I think the Civil Code, which is being created right now, will lay the initial foundation for exploring legal theory in Laos," Suda says hopefully.

07 | What Does "Only Eighteen Pages in One Year" Mean?

The first civil procedure flowchart, which was completed in 2012, has been compiled into a book, or "leaflet," of eighteen pages. This leaflet, which consists almost entirely of charts, took a whole year to complete.

The primary purpose of JICA's cooperation for legal and judicial development in Laos is to help Laotian judicial professionals improve their basic abilities as legal specialists. The results emerge in the form of the drafting of the Civil Code, as well as improvements in practical work processes, such as smoother, more standardized court proceedings. Nevertheless, it is still true that when the utmost emphasis is placed on "process," it is difficult for human resource development support to produce visible results, and the undertaking requires greater persistence and patience.

"This brings back many memories." A warm expression appears on Ishioka's face when he looks at the leaflet, which was completed quite some time ago. He recalls the discussions they had and the hard work they did back then.

> We spent an entire year producing just this one thing. This is something that no other donor would do. Other donors would be blamed for not producing more visible results, along the lines of, "Is this all you were capable of achieving in a year? What on earth were you doing?" Actually, this makes sense if the purpose of your assistance work is simply to produce project outputs such as textbooks and handbooks. We,

At a retreat

> however, believe that the most important part is the process of producing something through discussions between members.... Since our work is about developing human resources, even the best law articles will be pointless unless the Lao people really understand them.

The project holds a retreat several times a year in which project members leave the capital city of Vientiane, where each counterpart organization has its office, to stay in accommodations in the suburbs for several days and have SWG meetings there. This program has been launched to provide members with the opportunity to get away from their respective places of work to focus on project discussions.

Members of each group bounce ideas off each other, leaving their seats to work in front of a whiteboard, view tables shown on a screen, and so on. When one of the groups reaches a conclusion as a result of their heated debates, a round of applause erupts among the members. In such moments, it is not Japanese experts who are at the center of the discussions; they are just calmly observing the members from a distance. Suda believes that offering aid is "giving someone a supportive push." He says,

> All we do is guide the Laotian members back on track if their discussion begins to drift off topic. Our work is about making

> sure that they're on the right trajectory as much as possible, rather than providing input.... If we simply prop them up from below, the things that they accomplish can fall back to the ground once the support is gone. We should avoid this and give them a supportive push to help them develop the physical strength they need to stand on their own. I think this is exactly the approach adopted by JICA. With such support, they can walk further by themselves, and even run if they are lucky, even when nobody is there to push them. I think this is what capacity development[26] is all about.

26 See the Quick Guide to Japan's Cooperation for Legal and Judicial Development at the front of the book, page 11.

When Japanese members try to "guide the Laotian members back on track," however, it is often the case that the Laotian members have trouble understanding what the Japanese members are trying to get across, so it is difficult to convince them. In fact, the rate of change is far from fast. "It is sometimes difficult to witness visible changes in a short period of time, like a year or two, but even when things don't seem to me to be getting any better, advisory group members tell me that marked progress has been made compared to five or ten years ago. Meeting specialists see things on a longer timescale, and when they say that it reassures me that the capacity of Laotian members has been improving."

If the number of completed project outputs is a direct indication of the effectiveness of the project, it is visible to anyone and is easy to evaluate. When the effects are clear to see to those involved in the project as well, it is also easier for them to feel a sense of accomplishment. Nevertheless, the genuine outcomes of this project cannot be identified in terms of how many laws are established, how many books are published, and so on.

Ishioka declares, "Creating something tangible is not our main goal. In this regard, we are quite ready to accept whatever comes of the project." For her part, Maiko Amano,[27] a lawyer acting as a long-term expert, says, "Even if Japanese people feel that something is not legally right, I don't think that's a problem at all as long as the Lao people see nothing wrong there. After all, Laos is for the Lao people." The words of such long-term experts may sound as if they were detached from the Laotians.

27 Amano, a lawyer registered with the Saitama Bar Association, was stationed as a long-term expert in Laos from 2016 to 2017 after taking part in the JFBA program to assist the Lao Bar Association.

This, though, is precisely the result of them having a deep understanding of the goal of this support project being "human resource development," and completely respecting the Laotian members as independent decision makers. The important thing is that the Lao people should create what they consider is acceptable and adaptable to what Laos is today; the quality of project outputs is not what really matters. This is something they are prepared to accept.

"To tell the truth, I'm afraid that the quality of the outputs is pretty low," says Suda. "But that doesn't really matter, I suppose. After all, it's up to the Lao people to improve them later."

08 Japan Is a Family Member of Laos

When Japanese project members propose ideas or systems that are not familiar to Laos, it is rarely the case that they are turned down instantly, although sometimes the response may be "This is too early for Laos," or "Add a slight modification, and then it may be applicable to our situation." They are open-minded to whatever proposals come from Japanese members and are prepared to think critically about them. This is because of the successful precedents they have set in the past fifteen years, in which they have achieved success by accepting proposals that had not even been imagined in Laos before. For the Laotian side, however, just discussing the possibility of accepting a new way of thinking completely unfamiliar to them is a challenging task. Despite this, they show the courage to open themselves to new ideas, believing, "There is invariably some meaning behind what Japan proposes to us." What makes this possible is the solid relationship of trust that has built up over the years.

The core Laotian members who have been playing leading parts in the project all these years all say that they feel the warm disposition of Japanese aid workers and that they are like family.

One member, Nalonglith Norasing,[28] has been improving his abilities through having discussions with many Japanese experts and advisory group members. He is now demonstrating great

28 Norasing became director general of the Law Review and Assessment Department of the Laotian Ministry of Justice in 2017, after serving as head of legal affairs at the Ministry's Law Research Institute and director general of the Ministry's International Cooperation Department.

capacity in various fields as an ace member of the Ministry of Justice. When asked about his most memorable moment in the aid work he has been involved in so far, he answers,

> I have been working with Professor Matsuo for fifteen years now, but he has never said things like, "This is wrong. You should revise it." Even when the Laotian members say something wrong, the Japanese advisors and experts will not just dismiss it as wrong; they will kindly suggest better ideas, saying, "But you might as well give this a try," while praising and encouraging them. I think I have learned a lot from their consideration toward the feelings of others.... Sometimes Laotian members submit draft law articles with confidence, but the Japanese point out problems that we Laotians alone cannot notice. In those cases, they say things like, "You've done a good job, but this may actually have a negative impact on the economy." The experience of working together with such experts and advisory group members, who are intellectually inquiring hard workers, has been so inspiring and motivating that we've begun to feel the need to improve ourselves.

"What has struck me most is how Japanese advisors and experts treat Laotian members like family," says Ket Kiettisak,[29] deputy minister of justice. "They have always been concerned for Laos and want the country to develop and grow. They care not only about the current generation, but also about the future generations of Laos. They always work with us, eat with us, and talk to us candidly, and we can say anything to each other without holding back. This is another reason that we feel like family."

Ket Kiettisak

29 Kettesiak became deputy minister of Justice in 1998 after serving as a judge of the People's Supreme Court and then president of the Court. He retired in 2017.

Japan's cooperation has also brought about changes in the Lao people's attitude toward work. According to Laotian members, Japanese workers are "serious and strict," and "They always meet specified times and deadlines." Furthermore, "They establish a plan in advance and get their work done accordingly," and prioritize "attention to detail." Chomkham Bouphalivanh, the first director of the NIJ, says,

> Witnessing the Japanese way of working has brought me to realize that many Lao people are almost embarrassingly sloppy workers. In my opinion, it is a huge disgrace that Laotian members arrive late or do not work seriously when Japanese people go out of their way to support Laos in the legal sector.... I guess Lao people, who are now developing laws for their country, should start by establishing laws that govern themselves.
>
> I have learned numerous things, including lifestyle habits, work processes, management approaches, and research methods. The important thing is to work seriously to produce results, so that we can trust each other.
>
> Staff members have achieved remarkable growth by participating in this project. They always come back to their workplaces with a greater understanding and knowledge of law, as well as improved skills needed to get work done in a systematic fashion. Development of human resources in the legal and judicial sector can benefit the whole country of Laos.

In fact, many Laotian members have made remarks to this effect. Working together with Japanese members has brought about a gradual change in the attitude of Laotian members toward work, which, in turn, has been rubbing off onto others in their workplaces as well. Providing support to improve the capacity of people working in the legal sector contributes not only to increasing their knowledge and understanding of law, but also to enhancing their management skills, enabling them to work more efficiently.

09 Teaching People How to Catch Fish

"I have been involved with Laos for exactly fifteen years now and have been working with certain Laotian members the whole time. Seeing how much legal knowledge they have now, as well as how they discuss things now, convinces me that they have grown dramatically." This is how Hiroshi Matsuo feels after working for the project in Laos as a supporter for many years.

There were very few Lao translations of overseas laws and regulations, legal textbooks, or other informative materials in the early days of the project. Laotian members say that they were "hungry for information" since there were virtually no sources that they could consult for development of law articles, textbooks, and so on. This is the reason that the Japanese started by translating Japanese and other overseas information materials into Lao and providing them to the Laotians. "After all that they have been through," Matsuo says, "they are now able to independently search French and German laws, and laws from Thailand, Vietnam, and other countries, in addition to Japanese laws. They also review and compare them, and create law articles that suit the Lao people. At this point in time, they are now able to do these things. In other words, they have equipped themselves with tools to gather legal knowledge for themselves."

Furthermore, there are even times now when Laotian members take the initiative to propose that new regulations, or more detailed regulations, should be established for systems that are not stipulated in any Laotian laws or are only simply stipulated in Laotian laws. "They don't just make proposals; they make well-considerated proposals and raise really sharp questions. Frankly speaking, I was surprised to see them do this so naturally."

Matsuo thinks that this change is the result of the Lao people spending lots of time and effort developing legal textbooks and workbooks for themselves.

> This is presumably because they have begun to feel that laws are pointless unless they are applicable to, and useful in, real-life situations. It gives me the greatest sense of accomplishment to see the Lao people developing laws for themselves and becoming more and more enthusiastic about creating laws that they can really apply.

> The progress of law shows up in how laws are applied, rather than in something tangible, such as the number of laws that have been added. The project has many members who are judges. They study laws really carefully. For example, when I had difficulty understanding an article, it turned out that the Lao people had developed their own understanding of it, which the judges fully understood. They interpret laws in their own ways to fully understand them. Laotian judges and prosecutors, who are operators of the law, have made steady progress.

The prime purpose of JICA's aid activities is to "develop people in the course of creating things." Laotian members already know the real value and outcomes of this, which would never be gained through "aid activities targeted solely at producing things."

Khampha Sengdara, vice president of the People's Supreme Court, says with some pride,

> We have created drafts of the Civil Code and handbooks with the support of Japan. However, they are the result of our own thinking and production efforts, not what Japanese people have created for us. JICA's aid is different from that of countries that do nothing further once their projects are over. What sets JICA's aid apart is that it allows the Lao people to think independently and develop laws for themselves. The role of Japanese experts is to provide us with advice and point out problems. As such, it can be said that the Lao people have basically developed their laws themselves.

Viengvilay Thiengchanhxay,[30] dean of the Faculty of Law and Political Science of the National University of Laos, also describes his outlook for the future: "Japan referred to the opinions of many different sources when it first established its laws. We would like to make our own laws that are flexible to the times by applying the laws which we have established to real-life situations and making modifications where necessary."

Somsack Taybounlack, presiding justice of the People's

30 After working as a prosecutor at the Vientiane Prosecutor's Office and serving as vice dean of the Faculty of Law and Political Science of the National University of Laos, Thiengchanhxay, who has studied at Nagoya University, became dean in 2011.

Central High Court—projects the direction in which Laos and its laws are heading:

Viengvilay Thiengchanhxay

> Laws are for the good of people. The important thing is to listen to people, consider what kind of society it is that they wish to create, and establish laws that take this into account. At the same time, it is also essential for people to comply with laws once they are established. There are countries with very advanced laws and society, and Laos has yet to catch up with them. Even so, we should move forward step by step, without getting impatient.

Japan's cooperation focuses on increasing the abilities of the Lao people and guiding the country toward sustainable growth. To use Lao expressions, the key is to help Lao people "learn how to catch fish," rather than "be given fish caught by someone else." The fruits of such aid activities by Japan will stay in Laos forever. Chomkham Bouphalivanh, the first director of the NIJ, believes this is so.

> We do not see the support from Japan as support from just the Japanese government, but as support from all Japanese

JICA experts conferring with Mr. Somsack at the project office

people. We know that they are supporting us out of their taxes as friends. Of course, Japanese aid activities are limited in funds and time. There have been many aid projects implemented by other countries or organizations in the past in which no further progress was made once the projects were over. This Japanese project is different: we're sure that we can continue with our efforts after the project is complete. This is because our Japanese friends have always been supporting us, and have enabled us to do so. The laws and handbooks produced as part of the project will remain of value forever in the development of the Laotian legal system. Needless to say, we're going to make revisions as necessary to meet the needs of changing times and environment. Even after the completion of the project, we believe that Japanese expertise will stay with the Lao people forever in the form of the outcomes.

Hitoshi Kawamura

Laos project coordinator

PROFILE:
Became Laos project coordinator when the Project for Human Resource Development in the Legal Sector was launched in 2010. He is the man who is constantly working singlehandedly behind the scenes to ensure that everything goes smoothly.

Do you have any good anecdotes about the early days of the HR Development Project?

When long-term expert Osamu Ishioka started participatory discussion sessions, there was no whiteboard and there was nothing suitable to be found, so I had to rig up something myself. I agonized over what to make it with, but then I came across some PVC piping in town—the kind used in plumbing—and I thought to myself, "That's it!" I constructed a framework of pipes and fitted a plastic board into it. It was a nifty contrivance: it could be dismantled for carrying, and it came in really handy for making charts. Another fond memory is our first retreat. We spent the days in meetings and the evenings making merry, which transformed the mood of the project.

You've worked with a lot of long-term experts. Is there anything that particularly struck you about any of them?

I was struck by the way they tried to break the ice with the Laotians, even when they weren't discussing law. One evening during a party at a retreat, long-term expert Yoko Watanabe[1] gave a rousing rendition of the song "Space Battleship Yamato." Hiroyuki Ito,[2] who arrived later, sang a local folksong in excellent Lao. Both of them are serious, respectable people, so the Laotians were amazed to see them singing that way, which seemed so unlike their usual selves, and burst into applause. That was the moment when the Laotians and the long-term experts got closer to each other.

What place do your Laotian colleagues have in the project?

When I became coordinator in 2010, I took my time looking for staff. I didn't rush because I thought it was important to find highly qualified people of good character. The first people we hired were Manilay and Latthaya, who are still with us. They're both great assets to the Laos project. They do what needs to be done before we even tell them, which helps a lot. Treating local staff with respect so they stay with us for the long haul is vital to a project's success.

---

1 Watanabe was a prosecutor stationed in Laos from 2010 to 2011.

2 Ito, a prosecutor stationed in Laos from 2011 to 2013, is currently deputy director of the ICD.

Chapter 4

New Horizons, New Challenges —Indonesia, China, Uzbekistan, Nepal, Myanmar, Francophone Africa and Côte d'Ivoire

JICA's cooperation for legal and judicial development started widening its scope in response to particular circumstances in partner countries, along with the broadening of the geographical area covered, from the developing nations of Southeast Asia to the Côte d'Ivoire in Francophone Africa.

The center of Abidjan, Côte d'Ivoire's largest city
AFP-JIJI

Japan's cooperation for legal and judicial development, which started with Vietnam in the 1990s, began to expand in the 2000s to provide support to Uzbekistan, Mongolia, China, and other countries working toward becoming a democracy or a market economy.

As the number of targets expanded geographically to include countries like Indonesia, which had recovered from a currency crisis and was striving to reform its systems, and Côte d'Ivoire in French-speaking Africa, different kinds of activities were started to assist the legal and judicial development of each country. In fact, the scope of support has also been expanding to meet the different realities of each target country, along with the broadening of geographical coverage.

The Basic Policies on Legal Technical Assistance,[1] revised by the Japanese government in May 2013, state that the priorities shall include enhancing support in the area of economic law and assisting the creation of secure business environments to allow Japanese and other foreign companies to do business in developing countries with peace of mind, in addition to offering support concerning basic laws.

The policies also emphasize further enhancement of cooperation and coordination between implementation bodies, while placing importance on "Japan's additional economic cooperation through governance reinforcement."[2] "New emerging countries," such as Myanmar and Bangladesh, are also regarded as focal recipients of the cooperation alongside Vietnam, Cambodia, and other, more traditional target countries.

Mitsuyasu Matsukawa[3] is a judge who has been involved in the cooperation in this area in Cambodia and other countries as a professor from the International Cooperation Department (ICD),[4] Research and Training Institute, Ministry of Justice of Japan. He says,

> Indonesia is one of the countries that is particularly important when it comes to cooperation for legal and judicial development in the future.... About 90 percent of Indonesia's population is Muslim. Unlike Buddhism and many other religions, Islam is a set of laws in itself. As such, Indonesian people can

1 This policy document, which set the direction of Japanese government policy on cooperation for legal and judicial development, was adopted in April 2009 and revised in May 2013.

2 See page 57, note 26.

3 Matsukawa is a judge who supported efforts in legal and judicial development in several countries as an ICD professor in Japan from 2010 to 2012.

4 See inset, page 79.

feel torn between Islamic teachings and modern law. At the same time, there are Muslim people who regard Japan as one of the few possible partners with whom they can communicate. This, for example, means that taking advantage of experiences gained in Indonesia may help Japan approach Middle Eastern countries in the future. They are distant both geographically and culturally from Japan, making it difficult for the government to provide direct cooperation for legal and judicial development to them. It may also be possible for Japan and Indonesia to work together in some fields. If we can make this a reality in the future, I think it will set a new model for Japan's cooperation in this area.

Currently, Japan is facing a turning point in its cooperation for legal and judicial development. Providing developing Southeast Asian countries with "aid for modernization" in the area of legal and judicial system development is still an essential task for Japan, just as it was in the early days of the cooperation in this area. Underpinning this lies a "willingness to do what one can for others," which allows Japan to provide support without expecting anything in return. Nowadays, however, this alone is no longer sufficient to justify the effort: national interests matter as well. This is why one of the themes of the above basic policies, "assisting the creation of secure business environments to allow Japanese companies to do business in developing countries with peace of mind," has become part of Japan's focus.

Imagine that Japan and other foreign countries make investments or conduct business in a developing country whose laws remain underdeveloped. If a problem should occur, it might lead to grave consequences. Elimination of this risk is one of the prime advantages of working together with the target country to facilitate the development of its legal and judicial system. The resulting reinforced relationship with the country might also make it easier for Japanese companies to expand their businesses or investments into the country in the future. This strategic viewpoint is also incorporated into Japan's cooperation for legal and judicial development.

Of course, it would be inappropriate for Japan to focus only on its own advantages. A willingness to "do what one can for others" should always be the fundamental bedrock for Japan's cooperation; Japan should think together with the country receiving the aid about what it can do for them, and put it into action. As demonstrated in the "Myanmar" section of this chapter, Japan can build a win-win relationship with each target country by making legal and judicial system improvements in areas that are particularly likely to contribute to the Japanese economy while continuing to respect the spirit of "good old cooperation" as prosecutor Hiroki Kunii puts it.

Judge Matsukawa also says,

> Given the fact that the cooperation is supported by tax money paid by Japanese citizens, it is of course essential for the government to be accountable for the purpose of its activities. However, it has also been pointed out that too much emphasis in recent years has been placed on improving the investment environment. If too much attention were paid to improving the investment environment, what would the aid recipient think of that? They might suspect that Japan only provided them with the cooperation to make it easier for Japanese people to make money in their country, which I don't think would make them very happy. Nevertheless, this doesn't mean that we should criticize the investment environment improvement strategy itself. Nothing is wrong with a company pursuing its own corporate interests and social responsibilities at the same time. In the same way, the government need not choose between them: both are vital.

As Japan's cooperation in this field expands in terms of both geographic area and content, it is becoming increasingly necessary to gain the understanding of each recipient country by taking into account their own ways of doing things and their way of thinking in each area of support. Terutoshi Yamashita[5] says,

5 See page 79, note 57.

> While pursuing our ideals and setting high goals, we should conform to the measures of the recipient side, rather than

> forcing our way of thinking on them, in order to convince them. It's important to understand what they are really thinking and how they are feeling by asking them and collecting information and responding flexibly. It's only natural that opinions should differ and that they should have their own standpoints and the need to save face. We need to get over all of these issues and move forward, even if only by small steps. It may be impossible to score 80 or 90 out of 100 from the start, and they may not accept us immediately, but our efforts are sure to bear fruit over time.... Developing countries tend to jump to new, unfamiliar fields before laying solid foundations. Western donors are also likely to show an interest in such new areas. Nevertheless, your legal system development work will go nowhere unless the basic foundations are established. When people develop the basic thinking and reasoning skills required to foster laws and legal professionals, they can apply them to many other fields as well. This is what Western people don't teach, or fail to teach, and it's where Japanese aid work comes into play.

The core essence of Japan's cooperation for legal and judicial development, as previously described in the cases of Vietnam, Cambodia, and Laos, is present and vividly felt also in new recipient countries and new areas of support. This is the context in which we shall now examine the case of Indonesia.

PROJECT FACT SHEET

Indonesia

March 31, 2007–
March 31, 2009

Project on Improvement of Mediation System in Indonesia

COUNTERPART: Supreme Court

This project aimed to encourage reasonable, expeditious settlement of disputes by improving the running of the court mediation system. Specifically, assistance was provided in amending the Supreme Court rules, training mediators and promoting awareness and use of mediation procedures.

FY2009

Country-focused Training: Implementation of Court-connected Mediation

COUNTERPART: Supreme Court

Support was provided in improving training programs for mediators with the goal of promoting use of the court mediation system.

December 21, 2015–
December 20, 2020

Project on Intellectual Property Rights Protection and Legal Consistency for Improving the Business Environment

COUNTERPART: Supreme Court / Directorate General of Intellectual Property, Ministry of Law and Human Rights / Directorate General of Legislation, Ministry of Law and Human Rights

Assistance was provided in several areas: enhancing the quality of intellectual property examination by the directorate general of intellectual property of the Ministry of Law and Human Rights; strengthening action by the directorate and intellectual property rights (IPR) enforcement authorities against IPR violations; improving the Supreme Court's handling of intellectual property cases; and improving legal consistency in the drafting and vetting of business legislation (including IPR legislation) by the Ministry's directorate general of legislation.

©Rainbow/a.collectionRF/amanaimages

©Sybil Sassoon/Robert Harding/amanaimages

©Hideo Ishii/SEBUN PHOTO/amanaimages

INDONESIA

01 A Backlog of Unresolved Civil Cases

The Republic of Indonesia is situated in the southern part of Southeast Asia. The capital city of Jakarta is located on the island of Java. Straddling the equator, the country stretches east to west and is made up of some 13,000 large and small islands.

Even though seventy years have passed since the end of the Second World War, some laws rooted in the former Dutch colonial rule are still in effect in Indonesia. For example, no original civil procedure laws have been developed by Indonesian people themselves since the war: the country still uses Indonesian translations of the revised Indonesian Procedure Act and other civil procedure laws created in Dutch. These laws, however, do not function adequately to deal with the many different incidents and disputes arising in modern Indonesian society. In fact, there was a gigantic backlog of unresolved civil cases at Indonesian courts due to the slow speed of processing them and the huge number of appeals.

This is how Yoshiro Kusano,[6] a lawyer involved in JICA's cooperation for legal and judicial development, describes the situation concerning the legal system of Indonesia at that time:

> The dysfunctional legal system of Indonesia had begun to attract attention as a serious problem by the early 1990s. However, it was in 1997, when the devaluation of the Thai baht led to the Asian currency crisis, that the problem was officially pointed out by the international community. The crisis dealt a severe blow to the Indonesian economy, prompting the country to ask the World Bank for help. At this point, "transparency in the judiciary" was a requirement imposed on the country. The World Bank would offer loans to help Indonesia, but it needed to make sure that all

6 Kusano, a lawyer registered with the Tokyo Bar Association, is president of the Japan-Indonesia Lawyers' Association (JILA). After retiring from the bench, he became a professor at Gakushuin University Faculty of Law and Law School. He worked as advisor to the Project on Improvement of Mediation System in Indonesia.

its loans would be repaid and thought that it was necessary for Indonesia to reform its judicial system to guarantee the repayments. Meanwhile, momentum had already built among Indonesian people toward improving their legal system. Furthermore, Suharto's regime, which had gone on for thirty years, finally ended in 1998. This resulted in judicial system reforms, including amendments to the Constitution, becoming a priority task for the nation.

As part of these judicial reforms, Indonesia requested that Japan offer cooperation in this area in 2001, which Japan accepted. This was how Japan's cooperation for legal and judicial development for Indonesia got started, organized and implemented by JICA and the International Cooperation Department (ICD).[7]

7 See inset, page 79.

02 A Keen Interest in Compromise and Mediation

Kusano is a "master mediator," who played an important role in compromise and mediation in the past as a judge in Japan and wrote *Wakai gijutsu ron* (Technical theory on compromise) (Shinzansha Shuppan, 2003). After retiring, he became a professor of law at Gakushuin University and also works as a lawyer. Thereafter, in 2006, he began to involve himself in the JICA project.

From 2002 through 2006, five seminars were held in Japan to conduct comparative studies on the judicial systems of Japan and Indonesia by inviting legal professionals from Indonesia. The 2006 seminar exclusively targeted law professionals with a high degree of skill in drafting proposals and senior officials with the authority to make policy decisions in courts. They studied the kinds of compromise and mediation procedures used in Japanese courts, conducted mock conciliations, and compiled a collection of policy recommendations.

"The collection of policy recommendations revealed the keen interest that Indonesian judges had in Japan's compromise and mediation system," says Kusano.

Comparative seminar on judicial systems, December 2005

In fact, Indonesia also has a legal equivalent to the Japanese term *wakai* (compromise), *perdamaian*. Regardless of this, Kusano says, it was not applied often.

> Generally speaking, compromise was not very common among Indonesian judges. This was because, to their understanding, compromise was only possible before the first due date of the first-instance trial. Consequently, no compromise procedure was followed once the first due date was over, and Indonesian judges believed that compromise was impossible in appeals trials. Given the fact that there were no articles of law stipulating this, however, compromise was actually possible at any point in time. Nevertheless, it was a widely held belief among Indonesian judges that compromise should not be tried after the first due date.

Furthermore, the compromise and mediation system derived from common law, which the Supreme Court rules introduced in 2003 with the support of Australia, was failing to produce the expected results. As mentioned in chapter 1, legal systems are divided into British-based common law and European-based civil law (see page 47), and the law of Indonesia that was introduced from the Netherlands was civil law. This may be one reason that the common-law-based Supreme Court rules concerning compromise and mediation established with the support of Australia were incompatible with the judicial system of Indonesia.

Kusano points out, "It's often the case with common-law-based donors that they believe their common laws are the best and their systems should be transplanted as they are." By contrast, according to many, one characteristic of Japan's cooperation is that the donor explores realistic solutions together with recipients, saying, "Let's see what you can do. This may be difficult, but it may be more realistic for you." As such, it is understandable that Indonesian judicial officials, who were searching for quick solutions to unresolved civil cases in their country at that time, showed a keen interest in the conflict resolution system of Japan, which considered more appropriate solutions. As Kusano explains,

> Participating in training in Japan gave Indonesian judges a strong interest in the Japanese way of compromise, as compromise was possible at any point in time in Japan, regardless of due dates. Having learned that 30 percent of Japanese district court cases reached a settlement through compromise, they were eager to know more, saying, "Why is that possible in Japan? How does compromise work here?" While Indonesia also had compromise-related law articles similar to those in Japan, as well as its own common-law-based compromise and mediation system, Indonesian judges lacked the specific knowledge and skills required to go through actual compromise and mediation procedures. In fact, this was a major cause of the delay in popularization of compromise in the country.

03 The First Objective: To Amend the Supreme Court Rules

Under these circumstances, JICA launched the Project on Improvement of Mediation System in Indonesia in 2007 to introduce the Japanese way of compromise and mediation to Indonesia so that the country could resolve disputes more swiftly. The main objective of the project was to reduce the burden on

Preliminary survey team for the Project on Improvement of Mediation System in Indonesia (2006)

Indonesian courts by facilitating early resolution of incidents through agreements between the involved parties. The project's counterpart was the Supreme Court of Indonesia.

It was decided that the project would last for two years, from March 2007 through March 2009. The first goal was to revise the Supreme Court rules concerning compromise and mediation established with the support of Australia in 2003.

What was prioritized when JICA implemented the project? Kusano says,

> What the Japanese side kept in mind was that the cooperation should benefit not only judicial professionals in Indonesia but also the rest of the Indonesian population. To this end, the first thing for the Japanese and Indonesian sides to do was to develop an accurate understanding of differences between what was called *wakai* [compromise] or *chotei* [mediation] in Japan and what was called *mediasi* [compromise and mediation] in Indonesia. The important thing was to analyze the factors contributing to successful compromise and mediation in Japan and put our heads together to select elements that would be acceptable in Indonesia.

Japanese courts offer the option of following a *chotei* procedure to resolve a dispute, instead of conducting a lawsuit.

Chotei is a system by which mediation commissioners, who are selected from the general public, take part in the procedure together with judges to resolve the dispute based on talks between the involved parties. Being a less expensive alternative to a trial, it is a more accessible system for citizens. In Indonesia, by contrast, mediation was only possible after bringing an action to the court, and the litigant had to pay an additional charge to use a mediator (this is paid through state funding in the Japanese system). An important theme was for the two sides to understand these system and operational differences and work out a compromise/mediation system that would suit Indonesia.

04 | *Wakai* Goes Overseas

To this end, JICA decided to send lawyer Tamaki Kakuda[8] to work in Jakarta, the Indonesian capital, for two years from 2007 as a long-term expert. Kusano would back her up as a member of the Japanese advisory group. The goal for the first year was to amend the compromise- and mediation-related Supreme Court rules established in 2003. The core objective of the project for the second year was to implement training for Indonesian judges and court clerks, with the aim of providing technical education and promoting public relations.

8 Kakuda, a lawyer registered with the Kyoto Bar Association, provided frontline support in Indonesia as a long-term expert from 2007 to 2009.

First, three seminars were held in Jakarta to introduce Japanese *wakai* and *chotei* practices by inviting judicial professionals from Japan, as well as to discuss how the compromise- and mediation-related Supreme Court rules established in 2003 should be amended. Kusano recalls, "These seminars were productive in the sense that they effectively showed Indonesians the advantages of the Japanese *wakai* and *chotei* systems. They also provided opportunities for the two sides to exchange opinions as to which Supreme Court rules established in 2003 should be changed and what specific amendments should be made to them."

Besides the above, two seminars, each lasting for about two weeks, were also held in Japan. They included not only lectures but also study tours of Japanese judicial facilities, such as a court and bar association office, as well as mock *wakai* and *chotei* experiences. These worthwhile programs also helped create a stronger sense of solidarity among participants.

After the completion of these seminars in Indonesia and Japan, Kakuda held repeated discussions with an Indonesian working group in Indonesia regarding the revisions that should be made to the Supreme Court rules. As a result, the revised Supreme Court rules concerning the compromise and mediation system were established and enforced in 2008.

Kusano recalls, "I wasn't stationed in Indonesia myself. All I did was provide backup by taking some time out of my work schedule as a university professor to visit Indonesia from time to time. It was the expert Kakuda and ICD professors who actually took part in the seminars held in Indonesia and Japan and who did the real work of bringing about the revision of the rules by staying in Indonesia."

In this way, the amended Supreme Court rules were completed. The question now was how to make them known and put them to actual use in Indonesian courts. Both the Japanese and the Indonesians thought that training should also be provided to judges who were not members of the Indonesian working group, as well as to court clerks, in order to promote the amended rules and enable Indonesian judges to improve their compromise and mediation skills.

Until the rules were amended, court clerks had not been allowed to attend compromise and mediation proceedings in Indonesia. The Japanese insisted that court clerks in Indonesia needed to attend these proceedings to fulfill their duties, saying that "the amended Supreme Court rules would otherwise never go into common use, as the success of the Japanese compromise and mediation system is only possible due to the cooperation of court clerks." Thus, it was decided to organize the first joint training program for court judges and clerks in Indonesia.

However, because Indonesia is vast and has many islands, most judges and clerks found it difficult to attend the training. A commentary was compiled to facilitate smooth implementation of the amended Supreme Court rules, and a "mediator training" DVD was created to provide technical instructions for mediators. The content of this DVD was prepared through consultation between the Japanese and Indonesian sides. Real-life Indonesian judges appeared in the DVD, showcasing their considerable acting skills by simulating various problems that commonly occurred in Indonesia. The DVD has become an invaluable teaching aid that uses simulations of real-life cases to show learners how to carry out mediation proceedings and talks in a detailed, easy-to-understand manner.

Another noteworthy teaching aid was created in 2008 when Kusano was working for the project. It was an Indonesian translation of his book *Wakai gijutsu ron* (Technical theory on compromise) by Kusano. Interestingly, the Japanese word *wakai* was adopted as the title of the book.

Kusano looks back on those days: "This book is an abridged version of the original book, and some content that would be difficult for non-Japanese people to understand has been removed. The Japanese word *wakai* can be roughly translated as *perdamaian* in Indonesian, but we chose to name the book *Wakai* rather than *Perdamaian* because we wanted to distinguish between the two as used respectively in their two different societies, Japanese and Indonesian."

Indeed, the Indonesian *perdamaian* and the Japanese *wakai* are different in nuance; they are two different systems that have different penetration levels among their peoples. Kusano smiles and says, "In fact, now that the Japanese compromise and mediation system has become widely understood among Indonesian legal officials and other people, they commonly just use the words *wakai* and *chotei* quite casually among themselves."

05 | **Toward Greater Recognition and Wider Use of *Wakai* and *Chotei***

The Project on Improvement of Mediation System in Indonesia ended in March 2009. Needless to say, all projects end in due course. Given the fact that JICA's cooperation is funded by the Japanese government, it is only natural that its activities work

Instructional DVD for mediators

should be carried out intensively within a designated period of time. Once the prescribed work is completed, the rest should be left to the independent pursuit and self-help efforts of the recipient country.

This project by JICA made the compromise- and mediation-related Supreme Court rules established in 2003 more practical. It produced significant results for Indonesian legal professionals, who wished to reduce the number of unresolved cases by decreasing the number of incidents to be processed through trials, thereby alleviating the burden on courts.

Kusano voluntarily decided to continue traveling to Indonesia every year after the completion of the project to visit courts and other related places in the country. He laughs and says, "I was able to depend on research funds from the university, as I was still employed." Even after retiring from the university, however, he has continued to visit Indonesia every year.

In August 2012, Kusano founded the Japan-Indonesia Lawyers Association (JILA), an association of lawyers working to bridge the two countries. Kusano and Hikmahanto Juwana, a professor at the University of Indonesia, became president and vice president, respectively. In this way, the spirit of the cooperation, which Kusano had promoted within the framework of JICA, was passed down to the private sector.

JICA provided the cooperation for legal and judicial development that it was able to supply, and we have been providing what we can supply. There are some things that JICA can do that we cannot, and other things that JICA can't do but we can. I may only be able to travel to Indonesia once a year to visit the courts and educational institutions there, but I believe that can make a difference if my visit acts as an "anchor."

Every project is implemented within a preset timescale and budget. At the same time, some countries need to be prioritized over other countries as aid recipients. As described above, however, the fruit of JICA's cooperation has been passed into the hands of private-sector organizations and individuals to grow further. This is an effective performance indicator when considering the sustainability of outcomes from the cooperation in this area.

06 The Launch of a New Project

The year 2015 saw the launch of a new JICA Project, Project on Intellectual Property Rights Protection and Legal Consistency for Improving the Business Environment. The aim is to enhance the protection of intellectual property rights in Indonesia, while at the same time increasing the legal consistency of intellectual property rights-related laws in the country. The project period is to last for five years, from December 2015 through December 2020.

Before this project, JICA had already provided cooperation related to intellectual property rights to the Ministry of Law and Human Rights of Indonesia for more than twenty years, with support from the Japan Patent Office. The project has built upon the past achievements of such cooperation. Furthermore, as Japan and Indonesia had been maintaining a steady relationship in the area of the legal and judicial development since the end of the mediation system project, this new project was able to expand its targets to also cover the Supreme Court of Indonesia. Being a project that would not only contribute to the legal and judicial development in Indonesia but also assist the creation of secure business environments to allow Japanese companies to do business in developing countries with peace of mind, the project can be regarded as a model case of "strategic" cooperation.

PROJECT FACT SHEET China

November 18, 2004–November 17, 2009

Economic Legal Infrastructure Development Project

COUNTERPART: **Ministry of Commerce**

The first legal and judicial development project in China, conducted in partnership with the Ministry of Commerce (the equivalent of the Japanese Ministry of Economy, Trade and Industry). It assisted in drafting the Company Law, the Anti-Monopoly Law and marketing laws. The Company Law was amended in October 2005, and the Anti-Monopoly Law was enacted in August 2007.

November 1, 2007–October 31, 2010

Improvement of Civil Procedure Law and Arbitration Law Project

COUNTERPART: **Legislative Affairs Commission, Standing Committee of the National People's Congress**

The first legal and judicial development project in partnership with the legislative arm of the National People's Congress (NPC), the Legislative Affairs Commission of the NPC Standing Committee. It assisted in drafting the Civil Procedure Law, the Tort Liability Law and the Law for the Application of Law on Foreign-related Civil Relations. The Tort Liability Law was enacted in December 2009, the Law for the Application of Law on Foreign-related Civil Relations (private international law) in October 2010.

FY2010–2012

Country-focused Training: Judicial Capacity Building

COUNTERPART: **National Judges College**

This program was designed to help China improve its legal training institutions by educating participants about the corresponding institutions in Japan (law schools, the Legal Training and Research Institute program, training programs for judges and so forth).

June 10, 2010–October 31, 2013

Expert: Civil Procedure Law and Other Private Laws

COUNTERPART: **Civil Law Department, Legislative Affairs Commission, Standing Committee of the National People's Congress**

A JICA advisor helped draft amendments to the Civil Procedure Law, the Consumer Protection Law, the Inheritance Law and the Copyright Law in readiness for enactment. The Civil Procedure Law was amended in August 2012, the Consumer Protection Law in October 2013.

FY2012–2015

Country-focused Training: Administrative Procedure Law and Other Administrative Laws

COUNTERPART: **Administrative Department, Legislative Affairs Commission, Standing Committee of the National People's Congress**

Assistance was provided with drafting amendments to the Administrative Litigation Law, the Administrative Complaint Review Act, the Environmental Protection Law, the Food Safety Law and the Air Pollution Control Act. The Administrative Complaint Review Act was amended in November 2014, the Environmental Protection Law in April 2014, the Food Safety Law in April 2015 and the Air Pollution Control Act in August 2015.

June 25, 2014–June 24, 2020

Project on Legal Development for Improvement of Market Economy and People's Wellbeing

COUNTERPART: **Administrative Office, Legislative Affairs Commission, Standing Committee of the National People's Congress**

This project is designed to assist in drafting legislation that will embed China's economic reforms and guarantee and improve public welfare, as well as facilitate business for Japanese companies. Two to three laws are selected each fiscal year. Among the laws handled by the project to date are the Intellectual Property Law, the Civil Code and the Administrative Procedure Law. The general provisions of the Civil Code were enacted in March 2017.

CHINA

01 Development of Laws That Meet International Standards

China started to introduce capitalist market principles in 1978, and achieved dramatic economic growth in the 1990s under the "socialist market economy" model. While the amount of investment and trade skyrocketed, the country still did not have an adequate legal framework to guarantee fair and free socioeconomic activities. In 1999, China amended its constitution and declared that it would become a "nation governed by the rule of law." In 2001, China joined the WTO, resulting in increasing calls for the enforcement of international standards for a number of laws. Consequently, China set a target to establish the legal framework necessary for a market economy by 2010.

Although China studied the laws of developed countries to establish and revise its laws, the government was faced with many challenges in the course of drafting and amending these laws, as well as in applying and implementing established laws, due to a lack of human resources for legal system improvement and a delay in the development of human resources in the legal and judicial sectors. Under such circumstances, Japan began to plan for providing the cooperation for legal and judicial development to China.

While China's rapid economic growth continued, debate arose in Japan around the revision of Japan's ODA to China, resulting in the Ministry of Foreign Affairs of Japan developing a new aid policy for China called the Economic Cooperation Program for China in 2002. Following the 2001 entry of China into the WTO, one theme adopted by the ministry in this program was to support China's governance and legal system improvement as a part of Japan's ODA to China. This was because it was necessary for Japan to help China to improve its legal system so as to facilitate Japan's business expansion into China, which was making a shift toward a market economy.

Masato Watanabe[9] played a leading role in launching Japan's cooperation in this area as senior representative of JICA's China office. Looking back, he says, "Until then, we weren't involved in the legal system development of China. As such, we started by surveying Japanese companies doing business in China to determine whether there was a real need, and identify those needs. That was the state of things in 2001."

02 Both Japan and China Had Needs: The Official Launch of the "Economic Legal Infrastructure Development Project"

Sessions with the Japan-China Economics Association[10] and other related parties revealed that improving China's legal system was also a matter of great concern for Japanese companies that had large market shares in China. As Watanabe explains, "Some Japanese companies also expressed their opinions about the capabilities of Chinese judges concerning intellectual property rights. Many Japanese companies told us that fairer operation of laws would provide a greater sense of security to their company when conducting business in China. We learned that there was great demand from the Japanese side."

After that, Watanabe began to explore Chinese needs in 2002. He visited "every place that was likely to be relevant," including the Supreme People's Court,[11] the Supreme People's Procuratorate,[12] and the Ministry of Commerce of China,[13] together with Hitotsubashi University professor Chihiro Nunoi[14] and other experts. "The State Council[15] was preparing an amendment to the Company Law[16] at that time, and many other organs reacted favorably, saying, 'Although we have been hugely interested in Japanese economy-related laws ourselves, we had no direction. Japan's cooperation for legal and judicial development for China would be very much appreciated.'"

9 Watanabe worked on the legal and judicial development program in China as senior representative of JICA's China office from 2005 to 2008. He is currently on temporary transfer to J. F. Oberlin University, where he has a special professorial appointment.

10 A foundation incorporated in 1972 with the goal of promoting economic relations between Japan and China.

11 This is the highest of the people's courts. It is overseen by the National People's Congress.

12 This is the highest of the people's procuratorates, which prosecute criminal cases; it also acts as the state's legal watchdog. It is overseen by the National People's Congress.

13 The Ministry of Commerce is the executive arm of the State Council responsible for the economy and trade. The Chinese equivalent of the Japanese Ministry of Economy, Trade and Industry.

14 Nunoi is a jurist in commercial and corporate law. Professor at the Graduate School of International Corporate Strategy of Hitotsubashi University. An authority on corporate law in the EU, China, and other jurisdictions. Played a pivotal role in the Economic Legal Infrastructure Development Project in China.

15 The State Council is the chief administrative authority of the state, equivalent to the Japanese Cabinet.

16 This law regulates the establishment, organization, and equity of limited

liability and joint stock companies. Enacted in 1993 and revised with JICA's support in 2005, it underwent further revision in 2013.

These survey results indicated that both Japan and China had needs that could be addressed. In December 2003, China officially requested that Japan provide aid for the drafting and revision of China's company, anti-monopoly, and market and distribution laws, and technical cooperation in the area of the professional development of officials working for lawmaking and law-enforcement agencies. As a result, it was decided that cooperation work would be launched in April 2004.

Conference reviewing the results of the Economic Legal Infrastructure Development Project

This was how the Economic Legal Infrastructure Development Project was put into operation in the same year as the first full-scale cooperation for legal and judicial development in China.

Watanabe remembers a discussion regarding Japan's aid for the improvement of their company law at that time:

> One of the Chinese representatives said to me, "We've been studying Western laws, but our strongest interest has been in Japanese laws." They told me that they thought they could learn the most from the experience and knowledge of Japan, which had adapted laws taken from overseas to better suit its own needs. When we supported them in improving their company law, top-notch experts from Japan gave detailed explanations about what discussions, and what decisions, Japanese company law had gone through before it became what it is today. In other words, we assisted them by telling them what they really wanted to know themselves; "Like scratching an itch you can't reach," as the Japanese expression has it. As a result, our support was very much appreciated and characterized as "extremely helpful." We owe this to the passion and enthusiasm of those Japanese experts.

03 The Necessity for Long-Term Experts

The Improvement of Civil Procedure Law and Arbitration Law Project started in 2007. The counterpart to this project was the NPC Standing Committee Legislative Affairs Commission, and lawyer Takayuki Sumida[17] was sent to China as the first long-term expert.

"JICA thought that it was essential to start this project by stationing a long-term expert in China. Sending a legal specialist to China would enable JICA to identify local needs more accurately and accordingly design more effective training programs and seminars in Japan," says Akimitsu Okubo,[18] who began working for JICA's China office in 2006.

When the preliminary survey team of the project consulted the NPC Legislative Affairs Commission in June 2007, however, a huge difference in opinion was revealed between Japan and China as to the activities of long-term experts. While the Japanese side insisted on the necessity for a long-term expert, the Chinese side objected, saying that experts could visit China when they needed to. They didn't see why Japan needed to send an expert to be stationed long-term. The Japanese side said they wanted their long-term expert to be given a workspace inside the Civil Law Department,[19] as well as opportunities to join Chinese experts in discussions and meetings concerning the laws covered in the project. If the Chinese considered this inappropriate, then it was hoped they would at least consider sharing information. Nevertheless, the Chinese refused to give in and maintained a firm stance, saying that they could neither provide workspace for a long-term expert nor allow any foreign national to attend meetings held by the Chinese side. Apparently, their pride would not let them accept meaningful intervention by people from other countries in the development of laws forming the core of their country. While the Chinese side frowned on the acceptance of a long-term expert, Japanese members "did their utmost to convince the Chinese of the many advantages of having a long-term expert from Japan," according to Okubo.

Albeit slightly anxious, Sumida, the long-term expert, headed

17 Sumida, a lawyer registered with the Tokyo Bar Association, was stationed in China as a long-term expert from 2008 to 2010. He still works as a lawyer in the field of business law in China.

18 Okubo is a JICA staff member who worked on the legal and judicial development program in China as a member of JICA's China office from 2006 to 2010. He is currently director of the Law and Justice Team within the Governance Group in the Industrial Development and Public Policy Department.

19 This is the department of the Legislative Affairs Commission of the NPC Standing Committee that is responsible for civil law.

for Beijing, telling himself that the NPC Legislative Affairs Commission formed a core part of the state, so it was only natural for them to feel ill at ease if a foreign national were to intrude suddenly. Sumida laughs and says, "There may not have been unconditional welcome before I arrived there, but what actually awaited me were unexpectedly friendly people." As he was not permitted to be stationed inside the Civil Law Department of the NPC, he rented a small office elsewhere and worked with the NPC from there.

Sumida had studied in Beijing immediately after qualifying as a lawyer, so he had good Chinese skills as well. After returning from China, he had been working as a lawyer in Japan and had been involved in helping Japanese companies to expand their business into China. He says, "I learned through the Japan Federation of Bar Associations [JFBA] that JICA was looking for a legal specialist to work in China for its cooperation for legal and judicial development as a long-term expert. I found the job very exciting and applied." He had only been a lawyer for five years.

04 A Flexible Attitude Required to Respond to a Fluctuating Legislative Plan

As described above, Chinese members were initially not really certain about the appropriateness of accepting a Japanese expert into their country to be stationed for a long term. Okubo looks back on those days and says, "It was lucky that Sumida was such a young lawyer, because he gained lots of favorable attention from the NPC." According to Okubo, the most vital element of a good long-term expert is a friendly personality, which is even more important than specialist knowledge. "Sumida was a fluent speaker of Mandarin. Above everything else, however, I suppose that he blended in so well with Chinese members because he was young in age and agreeable in character."

Thus, Sumida was sent to China as a long-term expert to work for the project concerning the civil procedure and arbitration laws. Once a partial amendment to the Civil Procedure Law was completed in July 2007, however, the Civil Law Department began work on establishing the Tort Liability Law in 2008, while putting off the overhaul of the Civil Procedure Law. He recalls:

> The Civil Procedure Law was given particular importance in the legislative plan of the NPC. This is the reason that the Japanese side set up the project on the law. At this point in time, however, there was suddenly a need to provide support for the drafting of the Tort Liability Law, which was given an even higher priority. The Tort Liability Law is a set of rules concerning illegal behavior that corresponds to part of the Civil Code in Japan. In fact, it's completely different from the Civil Procedure Law. So we felt rather nonplussed at first.

Furthermore, the "Arbitration Law," which had also been given special importance, disappeared from the legislative plan, and was therefore moved far down in the order of priority. Consequently, work concerning the Arbitration Law also came to a standstill and remained incomplete.

Not even the Civil Law Department or the NPC Standing Committee Legislative Affairs Commission can control the schedule or priority of lawmaking. What is prioritized, and what the most pressing issue is, can change at a moment's notice in China. This meant that flexibility would be required of the Japanese side also. Says Okubo:

> It was customary, however, for JICA to manage its projects systematically by setting medium-term goals beforehand to be achieved in three to five years and implementing prescribed plans. As such, it was quite difficult for us to change direction each time the Chinese side told us, "*This* is now the most important theme." Nevertheless, we came to understand, through actually interacting with our Chinese counterparts, that we needed a certain level of flexibility to respond appropriately to such changes. In fact, JICA has adopted quite a different modus operandi in more recent projects.

Although several changes in direction took place during the

period in which Sumida was stationed in Beijing as a long-term expert between 2008 and 2010, China eventually established the Tort Liability Law. Meanwhile, activities like seminars in China and training programs in Japan were also proactively carried out, leading to an improved relationship between the Japanese and Chinese sides.

05 Overcoming the Anti-Japan Protests and Other Problems

Another lawyer, Hiroyuki Shirade,[20] was sent to China in January 2011 to provide cooperation in relation to the Civil Procedure Law and other civil and commercial laws. Like Sumida, Shirade was also publicly recruited by the JFBA. The Civil Procedure Law amendment work, which had been suspended, resumed after the establishment of the Tort Liability Law in 2009 and the Law for the Application of Law on Foreign-related Civil Relations in 2010. Shirade was put in charge of aid work for the improvement of civil and commercial laws reflecting the needs of China, while continuing to be involved in the Civil Procedure Law amendment work. Shirade recalls:

20 Shirade is a lawyer registered with the Osaka Bar Association. He has been involved in the legal and judicial development program in China as a long-term expert for more than six years (since 2011).

> While working mainly on the amendment of the Civil Procedure Law, I also became involved in the development of the Administrative Litigation Law and other administrative laws. Taking as precedent the way Chinese legislative needs

Chinese Civil Law Department seminar held in Kunming

Comparing amendments to the Chinese and Japanese civil procedure codes had fluctuated during the term of service of my predecessor, Sumida, a more flexible framework was adopted for me, providing a larger strike zone.

The amendment to the Civil Procedure Law was finally passed in August 2012. Immediately after that, the Senkaku Islands dispute broke out between Japan and China, resulting in anti-Japan protests in China.

I was living near the Embassy of Japan in Beijing at that time. The scale of the anti-Japan demonstrations increased day by day. There was a period of one month or so in which I was refused taxi rides for being Japanese and subjected to hostile glares at restaurants. While I can't say that the political situation between Japan and China did not affect our activities at all, we were steadily getting our work done despite all this. However, it was still true that we felt upset by how the Chinese media reported on this issue, and we took the utmost care not to let it adversely affect the Chinese staff of the China Office and Chinese members of the project.

Amid the surge in anti-Japan sentiment in China, Masayoshi Takehara,[21] who was a member of JICA China Office from 2009 through 2013, stayed in China. "The training programs scheduled to take place in Japan were canceled for the six months to a year following the large-scale anti-Japan demonstrations in 2012. Seeing what we had achieved through hard work to that point being suspended like that gave us a sense of crisis," recalls Takehara.

There was also a rapid increase in new types of issues and incidents in China, which was going through dramatic economic and social evolution. The most typical examples were environmental pollution and harm to consumers. While the new regime of China, which was launched in 2012 under the leadership of Xi Jinping, had "doubling incomes," "creating a beautiful China" and "constitutional commitment to the rule of law" as its slogans, serious environmental problems and harm to consumers increased.

21 JICA staff member Takehara worked on the legal and judicial development project in China as a member of JICA's China office from 2009 to 2013. He is currently director of Southeast Asia Division 2 in the Southeast Asia and Pacific department.

This was also when air quality became a matter of public concern in Japan. Under such circumstances, revision of the Environmental Protection Law suddenly became a higher priority in China. Consequently, Shirade was involved in the work of revising this legislation until the end of his term of service in China in October 2013.

Japan had suffered from severe pollution problems during its era of rapid economic growth, so it already had the experience of dealing with these problems from the perspective of legislation. Shirade says, "While Japan has faced and overcome many different challenges in a gradual manner over a period of forty years, China is faced with all of them at once and is required to deal with them at the same time." That being the case, there should be many aspects in which Japan can support China. According to Shirade, "It's also important that China should understand both the pros and cons of the processes followed by Japan, since Japan didn't overcome its environmental pollution problems overnight, as specialists from the Ministry of the Environment and researchers point out." Later, China adopted environmental principles suggested by Japan, such as "sustainable development," including for legislative purposes, and revised its Environmental Protection Law in April 2014.

06 | Paving the Way for Japanese Companies through Support Work

Shirade was sent to China again in 2014 to work as a long-term expert for the Project on Legal Development for Improvement of the Market Economy and People's Wellbeing.[22] The purpose of this project was to provide consensus-based support in legal areas of high concern to both Japan and China.

In fact, China now had the second largest GDP in the world, and growing numbers of Japanese people began to question why Japan was continuing to provide it with cooperation, wondering what the advantages of doing so were for Japan. Shirade explains,

22 This project was initially to last from 2014 to 2017, but it was then extended for three years, until June 2020.

The (revised) Basic Policies on Legal Technical Assistance, issued by the Japanese government in May 2013, stipulate that "Japan shall continue to provide support (to China) from the perspectives of facilitating smoother activities for Japanese companies and helping establish governance." In other words, the policies provide a clear response to the question whether Japan still needs to offer aid to China now that China has replaced Japan as the world's second-largest economy in GDP terms, by stating that helping China achieve further healthy growth as a market economy and improve its legal systems is essential for smoother corporate activities of Japanese companies. This understanding drove the launch of the project in 2014.

Watanabe, the former senior representative of JICA's China office, also says, "China is very special to Japan, completely different from other countries. After all, it is China that Japan needs to work with most in the area of cooperation for legal and judicial development."

The cooperation which Japan began to provide to China in 2004 has resulted in the establishment and revision of many laws related to business activities, including the Company Law, Anti-Monopoly Law, Tort Liability Law, Law for the Application of Law on Foreign-related Civil Relations, Civil Procedure Law,

A 2013 seminar on administrative law

Consumer Protection Law, Environmental Protection Law and Administrative Litigation Law.

According to Shirade, "New amendments to Chinese laws, for example the Consumer Protection Law, include boldly advanced provisions, which are sometimes surprisingly progressive even by Japanese standards. That being so, legal and judicial development projects can play another important role by making use of the outcomes through feedback into Japan, as a means of contributing to the national interests of Japan."

Watanabe points out, "For example, university academics and research institutes can maintain relationships with the Chinese side even after their JICA projects are over by continuing their exchanges with Chinese experts. One of the most significant outcomes of Japan's cooperation with China may be the creation of such connections between the two countries."

Here is what Sumida, the first long-term expert sent to China, thinks:

> When I was stationed in China from 2008 through 2010, I shared with Japanese related parties the recognition that we should provide the "support we can provide *now*." There are activities that were simply impossible twenty years ago and also activities that are unlikely to be possible twenty years later. My experience has taught me that the cooperation is subject to timing restrictions. So I think the important thing is to do what you can do, and do as much of it as possible *while you are able*. Even if there are no long-term experts from Japan in China in the future, the "Japanese way of thinking" might still underlie the thinking of Chinese people—Japanese people will have influenced in perpetuity how Chinese people think of the law. This should facilitate smoother Chinese investment activities abroad, as well as smoother investments from Japan and other countries in China. In my opinion, this will benefit both of us.

PROJECT FACT SHEET

Uzbekistan

August 30, 2005–
September 30, 2007

Project on the Commentary on the Bankruptcy Law

COUNTERPART: **Supreme Economic Court of Uzbekistan**

This project helped judges at the Supreme Economic Court write a commentary on Uzbekistan's Bankruptcy Law, so that bankruptcy cases would be properly handled by economic courts throughout the country. To promote better understanding of the bankruptcy system, this commentary was distributed not only to economic court judges but to anyone concerned with bankruptcy cases, including lawyers and financial institutions.

November 30, 2005–
December 31, 2008

Project for Legal Assistance for Improvement of Conditions for Development of Private Businesses

COUNTERPART: **Ministry of Justice**

This project, carried out in partnership with Uzbekistan's Ministry of Justice, sought to remove legal obstacles to free enterprise in the country. To that end it helped launch a public database of laws and assisted in the drafting, enactment, enforcement, and application of the Administrative Procedures Law and the Mortgage Act.

April 1, 2010–
September 30, 2012

Project for Improvement of Administrative Procedures for the Development of Private Sector Activities

COUNTERPART: **National Judges College**

Designed to stimulate private-sector economic activity in Uzbekistan and accelerate the transition to a market economy, this project, carried out in partnership with Uzbekistan's Ministry of Justice, assisted in drawing up an administrative procedures manual on the Law on Guarantees of Freedom of Entrepreneurial Activity. It also helped compile a model set of administrative regulations on the Licensing Act.

 UZBEKISTAN

01 A Country with Many *Oshin*-Loving Japanophiles

The Republic of Uzbekistan (hereinafter referred to as "Uzbekistan") declared independence in 1991, following the collapse of the Soviet Union. It has a population of about 30 million people in total; its sizable capital, Tashkent, is well known for having been the fourth-largest city within the Soviet Union, following Moscow, Leningrad and Kiev.

After independence, Uzbekistan made a gradual shift toward a market economy. Nevertheless, the vestiges of the planned economy, which had lasted for about seventy years, remained, and the country was criticized for not providing the necessary legal framework for private-sector corporate activities.

Katsuya Ichihashi,[23] trustee and vice president of Nagoya University and the former director of that institution's Center for Asian Legal Exchange (CALE),[24] spent seven months in Uzbekistan in 2002 to conduct research on the possibility of cooperation for legal and judicial development in the country. He recounts:

> The purpose of my visit to Uzbekistan was to look for the "seeds" of support; in other words to explore what support Japan could provide to the country. My impression was that Uzbekistan was a society that adhered strongly to traditional Asian cultural values, with particular importance placed on family and community ties. The Japanese TV series *Oshin* is extremely popular throughout Asia. I noticed that the people of Uzbekistan, particularly the women, showed great empathy toward the characters in the drama, and felt they could really relate to them. Immediately after the Second World War, a large number of Japanese prisoners of war were deported to this region. They are known to have worked very

23 Ichihashi, a jurist on administrative law, is trustee and vice president of Nagoya University and the former director of CALE. He studies the rule of law in Uzbekistan and other former Soviet states, and has been closely involved in efforts in legal and judicial development in Uzbekistan and elsewhere.

24 See inset, page 218.

hard in Uzbekistan. For example, when many old buildings collapsed in Tashkent due to a massive earthquake in 1966, those built by Japanese prisoners survived the disaster intact. This has also earned Japan respect from the Uzbek people. In fact, Uzbekistan has many Japanophiles.

OTHER ORGANIZATIONS INVOLVED IN PROMOTING THE RULE OF LAW

Nagoya University Center for Asian Legal Exchange (CALE)

Overview

CALE was established in 2000 to consolidate Nagoya University's efforts to support legal and judicial development and conduct legal education in Asia. It was reorganized in its present form in 2002. CALE's mission is threefold: to conduct theoretical research on the law and legal assistance programs in Asia; to train legal professionals in Asian countries; and to mentor global leaders who will contribute to Asia's development.

Main Activities

- Supporting JICA's legal and judicial development projects as a major Japanese partner.
- Accepting students from Asia under human resource development programs run by JICA and others.
- Conducting research on Asian law and legal development programs and publishing the results.
- Establishing research and education centers for Japanese law across Asia to teach Japanese law and research Asian law.
- Building a collaborative research network of Japanese and overseas institutions in the field of legal assistance and Asian law, and promoting cooperation across it.
- Publishing the journal *CALE News* and releasing research reports.
- Organizing research seminars, symposia, and international conferences.

Timeline

1990	The Asia-Pacific Region Studies Project is launched.
1998	Nagoya University's Graduate School of Law begins providing legal development assistance abroad.
1999	The school begins accepting students from overseas.
2000	The Center for Asian Legal Exchange (CALE) is established.
2002	CALE is reorganized in its present form under a Ministry of Education ordinance.
2005	CALE establishes the Research and Education Center for Japanese Law at Tashkent State University of Law, its first overseas education and research hub in Asia.
2006	The Research and Education Center for Japanese Law at the National University of Mongolia is established.
2007	The Research and Education Center for Japanese Law at Hanoi Law University is established.
2008	The Research and Education Center for Japanese Law at the Royal University of Law and Economics in Cambodia is established.
2012	The Research and Education Center for Japanese Law at Ho Chi Minh City Law University is established.
2013	The Japan Legal Research Center at the University of Yangon is established.
2014	The Laos-Japan Legal Research and Education Center is established at the National University of Laos. The Indonesia-Japan Legal Research and Education Center is established at the University of Gadjah Mada.

02 A Book of Commentaries Required for the Bankruptcy Law

JICA set out in earnest to provide the cooperation for legal and judicial development to Uzbekistan in 2005 with the aim of facilitating the economic growth of the country. The program was targeted mainly at laws concerning corporate activities.

One major target was the Bankruptcy Law. The Bankruptcy Law of Uzbekistan was first passed in 1994 and was largely revised in 2003. Although the law appeared to be better organized as a result of the 2003 revision, no dependable reference materials, guides, or other documentation for legal practitioners were available at that time, leading to different understandings of the law among different individuals. Consequently, there were no consistent bankruptcy proceedings. The resulting inappropriateness of bankruptcy proceedings, in turn, gave rise to the problem of inadequate protection of the rights of creditors and debtors.

An adequate law had already been established, but people found it difficult to make effective use of it. Under such circumstances, something needed to be done to make the law more practical and easier to use. One idea was to develop commentaries and guides about the Bankruptcy Law. This was the background that led the Supreme Economic Court of Uzbekistan[25] to

25 The highest of Uzbekistan's economic courts, which administer justice in economic cases. The Uzbek justice system has three branches: the economic courts, which are headed by the Supreme Economic Court; the regular courts, which are headed by the Supreme Court (with jurisdiction over civil, criminal and administrative cases); and the Constitutional Court.

The Supreme Economic Court of Uzbekistan

plan the creation of a book of commentaries (*Kommentar*). Japan decided to launch a project to support it.

03 Different Views of Commentaries

The "Project on the Commentary on the Bankruptcy Law of the Republic of Uzbekistan" was launched for a period of about two years from August 2005 through September 2007. The counterpart was the Supreme Economic Court of Uzbekistan. The creation of commentaries was carried out mainly by judges of the Supreme Economic Court who were handling bankruptcy cases, alongside lawyers, prosecutors, and staff members of national agencies who were involved with bankruptcy proceedings. Japan decided to join this initiative by assisting in compiling these commentaries.

It turned out, however, that the Uzbek and Japanese sides had totally different views on legal commentary. Kie Matsushima,[26] a lawyer who participated in this project as a long-term expert, witnessed the two countries' differences in perspective on what law was all about in the first place, as well as the cultural differences between the two countries.

26 Matsushima, a lawyer registered with the Tokyo Bar Association, was stationed in Uzbekistan as a long-term expert from 2006 to 2007. She has since continued to work in the field of law in Russia and Central Asia, including as a legal consultant based in Moscow.

> Our understanding was that commentaries should be a tool for making the law more practical for use by explaining it in a detailed, easy-to-understand manner. However, the Uzbek side did not think like that. In Uzbekistan, as in many other socialist countries, it's the norm to think of law as something you are not allowed to freely explain or interpret. As such, the commentaries they produced were nothing more than a directory showing what was written in each article. They were quite different from what we mean by a legal commentary.

How Matsushima ended up involved in the Uzbek project was a story in itself. She was first captivated by Central Asia because of the documentary TV series *Silk Road*, broadcast by NHK when she was in elementary school. After graduating from university, she began to study for the national bar examination, intending to work in Russia and Central Asia while developing a specialist career; she qualified as a lawyer in 2001. In those days, however, there were no Japanese lawyers based in Russia, and there was virtually no chance of a career opening for her there. Then she heard that the JFBA was reviewing the possibility of providing international legal support to Uzbekistan and put herself forward for it. Although a review was carried out, it led to nothing. Nevertheless, Matsushima learnt that JICA was at least considering providing cooperation for legal and judicial development to Uzbekistan in collaboration with the Ministry of Justice of Japan.

Matsushima joined the ICD[27] as a JICA training participant in 2004, on JICA's Customized Training for Experts Development[28] scheme. This was when she first became involved in the Bankruptcy Law project in Uzbekistan. She recalls, "I supported the creation of commentaries by basing myself in the ICD and traveling frequently between Japan and Uzbekistan in the first year of the project. I was stationed in Tashkent as a long-term expert for eighteen months after that."

27 See inset, page 79.

28 JICA conducts training programs for individuals interested in making an immediate contribution to its technical cooperation efforts and working in the international cooperation field in the future. Customized Training for Experts Development is one such program. It currently provides opportunities for short-term training at international agencies and universities outside Japan.

As mentioned above, however, it turned out that the Uzbek and Japanese sides had totally different views on legal commentaries. "The attitude of the Supreme Economic Court of Uzbekistan was that there was no need to change their traditional ways to create the kind of commentaries expected by the Japanese side. It seemed that they just wanted Japan to provide them with the funds they needed to print books of their commentaries."

Matsushima and other Japanese members did not agree with this. They thought that the Uzbek-style commentaries would not be sufficient to enable legal practitioners to accurately understand and apply the Bankruptcy Law. She explains,

> What we proposed was that prescribed forms and a process flowchart should be included, and that the concept of the Bankruptcy Law should be explained. We proposed the inclusion of Japanese-style legal commentary, with a definition of what Bankruptcy Law is in the first place, and when it's applicable, but initially, all of our proposals were turned down.

> The introduction of a flowchart met with particularly fierce resistance. Uzbek members said that a flowchart in a book of legal commentaries would feel as inappropriate as including a comic strip in a Japanese legal book. They also refused to use bullets to itemize lists. As well-educated people were expected to write in full sentences in Uzbek culture, they felt that it was vulgar to organize sentences into itemized lists to make them easier to understand.

Eventually, however, JICA told the Uzbekistan members that in order to meet the project objectives, they were obliged to create a book of commentaries that would be of practical use. With this, they obtained reluctant consent to introduce a flowchart.

04 We Are Heading Nowhere with Just Creation and Distribution

Three thousand copies of the book of commentaries, written in Russian, were printed in March 2007. While all that Uzbek members planned was to distribute the completed commentary book to judges and trustees, Matsushima and other Japanese members protested that this was insufficient. They said, "To encourage appropriate application of the Bankruptcy Law, the book needs to be promoted more widely, among companies and financial institutions, who are actual users, as well as lawyers, whom they consult." This marked the beginning of the second step of the project: "distribution and promotion of the book of commentaries." This step was set up in response to a need that arose in the course of supporting the creation of commentaries, rather than forming part of the original plan from the beginning. As this demonstrates, it is impossible to identify all needs at the planning stage: needs often arise naturally in the course of doing something.

The list of places where the book should be distributed included not only universities with law faculties, but also universities and other institutions teaching economics, management, and finance . In a nutshell, the places chosen were those where "future practitioners" were fostered. As part of the promotion activities, Matsushima came up with the idea of delivering regional seminars— in Samarkand, for example—to make quite sure that the book would not just be created and distributed and left at that.

Once the book of commentaries was distributed to these related organizations, things began to change. Bank employees and other, actual users of the Bankruptcy Law gave positive feedback such as "The flowchart is so helpful," and "It's easy to understand." Even the judges who had objected to the inclusion of prescribed forms saw the advantages when they actually used them. This feedback resulted in the release of a revised version with many additional forms in 2012. As the JICA project had already finished by this time, the necessary documents were mainly collected by judges of the Supreme Economic Court, using the follow-up scheme;[29] Matsushima, who had left Uzbekistan and was living in Moscow by then, also assisted them with the checking process.

The necessity for an "easy-to-understand and practical book of commentaries," which had been questioned at first, was also understood by the Uzbek general public once it was completed. Originally published only in Russian, it was later translated into Uzbek for provincial use. It has now been produced in four different languages, including English and Japanese.

Sharifzoda Sharipov,[30] a Tashkent-born employee of JICA's Uzbekistan office, saw the following sight one day:

> When I glanced out of the window of a bus, I saw a student walking along the street with the book of commentaries—the one we had produced in the project—in his hand. I was moved to realize that we were meeting the needs of people looking for an easy-to-understand guide to law.[31]

One characteristic of Japan's cooperation is that Japanese members put themselves in the shoes of the people in the target country, share present needs with them, encourage their independent efforts and work together on an equal footing. When Uzbek members said that it was unnecessary to make

29 A follow-up scheme is a program, conducted on a minimal budget, to ensure that the benefits of a project endure long after it is over.

30 Sharipov, a program officer at the JICA Uzbekistan office, has been working on the legal and judicial development program in Uzbekistan for many years, since his appointment in 2002.

31 Source: *JICA's World* no. 31 (April 2011): 21.

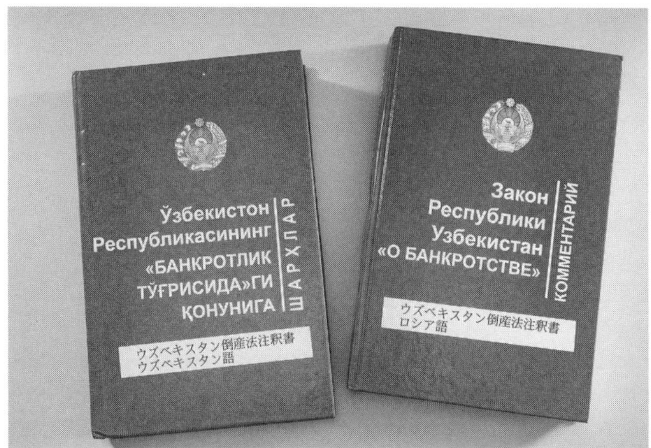

The commentary on the Bankruptcy Law, available not only in Uzbek and Russian but in English and Japanese as well

any changes to their book of commentaries, Japanese members demanded, "These changes will make the book more practical to judges actually using the law, and easier to understand also for the general public." This, however, could be seen as "unwanted advice."

Even so, through Japan's accumulation of experience and knowledge, there are things that have proved to be beneficial to recipient countries. If Japan knows that doing something can really help the target country, Japan should patiently persuade them. In fact, the resulting book of commentaries has been highly appreciated by Uzbek people and has satisfied Uzbek members as well. By doing things this way, a sense of accomplishment can be shared between both parties.

05 Cooperation for Legal and Judicial Development That Links "Old and New Mechanisms"

In addition to the Bankruptcy Law, Uzbekistan had quite a few other laws that needed to be improved; for example, those concerning administrative proceedings that were internally inconsistent or lacking in transparency. Katsuya Ichihashi, mentioned at the beginning of this section, says, "It's expected that an administrative procedure law will be established in Uzbekistan in the near future. The enforcement of that law will result in new needs, like support for the creation of another book of commentaries. We're hoping that we can provide the Uzbek people with as much support as possible as an educational institution through things like workshops and seminars."

According to Ichihashi, the development of laws in Uzbekistan is about "linking old and new mechanisms." He points out that the main challenge facing the legal and judicial development in the country is to enable a smooth transition and link the remains of the old systems from the Soviet era of the past with the new systems developed after independence. He also believes that, to overcome this challenge, it is vital to train legal specialists (academics, judicial professionals, and government officials); at the same time, it is also essential to develop young workers in the legal and judicial sectors. In fact, there have already been many cases in which those who have studied law in Japan, including those who have studied at Nagoya University, have later become young leaders in official and judicial circles after returning to Uzbekistan, assuming important positions like vice minister or supreme court justice.

Young bureaucrats and legal professionals who have studied law in Japan may contribute to "linking old and new mechanisms" through legal and judicial development in the future. If so, Japan can cooperate with the country in many different ways.

PROJECT FACT SHEET

Mongolia

March 1, 2004–
June 5, 2006

Legal and Judicial Development Support Plan

COUNTERPART: Ministry of Justice and Home Affairs

Working with the National Legal Center of Mongolia and the Supreme Court, a JICA advisor helped arrange the publication of civil judgments and aided the Ministry of Justice and Home Affairs in strengthening its legislative capacity. The advisor also helped the Association of Mongolian Advocates compile a directory of lawyers, publish its own magazine, and establish a legal advice and mediation center as it set about strengthening the organization.

September 15, 2006–
November 30, 2008

Legal Reform Support Project

COUNTERPART: Ministry of Justice and Home Affairs, Association of Mongolian Advocates

This project helped the Association of Mongolian Advocates strengthen its organization and arrange seminars for lawyers. It also assisted it in running its legal advice and mediation center and promoting awareness and use of the mediation system.

May 10, 2010–
November 9, 2012

Project for Strengthening the Mediation System

COUNTERPART: Supreme Court, Association of Mongolian Advocates

To lay the groundwork for the adoption of a court mediation system, this project provided technical support with a test run of mediation procedures in the pilot regions. It also helped train mediators, promoted awareness of the mediation system, strengthened the operational capacity of the Association's mediation center, and assisted with drafting a mediation law.

April 1, 2013–
December 15, 2015

Project for Strengthening the Mediation System, Phase II

COUNTERPART: Supreme Court, Association of Mongolian Advocates

Once the mediation law was enacted, assistance was provided with mediator training and institutional development to prepare the ground for rollout of the mediation system at trial courts throughout Mongolia.

MONGOLIA

01 Legal Inconsistency across a Vast Land

Mongolia once rose as one of the world's largest kingdoms, the Mongol Empire, under the rule of Genghis Khan, who conquered an immense area of land across the Eurasian continent. The country has vast plateaus of grasslands, as well as the enormous Gobi Desert, populated by only 3.18 million people, including nomads, who are spread out across an area about four times the size of Japan. Due to the fact that Mongolian wrestlers have been dominating the Japanese sumo scene, Japanese people are fairly familiar with the country.

However, Mongolia is faced with many challenges in the area of legislation. It ceased to be a socialist republic in 1992 and promulgated a new constitution, and since then it has enacted more than five hundred new laws in a short period of time. There were, however, many contradictions between these laws, as many of them were just advanced laws transplanted from other countries without much thought. Another major problem was that the country lacked resources in terms of workers who were able to make appropriate use of the newly established laws.

Under these conditions, JICA conducted a fact-finding survey in 2001 with the goal of providing the cooperation for legal and judicial development to Mongolia. After that, JICA implemented training programs related to land and NPO laws, mainly through Nagoya University, and sent two law professors from Nagoya University, Shigeru Kagayama[32] and Masanori Tanabe,[33] to Mongolia as short-term experts[34] in March 2003. The main objective was to carry out research to plan a support project.

32 Kagayama is professor emeritus of the Nagoya University Graduate School of Law.

33 Tanabe, a lawyer registered with the Aichi Bar Association, helped get legal and judicial development efforts off the ground in Mongolia as a long-term expert from 2004 to 2006.

34 See page 64, note 42.

02 Field Research to Find a Direction

Tanabe, a former participant in JICA's Customized Training Program for Experts,[35] had been looking for an opportunity to become involved in the cooperation for legal and judicial development in a developing country for a long time. He says,

> Nagoya University already had many years' history of involvement in the cooperation for legal and judicial development. I had long been interested in this area and had been asking the university to give me an opportunity to work in a developing country. Although I might possibly have been sent elsewhere, I eventually got the opportunity to go to Mongolia as a JICA legal advisor.

Having been asked by the vice minister of Justice and Home Affairs of Mongolia to "provide support for the drafting of a Security Execution Law" and "improvement of the corporation system," Tanabe arrived in Mongolia with great excitement. Once things began, however, these jobs were entrusted to donors from other countries, which dampened his early enthusiasm before anything really started.

"What on earth am I doing here?" he thought to himself. Directionless, Tanabe was at a loss as to what to do in Mongolia, where he was a stranger. Nevertheless, he could hardly return to Japan without achieving anything there. He set out to look for legal system improvement needs on his own; for example, through observing court proceedings and listening to local lawyers. As a result, he identified three themes, namely "enhancement of the Association of Mongolian Advocates," "disclosure of judgments" and the "mediation system."

Tanabe during his stint in Mongolia

35 The Customized Training for Experts, one of JICA's human resource development programs, is geared to individuals interested in making an immediate contribution to its technical cooperation efforts and working in the international cooperation field in the future. The participants, who may number from several to a dozen or more, gain a better understanding of development issues by completing the same curriculum together. They acquire new knowledge and refine their skills through case studies and group work. Currently the program takes the form of capacity-building training (see page 276). It differs from Customized Training for Experts Development (see page 221) in that it is conducted directly by JICA.

Incidentally, JICA's legal advisers are all required to be able to respond flexibly to shifting needs in their target countries by accordingly changing the support they provide. Therefore, Tanabe sought out new possibilities in his target country by acting flexibly in line with this policy. This, however, did little to help him through his emotional anxiety at that time: he was feeling as though he had been left standing alone on the vast steppes of Mongolia.

03 | Disclosure of Judgments as a Milestone

Masanori Tanabe recounts the beginnings of legal and judicial development in Mongolia:

> Despite its near eighty-year history, the Association of Mongolian Advocates was hardly functioning. We implemented training in Japan by inviting the vice minister of Justice and the chairperson of the Association of Mongolian Advocates to observe the activities of bar associations in Japan. As a result, they told us that some of the same activities could be carried out in Mongolia and they wanted to introduce them into their country. It was therefore decided that the Association of Mongolian Advocates would begin to work on preparing a membership list of the association, creating association newsletters for sharing of information between members, establishing a center for legal counseling and mediation services, and so on. Our first step was to feel our way to collect different seeds for needs. That was all we could do at that time.

In addition to the reinforcement of the Association of Mongolian Advocates, the publication of a casebook of court decisions is another area in which Tanabe feels significant results were achieved. The Supreme Court of Mongolia was particularly reluctant to disclose its decisions for reasons such as "Observing laws is all that matters for court decisions," and "Judgments made in other cases are irrelevant." Tanabe explains, "They didn't want to disclose their court decisions to the general public simply because the quality of their judgments was poor. Many of the decisions were affected by bribery, and in some cases, evidence and conclusions were poorly linked. This was the reason that they did not want the public to know about their decisions."

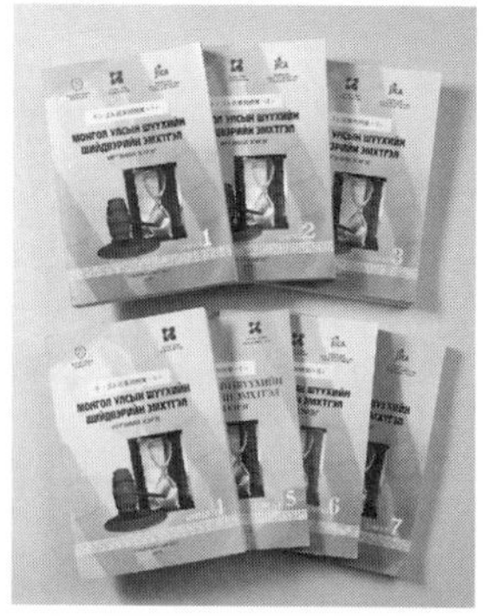

Casebook of court decisions

One aim in issuing a book to make judicial precedents widely known to the general public was to help reduce corruption in Mongolian courts, where indirect bribery was rampant. Tanabe patiently persuaded Mongolian lawyers and judges, saying, "Disclosure of court decisions is sure to lead to further development of Mongolia's judicial system." Consequently, the first casebook of court decisions in Mongolia, which was published in this way, has become widely used not only by lawyers and judges but also in universities and other educational institutions. Comments Tanabe:

> Today, all precedents are disclosed on the Internet. I believe that the publication of the casebook has played an important role in making this a reality. Given the fact that not all precedents are available online even in Japan, this is a remarkable achievement.
>
> One of the things I respect about Mongolian people is that they are always ready to acknowledge their mistakes when they realize they have made them, saying, "OK. That was my fault." In fact, it is unusual for Mongolian people to refuse to admit when they are wrong out of pride. Even when a quarrel arises, they'll normally apologize later. I feel that Mongolians are a dignified people.

04 Orange Peel and Orange Juice: Toward the Establishment of a Mediation Center

As part of the efforts to reinforce the Association of Mongolian Advocates, Tanabe also worked on establishing the Mediation Center, modeled after the Alternative Dispute Resolution (ADR) Centers run by Japanese bar associations. "What's called *chotei* [mediation] in Japan was not well known in Mongolia—or, rather, there was no term for the concept of mediation. So when you told them they could reach a resolution by talking it through, Mongolian people could not understand you in those days."

Tanabe used an allegory, the "orange peel and orange juice" story, to explain the concept. This analogy is widely told to explain mediation. Imagine two people fighting over an orange. One wants to squeeze the orange pulp to make juice, while the other wants to use the peel to make marmalade. If each one understands what the other person wants to do with the orange, both of them can fulfill their own goal through negotiation. This story shows that mediation is a means by which a third-party mediator asks the involved parties what each of them has to say and wants to do, thereby peacefully resolving the problem between them. Although there was no term for mediation in their language, Mongolian lawyers finally came to understand the mediation-based mechanism of reaching a compromise through this analogy.

The Mediation Center started as a small office, staffed by about ten lawyers at first. Tanabe stayed in Mongolia as a legal advisor until June 2006. After the establishment of a framework for the Mediation Center, the seeds planted by Tanabe were passed down to his successor Miha Isoi,[36] who was sent to Mongolia as a long-term expert in September of the same year.

36 See page 104, note 13.

05 From the Association of Advocates to the Supreme Court

The "Enhancement Planning Project for the Association of Mongolian Advocates" was launched in 2006, building upon the outcomes of Tanabe's previous activities. The project was aimed at protecting the rights and interests of general citizens by making higher-quality legal services available to them through reinforcing the functions of the Association of Mongolian Advocates. The activities of the Mediation Center, organized originally by Tanabe, however, did not go smoothly.

Nevertheless, judges of the Supreme Court of Mongolia who had observed the Japanese mediation system during training in Japan said, "We feel we definitely need to learn more about mediation." Thus, activities for promoting a mediation system in Mongolia continued at their request, and were shifted from the Bar Association to the courts.

This transition from the Bar Association to the courts marked a turning point for the promotion of a mediation system in Mongolia. Advancing from the Association of Mongolian Advocates, a relatively small organization, to the Supreme Court, an organization much larger in scale and wealthier in financial terms, resulted in rapid acceleration in the promotion of a mediation system in the country. Of course, another major factor was that the Supreme Court found it advantageous to introduce a mediation system to reduce its own burden, as it would no longer be necessary to resolve all disputes through trials.

06 A Mediation System Takes Root in a Short Time

In this way, the Project for Strengthening the Mediation System was launched in 2010, with the Supreme Court as a project counterpart (the Association of Mongolian Advocates also continued to act as a counterpart and participated in this project as well). Kazuto Inaba,[37] who was the leader of the Japanese advisory group at that time, says that, through the training provided in Japan to judges of the Supreme Court of Mongolia and other relevant people, he felt that the project was producing solid results.

For example, the training in Japan included mock (role-playing) mediation sessions concerning situations familiar to Mongolian people, such as troubles encountered in sheep trading.

37 Inaba is a professor at Chukyo University's Graduate School of Law and is a former judge. An expert in conflict resolution, including compromise and mediation, he has been closely involved in legal and judicial development projects in the field of compromise and mediation in Mongolia, Indonesia, and Nepal.

A mediation seminar in Mongolia

Inaba, who had learned mediation-related knowledge and skills in the United States, initially played the role of the mediator and demonstrated a mediation simulation with Japanese lawyers acting as parties involved in the dispute. The simulation was followed by a "review" of the mock mediation; Mongolian judges and other participants who had witnessed the mediation process as observers joined in this step. Inaba explains his view of the process:

> The comments Mongolian participants gave in the review process were specific, perceptive and creative. I learned many things from them myself. For example, I think they already had a mechanism by which a third party could serve as a buffer between Mongolian nomads involved in a dispute and resolve it through negotiations. I suppose it was just that the mechanism had not been systematized yet. In this regard, this experience has taught me that mediation is a universal system that can be established in any country.
>
> I believe it's a great achievement that the mediation system has taken root in Mongolian courts in a relatively short period of time. Given that basically only one expert at a time was stationed in Mongolia to run this project, its cost performance was very high. In my opinion, the project well deserves to be regarded as a successful example of JICA's cooperation for legal and judicial development.

07 | Moving Moments Experienced through Cooperation for Legal and Judicial Development

Another long-term expert working for the project, Hideo Oka,[38] an Osaka-based lawyer, stayed in Mongolia from 2010 through 2015, during which he worked on the drafting of a mediation law and so on. The two experts, Inaba and Oka, were awarded

38 Oka, a lawyer registered with the Osaka Bar Association, worked as a court secretary and a court clerk before qualifying as a lawyer. He was stationed in Mongolia as a long-term expert from 2010 to 2015.

the Most Distinguished Service Award by the Judicial General Council of Mongolia in October 2012 for their "outstanding contribution to courts." Displaying the medal, Inaba says,

> This is the medal of merit I received. It features the same design as the local mediator badge, with three arrows.... The announcement came as a total surprise to me, as I had not been given any notice beforehand. This is not unusual with Mongolian people, though. They always love to surprise others. They keep good news secret, and then please others with a nice surprise. Mongolians are people who like to see others happy.

Inaba and Oka were the first Japanese nationals to be awarded the Most Distinguished Service Award by the Mongolian courts. Although Mongolians are fond of awarding decorations, which may be a legacy of their socialist past, it is still a major token of honor. Gazing at his medal, Inaba says:

> A "surprise" is the astonishment arising when there is a departure from expected norms and comes about only because there is respect in the relationship. One doesn't just do dispassionately what's expected, but heads into unknown territory. Actually, I think the essence of cooperation may be found in this. That's how I feel.

With evident emotion, he continues:

> I understand from my own experience as a judge that judges think in similar ways regardless of the country. Mongolian judges are sincere, hardworking, and tolerant. In a nutshell, there is a way of thinking shared by many judges, and it resonated with me. Actually, it was a great pleasure for me that we were given opportunities to develop a deep understanding of each other through the law.
>
> For example, I'm always moved, almost to tears, when I say goodbye to Mongolian people at the airport after finishing a seminar in the country. It's not that I simply feel

sentimental; I think that the emotion comes from the satisfaction of knowing that we've been able to communicate our feelings to Mongolian people across national borders, as well as work well in cooperation with them to develop new systems for their country. Whenever I see their smiling faces before leaving Mongolia, I feel that all that I learned in the United States, and all that I've experienced in my life as a legal professional, have brought me to where I am right now. One of the best things about involvement in the cooperation for legal and judicial development is the process of experiencing such moving moments.

Tanabe, who started from nothing in Mongolia and explored project possibilities through trial and error on his own, quietly tells the following story:

When I was a legal apprentice, Shiro Muto[39] was sent from Aichi Prefecture to Vietnam to work as the first long-term expert in that country. In fact, I first became interested in the cooperation in this area through him. Although I haven't really been able to catch up with him yet, I feel I'm still following in Muto's footsteps, perhaps without even realizing it. I long to inspire younger lawyers myself, as Muto inspired me. This is what I am hoping to do.

I would also like younger people—for example, high school students interested in studying law in university—to know that their future judicial careers can open up the world to them and allow them to become involved in international projects, like legal and judicial development projects by Japan or the United Nations, rather than just working in Japanese courts.

39 See page 60, note 36.

PROJECT FACT SHEET **Nepal**

FY2009–2012

Country-focused Training: Seminars on the Civil Code and Related Laws

COUNTERPART: Supreme Court

Support was provided on drafting a civil code, preparing a commentary on the resulting draft, and improving the parliamentary briefing skills of Ministry of Law and Justice personnel.

FY2010

Country-focused Training: Comparative Research on the Criminal Justice System and Criminal Procedures

COUNTERPART: Supreme Court

A series of seminars was offered for the members of the Nepalese Criminal Law Reform and Improvement Task Force, which was then in the process of revising Nepal's criminal code. This was designed to enhance their understanding of the Japanese criminal justice system and Japanese criminal procedures.

July 28, 2010–August 31, 2019

Legal Support Advisor

COUNTERPART: Supreme Court, Ministry of Law, Justice and Parliamentary Affairs

JICA advisors dispatched in succession helped the Supreme Court of Nepal to implement the second and third five-year strategic plans for the judiciary more effectively and efficiently. The advisors also aided with the process of enacting and disseminating the Civil Code and with judicial mediation.

FY2012

Country-focused Training: Case Management Seminar

COUNTERPART: Supreme Court

These seminars were designed to educate participants about the case management system in Japan as a model for improving its Nepalese equivalent.

September 16, 2013–March 31, 2018

Project for Strengthening the Capacity of Court for Expeditious and Reliable Dispute Settlement

COUNTERPART: Supreme Court

This project aimed to enhance the function of courts in settling disputes expeditiously and impartially. To that end, it helped improve the system for managing contentious cases and encourage settlement of disputes by judicial mediation.

NEPAL

01 The Most Difficult Country in Which to Provide Cooperation for Legal and Judicial Development

"Nepal is the country to which it was most difficult to provide cooperation for legal and judicial development," says Hiroshi Matsuo,[40] a Keio University Law School professor who has been involved in the support of Nepal since the beginning.

In the South Asian republic of Nepal, political instability lasted for many years due to a civil war involving armed conflict with the Communist Party of Nepal (Maoist Center) from 1996 until 2006, when a comprehensive peace accord was finally signed. The country held a constituent assembly election in 2008. At their first sitting, the assembly decided to end the monarchy and shift to a federal democratic republic. At that point, the Nepalese monarchy, which had lasted for nearly 240 years, came to an end after more than a decade of civil war.

As Nepal set about working to reconstruct the country toward democratization and peace building, JICA began to make its move. Shiho Akamatsu[41] was working for JICA's Nepal office as a project formulation advisor in 2006 when the civil war ended. She was appointed to "conduct research to explore what kind of support JICA would be able to provide after the end of the conflict."

Looking back on those days, Akamatsu says, "I considered many different possibilities and explored what resources Japan had and what kind of support work would be most suitable to Japan."

One need identified in the research was the development of necessary laws for reconstruction of the country. In Nepal, there was a code of law known as the Muluki Ain, established about 150 years ago. The Muluki Ain contained both civil and criminal laws, including a civil code, a criminal code, a civil procedure act and a criminal procedure act. However, it was an outdated

40 See page 149, note 3.

41 Akamatsu worked on getting legal and judicial development efforts off the ground in Nepal as a project formulation advisor with JICA's Nepal office from 2006 to 2008. She is currently a program officer with the UN World Food Programme (WPF).

code incorporating the country's traditional ethics and did not appropriately reflect the rules of modern law. As such, it could not be regarded as an adequate system to guarantee the rights of Nepalese people. According to Akamatsu, Nepal fervently wished to overhaul its own legal system. She explains:

> In the immediate aftermath of a conflict, you are likely to want to organize short-term aid programs to produce quick results in order to alleviate the confusion facing the country at that moment. In fact, JICA implemented a program to assist the Constituent Assembly Election and other programs together with the Embassy of Japan. At the same time, however, we felt the need to provide cooperation for legal and judicial development to Nepal from a longer-term point of view as well, so as to help reconstruct the country.

One fundamental contributing factor in the outbreak of conflict in Nepal was discrimination based on regional disparities and class. Nepal has officially denounced the caste system as a form of social stratification. Nevertheless, the legacy of caste inequality persists in Nepalese society even today. This is why Nepal is the country to which it is the most difficult to provide the cooperation for legal and judicial development, as stated by Matsuo at the beginning of this section.

The fundamental goal of constitutions and other laws is to protect human rights and equality among people. How, then, can it be possible to promote the "rule of law" in a society in which human rights and equality are not actually guaranteed? This is where the challenge lies in Nepal.

02 Looking to Legal and Judicial Development Carried Out in Cambodia

Discussing Nepal, Akamatsu says, "There are apparent gender inequalities and class disparities in the society. Although the social advancement of women has seemingly been accelerated since democratization, it's actually difficult to radically change the customs and cultural traditions that have evolved over a long time."

Though Akamatsu was not a legal specialist, she began to see that the development of laws was essential for realizing democratization and peace building in Nepal, and for establishing new systems for the country. This was when she was invited for a meal with Nepalese Supreme Court Registrar Ram Krishna Timalsena,[42] who was engaged in the drafting of new civil and criminal codes at that time. Over *momos* (Nepalese steamed dumplings), Timalsena said, "I would like to discuss civil code drafts with Japanese experts. I've heard that Japan showed great respect for Cambodian culture when Japan provided civil code development support there. We're hoping that we can also maintain our cultural traditions while achieving modernization in the future. We'd greatly appreciate Japan's help in this important work."

42 Timalsena served as the Nepalese supreme court registrar from 2005 to 2011. He is currently executive director/principal of Nepal's National Law College.

Akamatsu communicated this enthusiasm on the part of the Nepalese directly to JICA's headquarters. "Development of laws is an essential part of creating a democratic and equal society. This is what Nepalese people are hoping for as well."

A Nepalese judicial official knew of Japan's achievements in Cambodia and requested expert advice from Japanese specialists. Furthermore, he accurately understood the attitude adopted by Japan toward its cooperation for legal and judicial development in other countries; he knew that Japan had been helping recipient countries develop laws by working together with them while respecting their cultural traditions, rather than just offering them money and goods. This fact attested to how far and wide the reputation of Japan's cooperation in this area, which the country had been providing to other countries since the 1990s, had reached by then.

03 Assisting the Drafting of a Civil Code to Support Democratization

Under such circumstances, JICA launched the Democratization Process Support Program for Nepal in 2009, under the slogan, "Creating systems to prevent Nepal from falling back into conflict."

The program started with the "Seminar on Democratization and Peace Building" held in February 2009. Japanese members, including Matsuo and Akamatsu, mentioned above, Taro Morinaga[43] and Naoshi Sato,[44] then began conducting the Preliminary Survey for the Democratization Support Program (Basic Law Support) in July of the same year. In this way, the program began to conduct field checking and research in Nepal to assess progress in the amendment of the civil code, confirm the roadmap for the legislative process following the completion of the civil code draft, and so on.

43 See page 81, note 63.

44 See page 164, note 16.

Matsuo, who joined this field research, says, "One major theme was how the triangle of politics, economics, and law should be established firmly at this stage, when the civil war had ended and the reconstruction process of the country was beginning."

Maiko Takeuchi,[45] who worked for JICA Nepal Office from 2009 through 2012 to assist the drafting of the civil code and other efforts, looks back on those days and says, "JICA had carried out the cooperation for legal and judicial development in Southeast Asia and Central Asia in the past, but this was the first time that JICA had ever provided cooperation to a South Asian country. We therefore started with very little information available to us, so in this regard, our work began through trial and error." According to Takeuchi, the Nepalese side requested assistance not only with the civil code but also about many different aspects of law. "For example, they were eager to know about Japan's high conviction rate when we provided them with training in Japan to introduce them to Japan's criminal system."

45 Takeuchi, a JICA staff member, worked on the legal and judicial development program in Nepal as a member of JICA's Nepal office from 2009 to 2012. She then joined the Law and Justice Team of the Governance Group in the Industrial Development and Public Policy Department before assuming her present post as deputy director of South Asia Division 4 in the South Asia Department.

While the reconstruction of Nepal required completion of many different tasks, Japan decided to provide the country with the cooperation mainly in the area of civil code drafting. Discussions between Japanese experts and the Nepalese Civil Law Reform and Improvement Task Force began, mainly comprising members from the Supreme Court and Ministry of Justice of Nepal.

Says Akamatsu,

A civil code is usually heavily affected by the country's customs and culture. Because of this, Japanese members found many parts of the civil code drafts prepared by the Nepalese Civil Law Reform and Improvement Task Force difficult to understand, and they struggled to see what was meant. As they read the drafts, the Japanese experts had to go through a painstaking process of asking the Nepalese side through teleconferences each time they had a question.

Takeuchi adds, "The civil code consists of about seven hundred articles. We created an Excel table for each of them, accompanied by comments from the Japanese side. The review process conducted with the Nepalese has also been recorded to show which recommendations from the Japanese side were accepted or turned down, and how the final version was completed."

04 Overcoming the Dissolution of the Constituent Assembly

The civil code draft was completed as the result of the training in Japan in August 2009, a seminar in Nepal in March 2010, and other activities. It was finally submitted to the Constituent Assembly in January 2011. In May 2012, however, the Assembly dissolved. Matsuo, sounding mortified, explains:

> The Constituent Assembly dissolved, as the stipulated time expired, before any discussions on the draft could be made. Consequently, the product of our years of effort was left unattended without producing any specific results. At any rate, the development of the new Constitution wasn't going smoothly. This experience has brought me to realize how difficult it is to establish new laws in the midst of political confusion.

This turn of events did not deter the team, however, who agreed to carry on with their efforts: "The Assembly may resume its work someday. Let's create commentaries on the articles of

Trainees in Japan keep abreast of developments on the ground via a teleconferencing system

the civil code for when that time comes." They decided to add commentaries to each article one by one, and had both the Japanese and Nepalese sides review them. This work continued even though there was no telling when their civil code draft would pass the Assembly and be established. Matsuo describes how they were feeling in those days:

> It was not easy for both of us and Nepalese members to keep up our motivation while caught up in the misery of uncertainty over what would happen next.... [Nevertheless,] we became excited once we began to discuss the articles, asking each other, "Why should this provision be put here?" or "What's the problem with this part?" Legal professionals tend to be argumentative. Nepalese ones were particularly so."

In this way, commentaries were added to all of the nearly seven hundred articles. What impressed Matsuo most at that time was the persistence of the Nepalese people. "They repeated discussions with patience and enthusiasm. I was impressed by the way they paid careful attention throughout the discussions."

Having finished the series of aid programs for civil code drafting, JICA began to support the improvement of systems for implementing laws as well; for example, by running a case-management seminar (training in Japan) in March 2013 to clarify what improvements should be made to the Nepalese case-management system by referring to the Japanese system.

The political situation finally began to improve in November of the same year. An election was held again, resulting in the resumption of the Constituent Assembly in January 2014. As deliberations took place toward the establishment of the Constitution, the draft civil code was further refined and submitted to the assembly.

Furthermore, the Project for Strengthening the Capacity of Courts for Expeditious and Reliable Dispute Settlement was launched in September 2013 (it lasted until March 2018). The aim of this project was to create guidelines for improving the case-management system to be introduced to courts across the country, while at the same time assisting in the development of teaching materials for training programs and other efforts to increase the rates of usage and implementation of the mediation system.

According to Matsuo, legal system development is an extremely artificial process; i.e., it is a process of making artificial interventions to change things that would otherwise remain unchanged forever, in order to fulfill the intentions and aspirations of the people. "While some people have no desire to change the status quo, others discuss better alternatives and make constant efforts to influence society. In my opinion, an important role of cooperation for legal and judicial development is to promote this process with the utmost caution, while paying careful attention not only to requests and support from society and practitioners, but also to possible side effects."

05 Political Implications of the Earthquake

While the political confusion still lingered, a gigantic earthquake with an estimated magnitude of 7.8 hit Nepal in April 2015, causing about 9,000 deaths and destroying 900,000 buildings. In the aftermath of the earthquake, JICA provided reconstruction aid in many different ways, including emergency assistance. As

Earthquake damage in the capital, Kathmandu

part of its assistance, JICA also implemented an "earthquake seminar" in Nepal in October of the same year. The seminar was jointly hosted by the Supreme Court of Nepal and JICA to provide Nepalese judicial and legislative professionals with knowledge about legal issues that could be caused by an earthquake, based on experiences gained from the Great Hanshin-Awaji and Great East Japan Earthquakes.

Although the disaster that claimed the lives of so many people was a devastating tragedy, it did provide an impetus for politics. After the launch of the Constituent Assembly in 2008, discussions had never gone very far due to enmity between political parties; the stipulated time period had been extended over and over again, and the establishment of the new Constitution had been put off. The huge earthquake in April changed this situation; the sentiment that confrontation between political parties should end immediately to focus on reconstruction suddenly gained momentum, resulting in an acceleration in the Constitution enactment process. After the seven years of confusion that had started in 2008, the new Constitution was finally established in September 2015. However, although a new administration was set up under the leadership of K. P. Sharma Oli in accordance with the stipulations of the new Constitution, the Indian border was closed due to political unrest, leading to a delay in the distribution of goods and severely affecting the lives of Nepalese people. Prime Minister Oli announced his resignation in July 2016; Pushpa Kamal Dahal was selected as the next prime minister in August of the same year and a new administration was formed.

Takeuchi, who went to Nepal as a member of the emergency relief team in the immediate aftermath of the earthquake, expresses her expectations as follows: "In the face of difficulty, Nepalese people can build stronger ties between themselves. I see them as patient people who have the strength to thrive on adversity. The new Constitution was established quickly after the earthquake. I'm hoping that a new civil code will be smoothly passed by the assembly in the same way."

06 The Largest Challenge Facing Japan's Cooperation for Legal and Judicial Development

Here is a story told by Matsuo about a person who had been involved in the civil code drafting process from the very beginning as a team member, "going through it all together" with Japanese members, and who later became de facto prime minister of Nepal:

> When a reelection was planned after the dissolution of the assembly, Khil Raj Regmi,[46] chief justice of the Supreme Court of Nepal, was appointed as the chairperson of the election management body, as he was regarded as neutral in the midst of fierce confrontation between political parties. Consequently, the reelection was implemented under his leadership as a de facto prime minister. In a televised address he made at the time, he said, "Nepal is now faced with an unprecedented situation in its history in which the country has neither Constitution nor Assembly. All we can do is to restore the power required to reconstruct the country and wait for a consensus to gradually form among the Nepalese people. That will be the starting point for our new nation-building journey."
>
> Being a judicial professional myself, I was impressed by

46 Regmi served as deputy registrar of the Supreme Court and chief judge of various appellate courts before serving as chief justice of the Supreme Court from 2003 to 2013. He also chaired the Nepalese Civil Law Reform and Improvement Task Force (see page 240).

> this message, which I thought deserved much respect. As he said, the role of the law is to encourage the gradual formation of consensus. My understanding is that it's precisely when the political process is stymied that the law really comes into play.

Even after democratization, Nepal is still a country in which caste-derived disparities are deeply rooted in people's daily lives, making it difficult to realize "equality," which is one of the principles of the Constitution. Is it really possible to contribute to creating a peaceful and equal society through the development of the legal system in such a country? According to Matsuo, this is perhaps the greatest challenge facing Japan's cooperation for legal and judicial development.

> At present, it is still difficult for Nepalese people to interact or marry across the caste boundaries. Under such circumstances, can our cooperation for legal and judicial development make a difference? Is it possible to realize the creation of an equal society, a guiding principle of the Constitution, using the law as a tool? These questions are arguably the largest challenges facing Japan's cooperation for the country. The basic philosophy behind the civil code is that all individuals are inherently endowed with equal rights. In my opinion, it's both challenging and worthwhile for Japan to provide support to get such laws to take root in Nepal and work together with Nepalese people to assist in their new nation-building process.

On September 25, 2017, an email popped up to tell Matsuo the following: "The long-awaited news is finally here; the civil code has passed the assembly today. I would like to share our joy with all of you." It was from Gopal Gurung,[47] a member of JICA's Nepal office who had been working together with him in civil code development support. Their eight-year cooperation reached a milestone on that day.

"Let's move further ahead." Gurung's message gave Matsuo fresh motivation for their next step forward.

47 Gurung is the program manager at JICA's Nepal office, which he joined in 2004 after working for an NGO. In this position, he has been playing a role in rebuilding the country after the civil war, including helping draft the civil code.

PROJECT FACT SHEET **Myanmar**

November 20, 2013–
May 31, 2018

Project for Capacity Development of Legal, Judicial and Relevant Sectors

COUNTERPART: **Supreme Court of the Union** **Union Attorney General's Office**

The first legal and judicial development project in Myanmar, Asia's last frontier. Working with the Union Attorney General's Office, which conducts judicial review of laws, and the Supreme Court of the Union, Myanmar's top judicial body, JICA took steps to upgrade the skills of those responsible for developing and implementing legislation. The goal was to enshrine the rule of law in that rapidly changing country, promote democracy and foster sustained economic growth.

MYANMAR

01 | The "Last Frontier" of Asia

"Hearing me speaking like this, now you understand how much I love Myanmar, don't you?" asked Hiroki Kunii[48] about half an hour into an interview. Kunii, who spent two years working on the cooperation for legal and judicial development as a JICA expert in Naypyidaw, the capital of Myanmar, says happily, "I feel that the mentality of Myanmar people is quite similar to that of Japanese people. We are both agrarian peoples. The experience of living in the country has brought me to like it even more." His enthusiastic tone of voice effectively communicates how attractive he finds Myanmar and its people.

48 Kunii, a prosecutor who supported efforts to support legal and judicial development in Myanmar as an ICD professor in Japan, was later stationed in Myanmar as a long-term expert (2014–2016).

The Republic of the Union of Myanmar, commonly known as Myanmar, is located in the western part of the Indochinese Peninsula in Southeast Asia. It launched a transition from a military junta government to a democratic one in March 2011. As a country with abundant natural resources that is in the process of turning into a market economy, it is often called the "last frontier" of Asia. It attracts worldwide attention from a business point of view, and many foreign companies are showing an interest in expanding their business into Myanmar. As the country has a larger area than Thailand—about 1.8 times the size

Seminar on the Company Law

of Japan—and a population of over 50 million people, it is seen not only as an important market but also as an economic base.

Nevertheless, Myanmar, which was under military rule for a long time, had many problems in its legislative and judicial systems. Many of its laws were transplanted from British India during the British colonial era and are still in use today. It is not difficult to imagine the range of problems that can occur when laws established more than a century ago continue to be used in their original form.

"While hundred-year-old laws remained unchanged and are still in use, the government overissued administrative orders instead of changing the laws themselves, resulting in contradictions within the laws and arbitrary legal practice without clear grounds. Although the country did have laws, we had to conclude that they were used in an extremely opaque manner," says Kunii. Under such circumstances, it was only expected that foreign companies should have reservations about expanding their business into Myanmar, despite having high expectations of finding huge business opportunities in the country.

In March 2012, the year following the announcement of the democratization of Myanmar, JICA launched preliminary research for the cooperation for legal and judicial development in the country. The aim was to examine possibilities of assisting Myanmar, which was regarded as a hugely promising destination for investment for foreign companies, with improvement of its legal environment. ICD[49] also began their research in the same year jointly with Keio University, for example by inviting the Chief Justice of the Supreme Court of the Union. JICA and ICD had repeated consultations with related Myanmar organizations, while sharing each other's research results to prepare for cooperation.

49 See inset, page 79.

JICA hosted a seminar on legal systems and corporate governance for public companies in Myanmar in August 2012, a seminar on privatization of state-owned enterprises in December 2012, and a seminar on commercial arbitration in Myanmar in April 2013. Then, in June 2013, it co-hosted a seminar entitled "Development and Challenges of Myanmar: What the Country Expects of Japan and Development of Laws" with the ICD and the International Civil and Commercial Law Centre (ICCLC),[50] for which it invited the attorney general of Myanmar to Japan.

50 See inset, page 275.

All these seminars were designed not only to be preparatory milestones leading to the future launch of a legal and judicial development project in the area of civil and commercial laws, but were also intended to make Myanmar understand the principle of Japan's cooperation: "Jointly carrying out research and other tasks with the recipient country, rather than just providing one-way assistance."

02 Exchanges with Japan Continued Even under Military Rule

An agreement on the Project for Capacity Development of Legal, Judicial and Relevant Sectors in Myanmar was signed between JICA and the Supreme Court of the Union[51] and the Union Attorney General's Office of Myanmar[52] in August 2013. After a year of careful preliminary research that began in 2012, it was officially decided that a project would finally start.

The aim of the project was to develop legal professionals for drafting and reviewing bills, as well as to improve the training systems for such legal professionals.

51 The Supreme Court of the Union is the highest of Myanmar's courts.

52 The Union Attorney General's Office is an administrative agency headed by the Union Attorney General, a member of the Cabinet. This body reviews legislation drafted by each ministry and handles prosecutorial matters at the federal level. It also provides legal advice to the legislature and the executive.

In the project, topic-specific working groups were formed by officers of our partners to have discussions with Japanese experts once every one or two weeks. For example, the legislative reviewing working group examined articles to make sure that they were all clear and consistent with other laws through detailed discussions.

These are the words of Kenta Komatsu,[53] a lawyer who was sent to Myanmar in January 2014 as a long-term expert. Komatsu, who specialized in corporate legal affairs when he was in Japan, says that he often finds these discussions with officers of our partners very constructive.

53 Komatsu is a lawyer registered with the Dai-Ni Tokyo Bar Association. After participating in efforts to support legal and judicial development in Myanmar and elsewhere as a senior advisor to JICA (2013–), he was stationed in Myanmar as a long-term expert (2014–2017).

Legal education deteriorated during the many years of military rule in Myanmar. As a result, the country does not have many legal practitioners equipped with an adequate knowledge of business-related laws, including company law and bankruptcy law. This is why we take various measures—for example, through using case studies—to make it easier even for those who have little work experience to understand such legal systems and to actively express their opinions, in addition to providing them with basic knowledge about them. When our partner officers ask precise questions about the information which we provide them and actively participate

Meeting of the working group on intellectual property law in Myanmar

in discussions, we can be sure that they have developed a deeper understanding of the officers and that we can more easily carry out the activities to follow. After all, it is when we have a fruitful discussion that I find my job rewarding.

Komatsu says that Myanmar government employees are very friendly toward Japanese people.

Japan has a long history of providing continued international cooperation to Myanmar even under military rule in the area of human resource development, even when the country was almost excluded from the international community due to sanctions imposed by Western countries. Japan also accepted many officers from Myanmar government agencies as international students. The mutual trust between the two countries is based on such ties. From an organizational point of view, however, I sometimes felt that Myanmar ministries and other organizations are too wary of foreigners. In fact, they even refused to disclose documents necessary for our project activities immediately after my arrival in Myanmar, which prevented us from effectively carrying out the project and put us in a quandary. However, we patiently explained to them our reasons while respecting our cultural differences. Today, growing numbers of government officers are beginning to recognize the need to ask a wide range of related parties for opinions while at the bill drafting stage.

03 | **Laws Matching the Speed of Democratization**

As described earlier, the legal system of Myanmar is characterized by its opacity; many of the laws transplanted during the British colonial era remain unchanged and are still in use, and those in top positions can decide how they should be applied; for example, through administrative orders. Komatsu points out, "The important thing is to make the extremely complex and opaque law system of Myanmar as concise and easy to understand as possible." At the same time, he says, "It's difficult to instantly overhaul the entire legal system through our cooperation. We have to gradually reform the system, step by step, tackling the problem areas whenever the Myanmar side sees the necessity in any given area." Needless to say, it is impossible to change a century-old legal system overnight.

Kunii, the prosecutor mentioned at the beginning of this section, was sent to Myanmar as a JICA project expert in May 2014, slightly later than Komatsu. After all the efforts he had made since 2012 to enable the successful launch of the project, traveling between Japan and Myanmar frequently, he had a special feeling about this project. Smiling, he says,

> When there was a need to send someone to Myanmar, I thought that no one was more suitable for the job than me, and I definitely did not want to see someone else working it. I arrived in Myanmar with such a strong sense of duty.
>
> For example, I've witnessed the rapid development of Yangon, the former capital of Myanmar. Growing numbers of people have begun to drive expensive imported cars, traffic has become more congested, and some companies have begun to make huge profits while others are still suffering from the poverty. In fact, the gap between the rich and poor and social disparities have been widening, causing inequality and distortion. I acutely felt that laws which had not previously existed in Myanmar needed to be developed, such as those concerning intellectual property rights. There are many things that Japanese legal practitioners can do for the country. The experience of actually living in Myanmar has brought this home to me.

04 Developing Accessible Laws

The Project for Capacity Development of Legal, Judicial and Relevant Sectors in Myanmar, which was launched in 2013, is still ongoing today. A new administration was formed in 2016 under the de facto leadership of Aung San Suu Kyi, and democratization of Myanmar seems to have been further accelerated. The most pressing issue for Myanmar at the moment is economic growth, and it is expected that demand for the development of laws in association with economic growth will increase in the future. Komatsu, who has continued his support activities in the country, says, "The important thing is how you can make the laws suitable for economic growth and the improvement of the investment environment as easy to use as possible in Myanmar."

He continues:

> As I see it, the chief characteristic of Japan's cooperation for legal and judicial development is that Japan first grasp the background of the legal issues and needs in the recipient country. Then it provides meticulous support to the point where the officials applying the laws drafted under that cooperation are sufficiently capable, so that those laws can be utilized as much as possible in the partner country. For example, when a Japanese project team is working on a bankruptcy law, members work together with the people who are actually going to use the law in the future, such as court officials, in order to complete the bill. If we don't adopt such kinds of methods, the resulting law may not suit the realities of the target country. Worse, it can even end up with the law falling completely out of use, as officials in charge have no idea how to apply it. This would make no sense at all.

05 | Short-Term Verification Needed

Kunii says that it is very difficult to determine when to stop providing support, not only in the case of Myanmar, but also in all legal and judicial development projects.

> Cooperation is not as simple as saying, "We have planned to create a specific number of laws, and as a result, this number

> of laws was developed." That's not the kind of work Japan aims to do. Needless to say, creating laws alone is not enough to ensure that the rule of law penetrates throughout the target country. In fact, the most important part is educating people. In other words, how you develop human resources who can make precise use of the laws? Given that the cooperation for legal and judicial development is part of Japan's technical cooperation with other countries, I believe that the final goal should be to increase the technical skills and abilities of people in recipient countries.

Evaluation of effectiveness, however, is even more difficult in the area of professional development.

> For example, while a ten-year interval may be appropriate for many other countries, it's necessary to review and verify the effects of our projects at intervals of about five years in Myanmar, given the speed of growth of that country. If we find that a particular change in direction is necessary, we should make modifications. There have been intensifying debates in Japan in recent years as to how Japan's cooperation to other countries can contribute to our own national interests. Under such circumstances, it's increasingly important nowadays to verify the cost performance of our projects at regular intervals. For example, the amount of investment from Japanese companies to Myanmar has doubled in five years. One factor contributing to the increase must be our cooperation for legal and judicial development to Myanmar—although there may also have been many others, such as infrastructure improvement. More and more investment from Japanese companies is expected in the future, so I think we should conclude that Japan needs to continue providing the cooperation in this field to countries that are promising investment targets for Japanese companies as part of its risk management.

This project also carried out training by inviting to Japan officers of the Directorate of Investment and Company Administration in the Ministry of National Planning and Economic

Development, which is in charge of drafting company law, and the Union Attorney General's Office, which is in charge of reviewing the draft. According to a participant from the Union Attorney General's Office, this training, including simulations of specific disputes, "has provided an opportunity to consider whether the existing draft articles for company law are genuinely appropriate." In addition, JICA began to examine the introduction of a mediation system with the Supreme Court of the Union in July 2016. As pointed out by Kunii, Myanmar is expected to become an increasingly attractive market for Japan in the future, so it is assumed that the cooperation should be periodically verified for cost effectiveness and last until the desired effects are achieved.

06 Insights, Knowledge, and Experiences as Outputs

After two years in Myanmar, Kunii returned to his original career as a prosecutor in Japan. However, he hopes to stay involved with Myanmar into the future, even if on a voluntary basis.

> I spent two richly rewarding years together with Myanmar legal professionals, during which I feel I was able to share with them what you could call a "legal mind," irrespective of the cultural and legal differences between the two countries. We've been keeping in touch even since I returned to Japan. For example, they've emailed to ask me for advice, and I've replied to them with my views. I've also been disseminating the insights, knowledge, and experiences I obtained through the project in many different ways, including contributing articles at the request of Japanese universities that teach the cooperation for legal and judicial development and joining the panel at the Conference on Technical Assistance in the Legal Field[54] to speak about Myanmar. It would have been a waste if I took part in a project but did nothing after I returned to Japan. Since I went to Myanmar on behalf of Japan, the insights and knowledge which I gained there can

54 This is an annual conference that has been jointly hosted by JICA and the ICD since 2000. Participants exchange information and engage in discussions on cooperation for legal and judicial development.

> also be regarded as an output for Japanese people. I think it's important for me to pass on what I've learned to someone else, even if in personal ways. I would also like to stay involved with Myanmar all my life, which I envisage as my life's work and my purpose in life.

Kunii also has something to say about how Japan should provide the cooperation for legal and judicial development in the future.

> I have no doubt that it's important to debate whether Japan's cooperation really contributes to our national interests. For a start, Japan's cooperation has always been carried out by people putting themselves in the shoes of people of the recipient countries and working together with them without expecting anything in return. You could call that "good old cooperation." Without this spirit, Japan could not have won the trust of so many different countries. We should never forget that. Although the economic situation of Japan has been far from good in recent years, I think that if Japan continues to provide cooperation to other countries , setting aside its own benefit, it's sure to have a positive influence on Japan's position in the international community. After all, we all want Japan to be seen as a country that is "there to help others."

When we asked Kunii what he had acquired through participating in the cooperation in Myanmar, he answered,

> This may sound like bragging, but the truth is, I think that the experience has broadened my horizons as a legal professional and given me a deeper perspective. It's brought me to realize that working inside the world of prosecution for many years gave me a narrow view of things, so I was almost ignorant of the real world. I feel that my involvement with Myanmar has changed me a lot. In fact, my family and peers also say that I'm kinder now. Working for the cooperation for legal and judicial development has the power to change people. This is the reason that I want to encourage all young

people interested in this field to go to Myanmar and different countries across the world. The first thing they should do there is to love the country and its people. In my opinion, that should always be the first step.

PROJECT FACT SHEET

Francophone Africa and Côte d'Ivoire

FY2013–2014

Country-focused Training: Training on Criminal Justice in French-Speaking African Countries I

FY2015–2017

Third-Country Training: Training on Criminal Justice in French-Speaking African Countries II

COUNTERPART: **The Ministry of Justice in each country**

This training program was intended for individuals working in the criminal justice field (police officers, prosecutors, and judges) in eight Francophone African countries: Côte d'Ivoire, Burkina Faso, Niger, Mali, Chad, Senegal, Mauritania, and the Democratic Republic of Congo. Carried out with the cooperation of the United Nations Asia and Far East Institute for the Prevention of Crime and the Treatment of Offenders (UNAFEI), the program was designed to develop the capacity to implement criminal justice procedures from investigation through trial. The FY2013–2014 training program took place at UNAFEI in Japan. The FY2015–2017 training program was held in Côte d'Ivoire to more effectively address the shared needs and challenges facing Francophone Africa and the Sahel.

December 8, 2014–
April 1, 2017

Legal Advisor

COUNTERPART: **Ministry of Justice**

The decade-long civil war that broke out in Côte d'Ivoire in 2002 seriously weakened the country's judicial institutions and its legal community. Impunity became rife, and public trust in the judiciary was shattered. A JICA advisor was therefore sent to Côte d'Ivoire to help ensure better delivery of legal services to the public, both by enhancing the skills of criminal justice professionals so that crimes would no longer go unpunished, and by improving access to justice.

CÔTE D'IVOIRE AND FRENCH-SPEAKING AFRICAN COUNTRIES

01 Toward Peace and Stability

What can be done to stand against the militant Islamists and organized crime that have been extending their influence in the Sahara Desert and surrounding regions, and to realize peace and stability there? Today, peace building is a critical and pressing issue for African countries.

A statement that neighboring countries in Africa are required to cooperate with each other to face this crisis and build peace across their borders was confirmed at the Fifth Tokyo International Conference on African Development (TICAD[55] V), held in Yokohama in 2013 .

In response to this move, JICA and the United Nations Asia and Far East Institute for the Prevention of Crime and the Treatment of Offenders (UNAFEI)[56] began in 2014 to provide Training on Criminal Justice in French-Speaking African Countries, targeted at eight countries, namely Burkina Faso, Chad, Côte d'Ivoire, the Democratic Republic of the Congo, Mali, Mauritania, Niger, and Senegal.

"The main goal of the training is to develop human resources in the criminal justice sector, in regard with implementation of procedure from investigation to trial.[57] The first and second training programs took place in Japan, and the third program in 2015 and more recent ones were hosted by Côte d'Ivoire."

These are the words of Wakaba Hara,[58] who was sent to Côte d'Ivoire in 2014 as a long-term expert. She became the first expert in the field of the law and justice sector to be sent from Japan to Africa. She had already had a colorful career as a legal professional: after accumulating practical work experience as a lawyer in international trade and other areas, she had been

55 TICAD is a conference on African development held since 1993 at the initiative of the Japanese government and co-hosted by the United Nations, the United Nations Development Programme (UNDP), the African Union Commission (AUC) and the World Bank. (Source: Japanese Foreign Affairs Ministry website)

56 See inset, page 261.

57 This comprises the entire sequence of legal proceedings under the criminal procedure code from when charges are filed until the case wraps up.

58 Hara is a lawyer registered with the Dai-Ichi Tokyo Bar Association. After working to promote access to justice in Japan at the Japan Legal Support Center, she was stationed in Côte d'Ivoire from 2014 to 2017 as a long-term expert in legal and judicial development. She is also a former guest senior advisor to JICA.

involved in many different activities, such as treaty development at the Ministry of Foreign Affairs, JICA's cooperation for legal and judicial development in Asia, and management of nationwide operation of services at the Japan Legal Support Center (Houterasu)[59] aimed at improving access to justice.[60]

Participants in this criminal justice training program included about thirty police officers, prosecutors, judges, and other judicial and legal professionals from the eight countries. Hara supported the implementation of preliminary research for the training, planning of program contents, organization of a follow-up reporting session, and so on.

In the course of the training, lectures were given not only by UNAFEI professors but also by relevant international experts in the field of criminal justice. Some local experts were also invited to the panel discussions in the program. The program ended with the adoption of an action plan for criminal justice process improvement by each country. At the same time, a joint declaration was issued to promote cooperation between these countries in the area of justice. The program has given the eight countries an opportunity to take a new step toward peace and stability, while building structures for cooperation between them.

59 This is a public agency with a mandate to help ordinary Japanese gain access to justice. Established in 2006 as part of a series of reforms to the Japanese judicial system, it operates a call center called Houterasu Support Dial, which provides information about the law and where to contact for advice.

60 Access to justice involves having recourse to the law as a citizen and being able to use the courts and other legal institutions. See the Quick Guide to Japan's Cooperation for Legal and Judicial Development at the front of the book, page 11.

02 Restoring the Ruined Credibility of Justice

Côte d'Ivoire, which hosted the criminal justice training, is a country faced with huge challenges, including those in the area of justice. Says Hara:

> Côte d'Ivoire is a lesser-known country to Japanese people, as it is distant from Japan geographically and culturally. It is also not a common tourist destination for the Japanese. Its largest city, Abidjan, however, used to function as an economic hub for West Africa. Each of the six largest Japanese trading companies has a branch in the city, in which the number of Japanese residents once peaked at nearly three hundred. However, the civil war that engulfed the country for about ten years from

2002 deeply paralyzed many legal institutions in the country, including the court and the prison. There was a particularly serious decline in the legal functions of the rebel-held territory, from which judicial and legal personnel had to escape. Consequently, the problem of impunity of criminals became prevalent, and public confidence in justice suffered greatly.

Restoring public confidence in justice is necessary in order to reconstruct a safe and stable society through the rule of law.

OTHER ORGANIZATIONS INVOLVED IN COOPERATION FOR LEGAL AND JUDICIAL DEVELOPMENT

United Nations Asia and Far East Institute for the Prevention of Crime and the Treatment of Offenders (UNAFEI)

Overview

UNAFEI, a training institute established in 1962 by agreement between the United Nations and the Government of Japan, is dedicated to promoting the sound development of criminal justice systems in the Asia-Pacific and other countries and strengthening cooperation among them. The United Nations Training Cooperation Department of the Research and Training Institute, an arm of the Japanese Ministry of Justice, runs UNAFEI's training and research programs in collaboration with the UN.

Main Activities

- Organizing international training programs and seminars for criminal justice professionals from various countries.
- Supporting JICA's legal and judicial development projects as a major Japanese partner.
- Conducting research on crime prevention and the treatment of offenders.
- Helping formulate and implement the UN's global policies on crime prevention and treatment of offenders in cooperation with the UN Office on Drugs and Crime (UNODC) and the UN Crime Prevention and Criminal Justice Programme Network (PNI).
- Releasing its research findings in print and other forms.

Timeline

1954	The first United Nations Asia and Far East Convention for the Prevention of Crime and the Treatment of Offenders adopts a resolution calling for the establishment of a UN regional training institute in Asia.
1961	The UN and the government of Japan sign an agreement establishing a UN regional training institute in Japan.
1962	UNAFEI is officially inaugurated and conducts its first International Training Course.
1970	The 1961 agreement is amended, with the government of Japan assuming full responsibility for UNAFEI's administration and finances.
1995	The number of international training courses and seminars conducted by UNAFEI reaches 100.
2013	UNAFEI takes over part of the task of helping Nepal reform its criminal justice system from the International Cooperation Department (ICD) of the Justice Ministry's Research and Training Institute.
2014	UNAFEI takes over part of the task of helping Vietnam improve its criminal justice system from the ICD.
2017	UNAFEI relocates to the International Justice Center in Akishima, Tokyo. As of October 1, 2017, over 5,500 criminal justice professionals from 138 countries and regions had attended UNAFEI training programs.

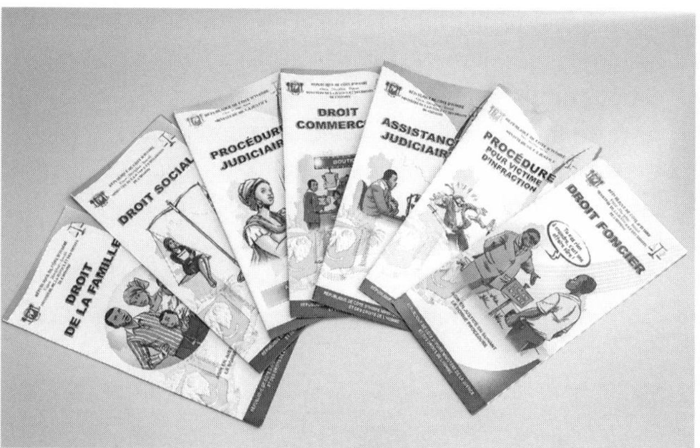

Pamphlets explaining the law and legal procedures in layman's terms

Côte d'Ivoire designated social stability and harmony as the most important goals of the reconstruction of the state's justice sector in its National Development Plan, and established a reform policy for the sector in 2013. Currently, reform is underway to reconstruct the country's judicial system, which was weakened by the civil war.

To achieve the goal of reconstructing a safe and stable society under the rule of law, it is essential to foster high-quality personnel in the legal and judicial sectors to restore public confidence in justice. In reality, Côte d'Ivoire only had a small number of legal professionals; at the same time, it was lacking an adequate availability of training programs for workers in the legal and judicial sectors. People's access to legal services is limited for various reasons, including their lack of information and knowledge about justice. In a nutshell, access to justice is not sufficiently guaranteed for all the people in the country. As such, the development of human resources in the criminal justice sector and the improvement of access to justice have been high-priority tasks for Côte d'Ivoire.

03 An Information Revolution Powered by Mobile Phones

As a way to improve access to justice, the Ivorian side requested that Japan establish a call center in their country. In response, Hara was selected for her expertise on access to justice and her experience in call-center management, and was sent to the country in 2014. She was assigned to what was then called the Ministry of Justice, Human Rights, and Public Liberties (hereinafter referred to as the "Ministry of Justice").

The Training on Criminal Justice in Francophone African Countries of 2015, which was implemented in Japan immediately after Hara's arrival in Côte d'Ivoire, also had the participation of people from the Ministry of Justice of Côte d'Ivoire, and, upon her proposal, included a small study tour of the Japan Legal Support Center (Houterasu). Houterasu was established as the core organization for the comprehensive legal support scheme proposed in the judicial system reform in Japan in the 2000s. As a result, various systems and initiatives—including operations related to civil legal aid and state-appointed legal assistance—that were traditionally implemented separately by different organizations such as bar associations, the Japan Legal Aid Association, and courts, including operations related to civil legal aid and court-appointed defense counsel, are now carried out in an integrated manner, with through Houterasu functioning as the center. One feature of this center that was emphasized most when it was first set up was the information service provided through multiple channels, including its call center and website. Hara describes this service as follows:

> Although bar associations across Japan have been offering legal counseling services, it's still quite a psychological barrier for ordinary Japanese people to use such services, as many of them feel awkward consulting legal professionals in person. The information provision service was launched to provide a more casual system that can encourage ordinary people to feel free to make legal enquiries by telephone or online.

61 Hassan, an investigator and later technical advisor with the secretariat of the Ivorian Ministry of Justice, has been the director of the secretariat's administration department since 2016.

Hassan Diane,[61] an Ivorian participant in the 2015 training program who was working for the secretariat of the Ministry of Justice as a senior official in charge of research and investigation, reported to the minister of justice about what he had observed in the study tour of Houterasu after returning from Japan. He compiled a plan for the establishment of a call center modeled after the Japanese system. Côte d'Ivoire already had a legal aid system derived from France that was implemented, albeit on a small scale, and managed by an office set up inside the Department of Civil and Criminal Affairs of the Ministry of Justice. Diane proposed that the call center should be established inside the Department of Civil and Criminal Affairs so as to allow the department to function as the center for access to justice for the time being. Meanwhile, plans should be made to establish an independent comprehensive support organization for access to justice, like Houterasu, in the future.

After some setbacks, it was eventually decided that the call center in Côte d'Ivoire would be set up inside the Department of Civil and Criminal Affairs to provide information to citizens, improving public access to legal services. Hara had been engaged in the operation of the Houterasu call center in a managerial position, and supported the establishment of infrastructure for the provision of services by taking the setup used in Japan and adapting it to suit the realities of Côte d'Ivoire. Despite its small scale, the center could provide more or less adequate legal information to meet the general needs of citizens.

Because it is still difficult to install land-based phone lines in Africa, the proliferation of mobile phones has resulted in an information revolution. The great majority of African people, including those living in rural villages, own mobile phones that allow them to make telephone calls despite not ever having had land lines installed in their homes. On the other hand, smartphones are still hard to come by for ordinary citizens. This is also a reason that the "call first" mechanism of the call center is considered to be the most effective, at least at the moment. Says Hara:

> In the next stage, the most important thing is to let people know that the call center exists. Even when a call center is

established, no one can call it if nobody knows its telephone number. Although running a TV advertisement requires the Ministry of Justice to secure a large budget, word of mouth and other analog communication methods are also effective in Africa. Being inspired by various distribution materials such as cards or leaflets prepared by Houterasu in Japan, we've firstly prepared a card to inform people of the telephone number of the call center. It is made in the same size as the Ivoirian ID card, based on a local staff member's idea. As often seen in Japanese information materials, the card features cartoons, drawn by a local illustrator, which make the information easier to understand and stand out to attract people's attention. Since Ivorian people love calendars, we've also created a calendar with the same design and information, and it was received very favorably. In addition, we've created a series of legal information leaflets which cover basic laws and procedures frequently asked about by people, by using the set of Q&As that had been developed for the call center. It was also modeled after leaflets used by Houterasu.

04 Precedent for Other African Countries

In December 2016, the call center opened inside the Ministry of Justice. It was established to receive enquiries from the general public about issues concerning laws, court proceedings, and so on. In a nutshell, it is a "legal information service." The information provided by the service consists of: first, information about legal issues and procedures, and second, information on the appropriate consultation desks for each user. Hara explains, "The Japanese Houterasu has prepared responses to about 5,000 frequently asked questions in the form of Q&A, and they are also available on its website. Following suit, we have prepared about 700 Q&A pairs to answer questions most likely to be asked in Côte d'Ivoire."

Results showed that the most common enquiries were those about family law issues, followed by criminal issues. Hara comments, "Family-related enquiries, for example about remedies against an unfaithful husband, are the most common in any country. The fact that criminal issues take second place, however, suggests that the society may not have become stable yet." The call center is staffed with two full-time operators and accompanied by a supervisor. "Houterasu in Japan receives about a thousand calls each day, which are answered by a maximum of sixty operators. Given the population of Côte d'Ivoire, which is about a fifth of Japan's, the call center needs to be staffed by a maximum of about twelve operators to receive 200 calls each day in order to provide the same degree of service available in Japan."

According to Hara, the role of the call center is to function as the first step toward resolution, rather than offering a final solution. In other words, it may not be possible to full resolve a problem by turning to the call center for help; it will be necessary to consult a legal professional or visit the court in person to follow the necessary procedures in many cases. However, contacting the call center can at least guide Ivorians toward the resolution of the problem by helping them take the right first step. Like many other developing countries, Côte d'Ivoire has many things to improve upon in the area of access to justice; for example, a lack of a sufficient number of legal professionals

The call center's two operators and their supervisor, Saboré Kourouma Guiro (second from left), Sub Director of the Department of Civil and Criminal Affairs

and the need to improve the operation of legal aid system. Making all these necessary improvements requires quite a sweeping level of reforms to be carried out in accordance with a medium- to long-term plan. It would take some time before call center users could be provided with a sufficient level of access to justice throughout all of their legal proceedings.

Nevertheless, it is still true that establishing a call center to improve access to justice is an advanced initiative in Africa and could be a precedent for other African countries. At the same time, it concretely contributes to achieving target 16.3 in the Sustainable Development Goals (SDGs)[62] adopted by the United Nations in September 2015: to "ensure equal access to justice for all." Côte d'Ivoire is expected to play a central role in the eight-country network of the Training on Criminal Justice while at the same time functioning as a hub in the area of justice (reflecting Abidjan's former status as an economic hub city).

62 The SDGs are a set of international goals for the years 2016–2030, superseding the Millennium Development Goals adopted in 2001. Consisting of 17 goals and 169 targets for achieving a sustainable world, they set out an agenda of issues to be tackled by both developing countries and developed ones.

The judicial system of Côte d'Ivoire is derived from France, the former colonial power; the country has also received aid for judicial system reform from France and other developed Western countries. On the other hand, Japan has its own unique experiences and knowledge, being a country that has learned from Western systems, and has been establishing and running systems in such a way as to suit its own culture and society, and meeting international standards. Hara describes the Japanese way of cooperation as follows: "If we share these experiences with African countries and help them design their own systems, by adequately adopting Western systems that really suit each country and run them in a sustainable manner, such cooperation must be welcome." The next task should be to accumulate these experiences.

05 | An Equal Relationship, Free from Historical Constraints

This was the first time that JICA sent an expert in the cooperation for legal and judicial development to a French-speaking African country. In this regard, this aid work is also expected to contribute to collecting information and accumulating experience in the area of law and justice in this region, for example as to what kind of medium- to long-term support should be provided and what possibilities there are. Another anticipated effect is contribution to economic activities of Japanese companies in African countries.

Hara's analysis is as follows:

> As observed in Côte d'Ivoire, France has accumulated an extraordinary level of experience through its relationships with its former colonies. In fact, it may not be easy for Japan to provide support that is as intrinsic and deep as that delivered by France to countries that have inherited French systems. At the same time, it can also be said that Japan has the advantage of being free from such historical constraints, which makes it easier for Japan to have equal friendly relationships with these countries.

If there is some kind of support that neither France, the EU, nor the USA, but only Japan can provide to Francophone Africa, how should Japan carry out such support in the future? Hara answers:

> Let's take the call center as an example. It cannot be denied that the Ivoirian side sometimes shows greater interest in material support, such as provision of PCs. At the same time, there are Ivorian people who are interested not in receiving material support, but in learning methods for improvement of critical skills and how to improve access to justice, and they are keenly aware of the significance of such learning. Nevertheless, even when they know how the systems and operations should be, it's no easy matter for them to actually change the status quo and carry out the necessary reforms on their own. Even if they could, it would take them a great deal of time.

Furthermore, there are times when I feel that many Ivorian people have a vague sense of trust toward Japan and the support provided by Japanese people, in a good way. This is another reason that I believe it's important for Japan to continue supporting recipient countries on an equal footing. The important thing is to never look down on others, and not to let others look down on you at the same time. I suppose this is the key to Japan establishing good relationships of trust, in its own way, with countries to which it provides support.

I was first posted to Côte d'Ivoire in December 2014, only two years after the end of the civil war. In Abidjan, the largest city in the country, you couldn't walk anywhere without seeing a piece of destroyed building all around, but I felt optimism and positivity in the people. The generation of Ivorians who remember Côte d'Ivoire's glorious days of dramatic economic growth in the 1980s are still in their working years, and are striving with great enthusiasm to restore what their country used to have. In fact, Japan's postwar history since 1945 might be the very best model for showing them that constructing systems for peace and social stability also lays the foundations for revitalization of all the economic activities of the country.

Additional Sidelights on Cooperation for Legal and Judicial Development

The Next Generation
Asian Students Studying Law in Japan

What motivated you to study law in Japan? How do you plan to apply what you've learned in the future?

Chin Mony

Staff member, Cambodian Ministry of Justice
Second-year student, master's program, Nagoya University Graduate School of Law

What really struck me when I came to Japan was the pervasiveness of the attitude that laws and rules are to be obeyed. The way people here are so punctual about time is a case in point. I want to cultivate that attitude in Cambodian society. One day I'd like to assume a leadership role at the Ministry of Justice and ensure that the law is properly enforced in Cambodian society—and rid the country of corruption.

Try Bakleang

Graduate of the Royal University of Law and Economics, Cambodia
Second-year student, master's program, Nagoya University Graduate School of Law

When I was studying at the Research and Education Center for Japanese Law at the Royal University of Law and Economics in Cambodia, I became interested in learning about the Cambodian Civil Code and its model, the Japanese Civil Code, from a comparative law perspective. My thesis topic is the protection of trust in nonsubstantive real-estate registration. When I graduate, I hope to become a scholar in Cambodia and research civil case law. I'd also like to write a book explaining the Cambodian Civil Code to people in layman's terms.

Nguyen Tuan Linh

Staff member, Vietnamese Ministry of Justice
Second-year student, master's program, Nagoya University Graduate School of Law

I work in the field of intellectual property rights at the Vietnamese Ministry of Justice. The Vietnamese intellectual property law is coming up for revision in a couple of years, so I've come to Japan to learn about the corresponding Japanese legislation. My Japanese still isn't very good, so my personal goal is to become more proficient in the language. One day I hope to occupy a senior position at the Ministry of Justice and further advance cooperation between Japan and Vietnam.

Tuong Thi Tu Hoai

Graduate of Hanoi Law University
First-year student, PhD program, Nagoya University Graduate School of Law

I graduated from the Research and Education Center for Japanese Law at Hanoi Law University, and I decided to study in Japan because I was interested in doing in-depth research on the Japanese Civil Code. Right now, I'm learning about the system of prescription in Japanese civil law. I'd like to become a professor at my alma mater once I graduate. By teaching Vietnamese and Japanese law from a comparative perspective, I hope to produce students with the ability to ask themselves how to solve the challenges facing Vietnamese society.

Chapter 5

The Future of Legal and Judicial Development

Japan has been working on cooperation for legal and judicial development abroad for twenty years. While its efforts have achieved much, they have also brought new challenges to light. Today more young Japanese than ever are interested in working in this area. What new goals should JICA's program pursue as it enters its second generation?

The bustling streets of Yangon, Myanmar's former capital

01 The Results of "Twenty Years of the Cooperation for Legal and Judicial Development"

The previous chapters have described the progress of Japan's cooperation for legal and judicial development over the years, from the start of the first project in Vietnam (chapter 1) to providing support to countries all over the world, such as Africa (chapter 5). Through repeated trial and error, these activities have produced a wide variety of results for each recipient country, such as the revision of the Civil Code of Vietnam, establishment of the Civil Code and Civil Procedure Code of Cambodia, and creation of the Laotian civil and criminal procedure flowcharts.

Let us shift gears this chapter and look at what the results of cooperation for legal and judicial development have brought to JICA and Japan, as well as outcomes produced internationally, to consider the future of the cooperation in this field.

OUTCOME 1
Establishment of a new field of "technical cooperation"

According to Ken'ichi Tomiyoshi,[1] senior vice president of JICA, the most significant outcome is that the legal and judicial development has become clearly defined as part of Japan's "ODA-based technical cooperation."

1 Tomiyoshi oversaw assistance programs in the governance field, including legal and judicial development, as vice president of JICA from 2015 to 2017.

Until the early 1990s, it was unimaginable for Japan to provide ODA to developing countries in the form of assistance in drafting legislation, developing human resources in the legal and judicial sectors, and so on.

Ken'ichi Tomiyoshi

Thanks to the hard work of many people involved in legal aid activities, the legal and judicial development has grown in importance as an area of assistance, to the extent that it's now regarded as an essential pillar of international cooperation. The Development Cooperation Charter,[2] which was

2 See page 57, note 25.

approved by the Cabinet in February 2015, also cites the "rule of law" as "the key to realizing an equitable and inclusive society." Furthermore, the Sustainable Development Goals (SDGs)[3] adopted by the United Nations in September of the same year promote the rule of law (target 16.3) as well. Under such circumstances, I think that it has been an extremely significant achievement that legal and judicial development has been established as a new area of Japan's international cooperation.

3 See page 267, note 62.

OUTCOME 2

Establishment of the "all-Japan approach"

When JICA started the first project in Vietnam in 1996, only one long-term expert, a lawyer, was posted to the country. Later, a system was developed to send suitable staff members from the three branches of the legal profession to meet actual local needs: judges (including former judges), prosecutors, and lawyers. This was done through the establishment of the International Cooperation Department (ICD)[4] and the Research and Training Institute, assistance from the Ministry of Justice, the involvement of courts in the project activities, cooperation with the Japan Federation of Bar Associations (JFBA), and so on. Furthermore,

4 See inset, page 79.

The Conference on Technical Assistance in the Legal Field

in addition to jurists (legal scholars), Japanese advisory groups are now made up of a wider variety of people, including judges (or former judges), prosecutors, and lawyers. The result is the current style of Japanese cooperation for legal and judicial development, in which Japanese judges (or former judges), prosecutors, and lawyers play central roles in cooperation with courts, prosecutor's offices, and bar associations respectively in their target countries, so that the concerns and experiences held in common among practitioners can be shared in these sectors, while at the same time they work in coordination with experts in other positions.

Hiroshi Matsuo,[5] professor of law at Keio University, who has been involved in this field since 2002, mainly in Laos, has been conducting theoretical research on this topic. He describes how significant it is for people from the three branches of legal professions, as well as jurists, to work together as members of the same advisory groups. "There is not a single 'right' answer in law. Take the civil code, for example. It's divided into a large number of different fields, and there is a room for interpretation of each provision. This is why it's essential that multiple perspectives should be reflected in cooperation for legal and judicial development, not just the opinion of a single expert."

5 See page 149, note 3.

From going through these processes, JICA, the Ministry of Justice (and courts), the JFBA, Nagoya University and other research institutes, and individuals with specialist knowledge and experience in a variety of fields are providing cooperation in close coordination and collaboration with one another. In addition, the International Civil and Commercial Law Centre (ICCLC),[6] a private-sector organization, has also been supporting JICA in hosting advisory group meetings and accepting overseas training participants in Japan, and the like. This "all-Japan approach" is what enables the provision of quality support in activities for the target countries and training programs in Japan.

6 See inset, page 275.

Furthermore, the creation of this style has revealed advantages that were not expected at the beginning of the activities. One is greater awareness of the law of Japan. Matsuo explains, "As we repeatedly discuss the laws and regulations of the

OTHER ORGANIZATIONS INVOLVED IN COOPERATION FOR LEGAL AND JUDICIAL DEVELOPMENT

International Civil and Commercial Law Centre (ICCLC)

Overview

The International Civil and Commercial Law Centre (ICCLC) is a private-sector Japanese foundation that participates in efforts to aid and assist the Asian countries in developing their respective legal infrastructures. It also engages with counterparts outside Japan by organizing symposia and seminars, conducting research, and sharing information in order to reach a better common understanding of the legal system as it applies to cross-border economic transactions.

Main Activities

- Supporting JICA in accepting trainees from abroad and organizing advisory group meetings as a major Japanese partner in JICA's efforts in legal and judicial development.
- Organizing the Japan-China Civil and Commercial Law Seminar and lectures and seminars on other subjects.
- Carrying out research on Asian countries' civil and commercial legislation.
- Publishing the journal *ICCLC* and the newsletter *ICCLC News*, and issuing research reports.

Timeline

1996	Meeting of founding members; the ICCLC is established with the approval of the Japanese Minister of Justice; applies to register as a foundation; holds its inaugural board meeting and founding ceremony; initiates assistance to Vietnam and Cambodia.
1998	Is licensed by the minister of justice as a special public interest promotion corporation; initiates assistance to Laos and Indonesia.
2001	Initiates assistance to Uzbekistan.
2004	Initiates assistance to Mongolia.
2007	Initiates assistance to China.
2009	Initiates assistance to Nepal.
2013	Is licensed by the prime minister as a public interest incorporated foundation and re-registers as such; initiates assistance to Myanmar.
2016	Wins the JICA Recognition Award in the 12th JICA President Commendation.
2017	Awarded the Japanese Foreign Minister's Commendation.

target country with associates from that country, we sometimes noticed weaknesses in the law, or legal studies, in Japan."

Another benefit is the rediscovery of one's identity as a legal professional. Judges (and former judges), prosecutors, and lawyers are given the opportunity to re-identify themselves as "individuals in the discipline of law" by leaving their positions in Japan and conducting extensive discussions with legal professionals in their target recipient countries.

Jurists are no exception. Matsuo says:

> Cooperation for legal and judicial development has begun to surface in discussions at academic conferences in Japan in recent years. There's no doubt that this subject has been

> attracting increasing attention. In fact, some jurists [legal scholars] have started to call for the outcomes of Japan's Civil Code development support programs in Vietnam and Cambodia to be reflected in the revision of the Civil Code of Japan itself. I'm hoping that we can explore even better legislative systems together with aid recipient countries through mutual learning in the future.

The invaluable experiences that they have acquired in their target countries are sure to be put into practice in Japan, resulting in positive effects to the law and legal system of Japan in the future.

OUTCOME 3

Development of next-generation leaders for the cooperation for legal and judicial development

Human resource development efforts in the area have also become increasingly organized over the past twenty years. Akimitsu Okubo[7] is director of the Law and Justice Team, and has been providing cooperation for legal and judicial development as a JICA staff member since 1998. He describes the current state of human resource development at JICA:

> Every August, JICA implements capacity-building training with the aim of developing human resources[8] who will be able to play leadership roles in the world of cooperation for legal and judicial development. In a nutshell, it's a "dojo" for cooperation for legal and judicial development. Practitioners in the discipline of law, consultants, think-tank employees, and researchers involved in international cooperation all participate in this training. It provides them with the opportunity to gain the knowledge and experience required for working in international cooperation, mainly in the field of legal and judicial development, but it also offers basic knowledge about the activities of JICA, aid trends, project management, and so on. Furthermore, participants are required to be proactive in discussions, rather than just passively listening to

7 See page 208, note 18.

8 For further information on JICA's human resource development programs, see page 221, note 28 and page 228, note 35.

Capacity building training

lectures. Many former participants are now playing important roles in the field.

Similar training is provided also by the ICD. The Training Seminar for International Cooperation Human Resource Development, hosted annually by ICD since 2009, aims to allow participants to develop a deeper understanding of international aid by getting them to actually experience working in the field of cooperation for legal and judicial development.

In addition, JFBA also began a training program for lawyers interested in the field in 2012, titled "Next-generation International Legal Support Training for Lawyers." This program, which uses a teleconferencing system to link bar associations in different parts of Japan, has been attracting the attention of many lawyers across the country, particularly young ones.

Furthermore, cooperation for legal and judicial development has been drawing attention from a wider range of people in recent years. Universities and law schools have set up new courses like "Law and Development Studies"[9] and "Cooperation for Legal and Judicial Development,"[10] resulting in increasing numbers of students becoming interested in this area.

Katsunori Irie,[11] a lawyer and JICA senior advisor who is currently stationed in Laos as a long-term expert, says:

9, 10 While there are not precise definitions for "Law and Development Studies" and "Cooperation for Legal and Judicial Development," in general usage both refer to the study of how the development of legal and judicial infrastructure in developing countries contributes to social and economic progress. Theoretical aspects as well as methodologies of cooperation are often discussed in the context of development law studies.

11 See page 154, note 8.

> There have been a lot of public relations activities related to cooperation for legal and judicial development for students recently. For example, Nagoya University, other educational institutions, JICA, ICD, JFBA and other related parties have jointly hosted seminars and symposiums. JICA's senior advisors, including me, have also been trying to make more students interested in this field; for example, by giving lectures on the topic in universities and law schools, and by interacting with students when running symposiums. I feel that students nowadays realize from an early stage that cooperation for legal and judicial development is a possible career path for lawyers. Moreover, non-legal-profession employees of private companies also participated in a symposium related to such cooperation that I attended recently. In this way, the broadening of professionals interested in the field is resulting in increased understanding among the general public in Japan as a whole. We're thinking of further promoting our partnership and coordination with universities and law schools in the future from a long-term and comprehensive point of view.

12 See page 60, note 37.

Masanori Aikyo,[12] an expert on Vietnamese law who has been behind the cooperation for legal and judicial development of Japan since the very beginning, points out that more emphasis should be placed on the development of jurists and practitioners specializing in Asian laws in the future. He also applauds the increase in Japanese students interested in the laws of Asian countries and the cooperation in the Asian region over the past twenty years.

> In my opinion, one thing that differentiates Japan's cooperation for legal and judicial development from other aid organizations is that, on top of learning the languages of their target recipient countries, learning to understand their cultures and customs, and of course their laws, Japanese experts work together with the people in these countries. We shouldn't forget that behind this effort were Japanese researchers, particularly those at Nagoya University, who specialized in the

laws of Asian countries. They are few in number, but they are specialists in this area. Now that public attention toward this area is increasing, the number of students interested in studying Asian laws is also growing. Currently the ASEAN Community is working toward "Unity in Diversity," so I think it's becoming increasingly important to foster researchers who understand the languages and laws of their target countries, and seriously work on comparative studies of Asian laws in order to produce the next generation of experts for cooperation for legal and judicial development.

OUTCOME 4

Building a "Relationship of mutual trust" with the target country: From aid to partnership

"Legal and judicial development" is a task that each sovereign nation should undertake for itself. It is an endless challenge to establish laws, reinforce the functions of organizations that apply those laws, and improve access to justice, in aiming to become an ideal nation.

By contrast, goals and deadlines are set when providing cooperation for legal and judicial development. The cooperation provided to a country through ODA ends once an appropriate environment is established. That is when they can carry out legislative reform and foster human resources in the legal and judicial sectors themselves from then on, and the necessary human resources in place to play core roles.

With this in mind, what relationship will Japan have with a target country that has "graduated" from the ODA-based cooperation for legal and judicial development? Miha Isoi,[13] who has worked as a long-term expert in Mongolia and Cambodia, is currently engaged in this area as a JICA senior advisor. She describes the kind of cooperation that can continue after the completion of a project, using Mongolia as an example:

13 See page 104, note 13.

> Our cooperation for legal and judicial development in Mongolia ended at the end of 2015. Interested members of the Association of Mongolian Advocates, however, have

continued to personally apply and come to Japan every year since 2013 to learn about Japanese systems, paying all of their expenses themselves, including costs for travel, accommodation and translation/interpreting. The JFBA is the Japanese host for them, and JFBA volunteers give lectures and work to make the necessary arrangements for study tours and other programs. One advantage of volunteering like this is that volunteers can collect information about recent developments in the evolution of Mongolia's legal system. In fact, I've also joined them to help receive the participants. In my opinion, the continuation of these exchanges attests to the solid relationship of trust established between the two countries through the cooperation for legal and judicial development.

These kinds of exchanges have begun early during technical cooperation projects, not only in Mongolia but also in other countries. For example, the Bar Association of the Kingdom of Cambodia and the JFBA signed a memorandum of friendly mutual cooperation in 2000, based on which the two organizations are expected to maintain exchanges in the future. Another example is the exchange project between the Supreme People's Procuracy of Vietnam and the Ministry of Justice of Japan, which already has quite a long history; the Supreme People's Court of Vietnam has been gathering information about the judicial

Members of the Association of Mongolian Advocates in Japan

system of Japan by visiting the country at its own expense. Yet another example is Indonesia. As outlined in chapter 4, lawyer Yoshiro Kusano[14] established the Japan-Indonesia Lawyers Association after the completion of JICA's Project on Improvement of Mediation System in Indonesia in order to pass on to people in the private sector the relationship of trust that had been nurtured through the project.

14 See page 193, note 6.

It can be said that the completion of support is the first step into a journey toward equal partnership between the recipient country and Japan, and is a new starting point for mutual exchanges.

As vice president of JICA, Tomiyoshi is hoping that countries that "graduate" from aid will become Japan's partners and join Japan in providing cooperation for legal and judicial development to other countries in the future. "For example," he says, "Vietnam has experience in developing its own legal system 'independently and from scratch' with the advice of Japan and other countries, and has already produced quite a number of highly capable experts. I'm hoping that these individuals will make the most of their experience and play important roles as powerful partners of JICA in the future."

Such activities have already begun to take place. For example, members of the sub-working group on the Criminal Procedure Code in Laos were invited to Vietnam in 2013, as part of JICA's project activities, so that lessons learned from the Vietnamese experience could be shared with Laos; Vietnamese practitioners taught the training sessions, as well as conducting other activities. Then in 2017, the director of the Department of Economic and Civil Law of Ministry of Justice of Vietnam, along with other representatives from Vietnam, visited Laos to hold a joint civil law seminar with the Laotian members who were drafting their civil code at that time.

In this way, former "donor" and "recipient" countries can join forces to assist another developing country in establishing and improving its laws. When the number of partner countries like Vietnam increases in the future, cooperation for legal and judicial development will surely become a more sustainable pursuit with greater diversity and depth, capable of meeting a wider range of needs.

02 Future Challenges for the Cooperation for Legal and Judicial Development

Japan established the "Japanese style" of cooperation for legal and judicial development, which is different from that adopted by the government of any other country, or any aid agency, over the past twenty years. What are the objectives of Japan's cooperation for legal and judicial development for the future? Different organizations and individuals with a wide variety of experience in the field have their own different thoughts.

CHALLENGE 1

Deepen public understanding of the cooperation for legal and judicial development

As long as the cooperation for legal and judicial development is financed by Japanese taxpayers, it is essential to gain their understanding and support. Kohei Sakai,[15] former director of ICD, asserts that it is necessary to make the significance of the cooperation understood by the general public in order to achieve this objective. Says Sakai:

> Japan's cooperation for legal and judicial development has produced significant results so far, thanks to the devoted efforts of many jurists and practitioners. I believe that the Ministry of Justice of Japan has also played an important part as a member. At the same time, however, I also feel that we have only made limited efforts to communicate information to people using easy-to-understand language to gain their understanding with regard to the cooperation in this area. ICD was based in Osaka for seventeen years from 2001, but in October 2017 it was relocated to the city of Akishima in the Tokyo region. Before leaving Osaka, I visited leading business people in the city to offer them my sincere thanks

15 Sakai is a prosecutor who became director of the International Cooperation Department (ICD) of the Ministry of Justice Research and Training Institute in 2015. He is currently director of the Institute's First Training Department.

for their ongoing support. I was shocked when they often reacted with, "Cooperation for legal and judicial development to developing countries? I never knew that the Ministry of Justice has been doing that."

Sakai argues that the results of Japan's cooperation for legal and judicial development should be more proactively communicated; for example, by launching a special website to provide information about the current status of Japan's cooperation, the legal system of Japan, how it is actually used, and so on, in English, as well as through public relations activities inside Japan. He elaborates:

> When the legal system of a developing country is improved, it becomes easier for companies to expand their business into the country. Another clear contribution to the national interests of Japan is that with the deepening of trust between Japan and each recipient country, a greater number of people who are knowledgeable about Japan or have friendly feelings toward Japan emerge in central government and business circles in the country. Unlike "hard" or material aid, such as the construction of bridges and ports, the export of soft infrastructure like legal and judicial development rarely produces results that are immediately visible. It takes longer for the results to become apparent. For this reason, it's all the more important to consistently communicate the significance of these projects to the general public.

CHALLENGE 2

Efforts to increase Japan's international presence

Some people involved in cooperation for legal and judicial development also argue that it is important to encourage greater public understanding of the project, not only within Japan, but also abroad. Akio Morishima,[16] who played a pioneering role in the project, passionately advocates the need for strategy and assertiveness.

16 See page 45, note 2.

The first thing to do is accurately evaluate what Japan has done so far and, accordingly, consider what strategy Japan should take. In the future, if Japan accepts requests from countries under different conditions and provides aid to them, will it be appropriate for Japan to adopt the same approach as in the past? What standards should be used to prioritize potential recipient countries and aid programs, given Japan's limited aid budget? A clear strategy for the cooperation for legal and judicial development must be established. Once that is done, it's also important to translate the strategy into English and publish the information. Otherwise, JICA, the Ministry of Justice, and researchers—including me—might just end up celebrating our achievements among ourselves, telling each other what a great difference we have made. This would not have any particular meaning in the outside world, particularly outside Japan. In fact, despite the fact that Japan has been allocating significant funding for ODA, surveys have shown that only about 10 percent of young overseas respondents were aware of it. Cooperation for legal and judicial development is not the kind of work that can be completed in ten years, or even in twenty years. Sustainability requires strategy and assertiveness.

A symposium co-hosted by the UNDP and JICA

Akimitsu Okubo, who worked for JICA in China, takes this seriously, and expresses his thoughts on the future direction of Japan's cooperation for legal and judicial development:

> It's a remarkable achievement that we have strengthened our relationship with the Rule of Law team at the UNDP (United Nations Development Programme).[17] JICA co-hosted the first joint symposium with the team in New York in December 2016. We're thinking of regularly co-hosting symposia in the future as well. I believe that it's hugely important for Japan to raise the profile of its cooperation for legal and judicial development through international organizations. To achieve this objective, I'm hoping that we can further reinforce this connection in the future. The goal of initiatives like this is to introduce our work in this area to other countries, thereby making Japan's strong commitment in this area widely known across the world. In my opinion, this will bring about an extremely positive effect not only in building new relationships between donors, but also in discovering new needs in developing countries. It's often pointed out that Japan's profile is low, despite the large sums it contributes to international organizations. I believe that one solution for improving Japan's international presence is for JICA to raise the profile of Japan's international contributions through engagement with the United Nations.

17 See page 47, note 7.

CHALLENGE 3

Summarize all past experiences to provide more strategic support

The importance of strategy is also pointed out by Keio University professor Hiroshi Matsuo.

> Japan's cooperation for legal and judicial development requires big-picture strategy. For example, what is the final goal? What means should be adopted to achieve that goal? While one strength of Japan's cooperation is that Japan respects the ownership[18] of each country receiving support,

18 See page 72, note 51.

a weakness is that Japan tends to respond to the fragmented needs of each target country on demand. Before anything else, however, it's necessary to thoroughly debate and clearly answer the question of what Japan aims to do through its cooperation. There are also many other important questions that need to be fully discussed beforehand, such as whether Japan should set up a special headquarters for cooperation for legal and judicial development, and if so, where the headquarters should be established. Another question is what should be done to build an "all-Japan" framework together with more cooperative organizations to carry out activities in a consistent and incremental fashion? We have already gained invaluable experience through repeated trial and error. I believe that now is the time to take advantage of these experiences and undertake serious efforts to make Japan's cooperation more strategic, with specific goals in mind.

In response to the suggestions above, Toshiyuki Nakamura,[19] director general of JICA's Industrial Development and Public Policy Department, points out that the current moment, the twentieth anniversary of Japan's cooperation for legal and judicial development, is a great opportunity to call for debate around national strategy.

19 As director general of JICA's Industrial Development and Public Policy Department since 2017, Nakamura is responsible for all aspects of assistance in the governance field, including cooperation for legal and judicial development.

In its early days, Japan's cooperation for legal and judicial development was launched to support countries that were undergoing a change in system, like Vietnam. The goal of the aid was clear at that time. Twenty years later, however, the number of target countries for cooperation has increased and the goals have diversified. It's high time that we begin discussions about what kind of cooperation Japan should provide in the future based on these facts. The important thing is that the discussions need to be more advanced than just meetings involving the organizations and individuals that

Toshiyuki Nakamura

have actually been engaged in the project in the past, such as the Ministry of Justice, jurists, and JICA. They should be held in a comprehensive context, taking into consideration policies such as the National Security Strategy that was adopted by the Cabinet in December 2013. In June 2017, the Liberal Democratic Party's Research Commission on the Judiciary System recommended to the Japanese government that Japan should place emphasis on "justice affairs diplomacy" by introducing Japanese-style legal systems to countries in Southeast Asia and elsewhere. The commission also recommended establishing a headquarters for this initiative inside the Ministry of Justice, and developing internationally-minded experts in the legal and judicial sectors. I think that Japan's strategy in the areas of diplomacy and security, as well as its vision for "the century of Asia," should also be reflected in discussions about where the country's cooperation for legal and judicial development should be heading in the future.

03 The Results of Cooperation Proliferate

The ultimate goal of JICA's cooperation is to deliver the results of its aid to every individual in the country being supported. In this regard, the completion of a project is none other than a new starting point. Cooperation can be said to have produced results only when professional personnel fostered through JICA projects have successfully established laws and legal systems that are reflected in the daily lives of their compatriots, and there is a clear course for the proper protection of the human rights of each and every citizen of the target country.

Today, it is becoming increasingly common for former JICA project members to voluntarily carry out their own activities that build on the project's achievements.

An example from Cambodia illustrates this. One challenge in Cambodia is to make sure that the Civil Code and the Civil Procedure Code, which have been established with the support of a JICA project, are commonly and appropriately used in people's

A Contribution of Law seminar

daily lives. This is the reason that JICA launched the Legal and Judicial Development Project (Phase V) in April 2017 with the goal of promoting broader and more appropriate implementation of the Civil Code and Civil Procedure Code.

Iv Poly[20] and Tep Bophal,[21] a married couple, are both lawyers and members of the Bar Association working group of the JICA project. They voluntarily began providing seminars on the Civil Code and the Civil Procedure Code to students and young lawyers in 2015. Since 2016 they have expanded this activity by involving employees of the Ministry of Justice of Cambodia, judges and Japanese experts, and staff members of the JICA project in order to promote wider implementation of the Civil Code and Civil Procedure Code. They were also part of the Project for Legal and Judicial Cooperation for the Bar Association of the Kingdom of Cambodia (which took place from 2007 to 2010), and were engaged in the creation of the Prerequisite Fact Handbook and other activities. They describe this promotional activity as follows:

> We started our own activity, titled "Contribution of Law," in March 2015. We collected a fee of about five dollars each from students and young lawyers to rent a venue and host a seminar for them. We have also printed informative materials at our own expense to distribute to seminar participants.

20 Poly is a Cambodian lawyer who has been practicing since 2008, when he graduated from the Center for Lawyers Training and Professional Improvement (LTC) of the Bar Association of the Kingdom of Cambodia (see page 127).

21 Bophal, a Cambodian lawyer, has been practicing since 2007, when she graduated from LTC.

These seminars are taught not only by us, but also by other working group members of the JICA project—whom we ask for help. In addition, Japanese experts sometimes join us to give lectures and answer questions raised during lecture preparation. Although many Cambodian lawyers and students are eager to learn more about the Civil Code and the Civil Procedure Code, there are not enough opportunities or learning materials available to them at the moment. The Civil Code and Civil Procedure Code need to be made known and accessible to more people.

With activities like these, the main cog that was put into motion through the cooperation for legal and judicial development of Japan is now, in turn, beginning to make a large number of smaller gears turn.

04 Young People Expected to Become Next-Generation Leaders of Cooperation for Legal and Judicial Development

A five-day training course titled "Capability-Building Training 2017: Cooperation for Legal and Judicial Development Course," took place in a seminar room of the JICA Research Institute in Ichigaya, Tokyo, in August 2017.

The following interviews were conducted on the final day, on which a group exercise titled "Let's Plan a Project" took place. The theme was cooperation for legal and judicial development conducted with the government of an imaginary country named Nurasia. In the first half of the exercise, each group of participants considered what problems should be resolved in the country, what targets should be set for the project, and so on, based on basic information and research on the target country, including its domestic situation. In the second half, each group translated the results of their discussions into specific goals for the cooperation for legal and judicial development in Nurasia, discussing how they should combine a wide variety of resources—for example the provision of long-term experts, the establishment of an advisory group, and the implementation of seminars in Nurasia—to assist the country in an efficient and effective manner. Lastly, they developed a plan for the overall project. This seminar took an extremely practical approach.

One of the participants, Hikaru Kagami, is a lawyer running a community-based legal firm in Togane City, Chiba Prefecture. As a university student, he visited "Smokey Mountain"[22] in the Philippines. The experience prompted him to explore the question: "Is there anything I can do to help improve human rights conditions?"

22 "Smokey Mountain," a landfill site in northern Manila, was so called because of the constant plumes of smoke that rose from the garbage as it spontaneously caught fire. People settled there to scrape together a living by scavenging for anything of value, creating what came to be known as East Asia's largest slum.

With this question in mind, he participated in a summer school held at Nagoya University's Center for Asian Legal Exchange (CALE), which introduced him to cooperation for legal and judicial development, sparking his interest in this area.

> I already had a desire to be involved in international cooperation in one way or another. Participation in the summer school, however, has made me more aware of what kind of work I really want to do, as the approach of understanding the realities of the target country, and thinking and working together with local people to solve problems, resonates with me powerfully. I'm currently working in what is called a "legally underserved" region that faces a shortage of lawyers. I'm hoping that I can take advantage of this experience in the future to make some contributions in areas like improvement of civil proceedings and access to justice.

Prosecutor Fumie Fukuoka has been in charge of Cambodia as an ICD professor since April 2017. She was first introduced to cooperation for legal and judicial development when she attended a lecture by a more experienced member of ICD in the post-adoption training, which left a lasting impression on her.

> It was a lecture by Noriko Shibata,[23] who was stationed in Cambodia as a long-term expert for about two years from 2006 to 2008. I was so excited about the duties in my job as a prosecutor at that time—investigations and trials and such—that I wasn't immediately interested in working in

23 See page 126, note 53.

> cooperation for legal and judicial development. After about ten years of working as a prosecutor, however, I gradually became increasingly keen to challenge myself in an international field of work. So I requested a transfer to ICD.

At present, Fukuoka is in charge of Cambodia, and teaches in seminars in Cambodia as a short-term expert. She says that participating in capacity-building training has enabled her to rediscover the significance of working in cooperation for legal and judicial development.

> Cooperation for legal and judicial development is not merely about assisting other countries in creating and applying their laws and systems. It consists of a wider range of activities designed to make sure that people in each recipient country can lead safer and happier lives by making the most of the laws and systems. It's about establishing a relationship of trust with people in these countries, each with their own languages and cultural backgrounds different from yours, through patient communication, and cooperating to create legal systems that will lay the foundations for their lives. The results bring about the happiness of the people... I can't think of a job more rewarding or inspiring.

At 4:30 in the afternoon on the final day of the capacity-building training, when the participants had completed all the programs of the course, the final assignment was given to them. Keio professor Hiroshi Matsuo, first mentioned in chapter 2, had repeatedly asked his students and training participants to do this same assignment in the past, in JICA's capacity building training programs and in his lectures on Law and Development Studies. Each participant was asked to fill in the blanks to complete the following English sentences, which are inscribed on the gravestone of Kanzo Uchimura, a renowned Christian thinker and author.

I for Japan.
Japan for the world.
The world for ___.

And all for ___.

Participants wrote different words—"love," "peace," and so on—in the blanks. No matter what word they chose, however, the assignment filled them with positive energy.

05 The Aims of JICA's Cooperation for Legal and Judicial Development: A New Stage

24 See page 188, note 1.

The document for Basic Policies on Legal Technical Assistance[24] was revised by the Japanese government in May 2013 to state that "Japan shall enhance support in the area of economic law and assist the creation of secure business environments to allow Japanese and other foreign companies to do business in developing countries with peace of mind, from cross-sectional perspectives, in addition to offering support concerning basic laws." The policies also emphasize further enhancement of cooperation and coordination between implementation bodies, with importance placed on Japan's economic cooperation through governance reinforcement and contribution to achieving international development goals.

The ultimate goal of cooperation for legal and judicial development is not the creation of good laws and systems, however. It needs to aim to achieve higher-level development goals while encouraging alignment with other areas of cooperation, so as to help people lead safer and richer lives.

Toshiyuki Nakamura, mentioned earlier, describes how Japan should provide cooperation for legal and judicial development in the future:

25 See page 57, note 26.

> The goals of the cooperation implemented by JICA as part of ODA programs have been and always will be to assist the self-help efforts of developing countries based on good governance,[25] and also to contribute to the creation of the legal systems and the fostering of the human resources that lay the foundations for development of the country. In this regard, the most important area of cooperation, without doubt, should be cooperation concerning the basic rules governing

social life, such as the Civil Code and the Civil Procedure Code. This is an area in which significant results can be achieved only after a medium- to long-term period of cooperation. I believe that only aid agencies like JICA, which work in tandem with respective recipient countries to support their self-reliant efforts, can carry out this mode of cooperation and help countries lay the foundations for their society.

At the same time, it's also true that the economic growth of target countries is resulting in increasingly diversified development needs in these countries. In fact, JICA is aware of the need to respond to these shifting needs. When implementing cooperation in the area of economic laws, it's essential to work in collaboration with the Japanese companies and private-sector organizations that are the "end users," and reflect their knowledge and skills in the activities. In addition, it's also vital to pay due attention to criminal laws in order to make sure that economic laws are properly used. While JICA has mainly been providing aid to Asian countries so far, it should pay greater attention to different regions outside Asia in the future. In this way, cooperation for legal and judicial development is expected to play a growing role.

What changes can the Japanese approach to cooperation for legal and judicial development bring to developing countries, and how can it change the world? These questions have not yet been answered. Even so, there is no doubt that Japan's cooperation has produced significant results in many countries and has succeeded in garnering the confidence of many people within the space of just twenty years. Japan must build on its achievements and trust from its partners to make the most of its strengths and meet ever-shifting development needs. Cooperation for legal and judicial development has an important role to play as a form of international contribution that Japan can present to the world with pride.

A new stage in the project has been ushered in, and it will go further, building upon twenty years of achievements.

List of Interviews

*Affiliations are those at the time of the interview; only those relevant to cooperation for legal and judicial development are given.

JAPAN (IN JAPANESE SYLLABIC ORDER)

Akimitsu Okubo—JICA staff member (director, Law and Justice Team, Governance Group, Industrial Development and Public Policy Department; former member of the China Office)

Akio Morishima—Professor emeritus, Nagoya University; leader, JICA Joint Research Group on the Vietnamese Civil Code; leader, JICA Joint Research Group on the Cambodian Civil Code

Atsushi Kamiki—Lawyer; former JICA long-term expert in Cambodia

Ayako Tamiya—Lawyer; former JICA long-term expert in Cambodia

Emi Aizawa—JICA staff member (former member of the Cambodia Office)

Emiko Kanetake—Judicial scrivener; advisor to the Cambodian Ministry of Land Management, Urban Planning and Construction; former JICA long-term expert in Cambodia

Hajime Kawanishi—Prosecutor; JICA long-term expert in Vietnam

Hideaki Matsumoto—JICA staff member; former member of the Laos office

Hiroki Kunii—Prosecutor; former JICA long-term expert in Myanmar

Hiroshi Matsuo—Professor, Keio University Law School; JICA Laos project advisor; JICA Nepal Civil Code advisor

Hiroshi Suda—Prosecutor; JICA long-term expert in Laos

Hiroyuki Ito—Prosecutor; deputy director, ICD; former JICA long-term expert in Laos

Hiroyuki Shirade—Lawyer; JICA long-term expert in China

Hitoshi Kawamura—JICA long-term expert in Laos

Ikufumi Niimi—Professor, School of Law, Meiji University; member, JICA Joint Research Group on the Vietnamese Civil Code; member, JICA Joint Research Group on the Cambodian Civil Code

Issei Sakano—Consultant, United Nations Office on Drugs and Crime (UNODC); former JICA long-term expert in Cambodia; former JICA long-term expert in Myanmar

Jun Uchiyama—Prosecutor; JICA long-term expert in Cambodia

Kaoru Obata—Professor, Nagoya University Graduate School of Law; director, CALE

Katsunori Irie—Lawyer; JICA senior advisor

Katsuya Ichihashi—Trustee and vice president, Nagoya University; former director, CALE; former JICA Uzbekistan project advisor

Kazuo Sakakibara—Prosecutor; former director, General Affairs and Planning Department, Research and Training Institute, Ministry of Justice

Kazuto Inaba—Professor, Chukyo University Graduate School of Law; former judge; former JICA Mongolia project advisor

Ken'ichi Tomiyoshi—Vice president, JICA

Kenta Komatsu—Lawyer; JICA senior advisor; former JICA long-term expert in Myanmar

Kie Matsushima—Lawyer; former JICA long-term expert in Uzbekistan

Kimitoshi Yabuki—Lawyer; former chairman, JFBA International Exchange Committee

Kohei Sakai—Prosecutor; director, ICD

Maiko Amano—Lawyer; JICA long-term expert in Laos

Maiko Takeuchi—JICA staff member; former member of JICA Nepal office

Masanori Aikyo—Chairman, Board of Trustees, Aichi Public University Corporation; professor emeritus, Nagoya University; former director, CALE

Masanori Tanabe—Lawyer; former JICA long-term expert in Mongolia

Masanori Tsukahara—Lawyer; JICA long-term expert in Vietnam

Masato Watanabe—Professor, J. F. Oberlin University; former JICA technical cooperation advisor in China

Masayoshi Takehara—JICA staff member; former member of the China office

Michiaki Ozaki—Lawyer; former prosecutor; former director, ICD

Miha Isoi—Lawyer; JICA senior advisor; former JICA long-term expert in Mongolia; former JICA long-term expert in Cambodia

Mitsuyasu Matsukawa—Judge; former ICD professor

Morio Takeshita—Professor emeritus, Hitotsubashi University; leader, JICA Joint Research Group on the Cambodian Civil Procedure Code

Naoki Sakai—Judge; JICA long-term expert in Vietnam

Naoshi Sato—Lawyer; Legal Advisor to JICA; former JICA long-term expert in Vietnam; former JICA senior advisor

Noriko Shibata—Prosecutor; former JICA long-term expert in Cambodia; former deputy director, ICD

Osamu Ishioka—Lawyer; JICA long-term expert in Laos

Sadao Matsubara—Lawyer; former prosecutor; former JICA long-term expert in Cambodia

Shiho Akamatsu—Programme officer, UN World Food Programme (WPF); formerly project formulation advisor with JICA Nepal Office

Shiro Muto—Lawyer; former JICA long-term expert in Vietnam

Sumiko Sekine—Judge; former ICD professor

Svay Leng—Khmer interpreter

Takako Tsukabe—Prosecutor; JICA long-term expert in Vietnam

Takayuki Sumida—Lawyer; former JICA long-term expert in China

Takeshi Matsumoto—Prosecutor; former JICA long-term expert in Vietnam

Takeo Kosugi—Lawyer; former judge; board member, ICCLC

Takeyoshi Hongo—Lawyer; former prosecutor; auditor, ICCLC

Taro Morinaga—Prosecutor; former JICA long-term expert in Vietnam; former deputy director, ICD; deputy director, UNAFEI

Terutoshi Yamashita—Notary; former prosecutor; former director, ICD

Tomohiro Nakajima—Judge; Former JICA long-term expert in Vietnam

Toshiyuki Nakamura—JICA staff member (director general, Industrial Development and Public Policy Department)

Tsugunori Teramoto—JICA long-term expert in Vietnam

Wakaba Hara—Lawyer; former JICA long-term expert in Côte d'Ivoire

Yasuhiko Tsuji—Prosecutor; JICA long-term expert in Cambodia

Yasuhiro Kudo—Prosecutor; former JICA long-term expert in Laos

Yoichiro Shinoda—Lawyer; JICA long-term expert in Cambodia

Yoko Obata—Lawyer; former JICA long-term expert in Vietnam

Yoshinobu Ikura—JICA staff member (former director general of JICA's Industrial Development and Public Policy Department)

Yoshiro Kusano—Lawyer; former judge; former JICA Indonesia project advisor

Yoshiko Homma—Professor, Soka University Law School; lawyer; former JICA long-term expert in Cambodia

Yoshitaka Watanabe—Staff member, Ministry of Justice; former ICD professor

Yuko Kawaguchi—JICA long-term expert in Cambodia

Yosuke Kobayashi—JICA staff member; former member of JICA Vietnam Office

VIETNAM

Dang Hoang Oanh—Deputy director-general, International Cooperation Department, Ministry of Justice

Dinh Thi Bich Ngoc—Former specialist, International Cooperation Department, Ministry of Justice

Dinh Trung Tung—Former vice minister of justice

Ha Hung Cuong—Former minister of justice

Le Thanh Long—Minister of justice

Luu Tien Dzung—Lawyer; director of the International Cooperation Department of the VBF

Ngo Cuong—Director, International Cooperation Department, Supreme People's Court

Nguyen Thi Thu Ha— Staff member, JICA Vietnam project office

Nguyen Tuan Khanh—Chief of the office, Hai Phong People's Procuracy

Nguyen Tuan Linh—Student at Nagoya University; staff member, Ministry of Justice

Tran Ngoc Thanh—Staff member, International Cooperation Department, Supreme People's Court

Tran Nguyet Anh—Program officer, JICA Vietnam office

Tuong Thi Tu Hoai—Student at Nagoya University

Vu Thi Hai Yen—Deputy director-general, International Cooperation Department, Supreme People's Procuracy

Vu Van Moc—Former director-general, International Cooperation Department, Supreme People's Procuracy

CAMBODIA

Bun Honn—Lawyer; former president of the Bar Association of the Kingdom of Cambodia

Chan Sotheavy— Secretary of State, Ministry of Justice

Chhorn Proloeung—President, RAJP

Chin Mony—Student at Nagoya University; staff member, Ministry of Justice

Kim Sathavy—Supreme Court judge

Leang Monirith—Assistant secretary, Ministry of Land

Lim Voan—Secretary of state, Ministry of Land

Luy Channa—Rector, RULE

Nget Naroth—Student at RSJP

Phok Phira—Program officer, JICA Cambodia Office

Try Bakleang—Student at Nagoya University

You Bunleng—President, Appeal Court

LAOS

Chomkham Bouphalivanh—Director, National Institute of Justice

Ket Kiettisak—Deputy Minister of Justice

Ketsana Phommachane—Director general, Department of Legal Affairs, Ministry of Justice

Khampha Sengdara—Vice president, People's Supreme Court

Khamphay Xayasouk—Deputy head, Technical Division, Judicial Research and Training Institute, People's Supreme Court

Latthaya Kho—Staff member, Laos project office

Manodeth Chounthavong—Former staff member, Laos project office

Nalonglith Norasing—International Cooperation Department, Ministry of Justice

Nyvanh Somsengsy—Lawyer

Phetsamay Xaymoungkhoune—Deputy director, National Institute of Justice

Somsack Taybounlack—Presiding justice, People's Central High Court

Viengvilay Thiengchanhxay—Dean, Faculty of Law and Political Science, National University of Laos

Vilay Langkavong—Head, Political Science Department, Faculty of Law and Political Science, National University of Laos

Xaysana Khotphouthone—Deputy supreme people's prosecutor

Afterword

This book, we hope, has given you an idea of the Japanese approach to cooperation for legal and judicial development. We put it together out of a desire to look back on the history of Japan's efforts in this area as we marked a significant milestone—the twentieth anniversary of the commencement of JICA's legal and judicial development program in Vietnam—and the wish to share it with a wider audience.

In compiling this book, we had two things foremost in mind.

First, we wanted to inform as many readers as possible about Japan's efforts in legal and judicial development and arouse their interest. We have accordingly done our best to avoid arcane terminology and to use plain language, and to produce an engaging read, even for those completely new to the subject of international cooperation and legal and judicial development.

Second, we wanted to chronicle Japan's efforts to support legal and judicial development to date by leaving a living, breathing record of the hard work and dedication, the struggles and triumphs, of the players involved, both in Japan and its partner countries, and the lessons they learned.

To that end, we interviewed more than a hundred people who had been involved in the program, asking them to recount their experiences one by one. They talked about things that you would never learn from reading a dry report, like their passion for the task, the drive that kept them going, and the emotions they felt. The more you get to know about promoting the rule of law, we felt as we listened, the more fascinating it becomes.

We spent more than a year working on the manuscript, determined to present the story as precisely and straightforwardly as possible. But there were so many wonderful anecdotes to choose from that writing and editing the book proved no easy task. We regret that, owing to limitations of space, not every anecdote could be included. Still, we are convinced that the Japan's cooperation for legal and judicial development would not be where it is today without the hard work and input of the entire cast of characters, including those we were unable to mention in this book.

Our heartfelt thanks go out to everyone who has been involved in the cooperation to date or who helped us with this book, including those we could not interview due to time constraints.

Cooperation for legal and judicial development is an unusual enterprise in that it relies solely on the medium of words to influence the central organs of the state—the justice ministry, the supreme court, the national assembly. For us at a personal level, the task of producing this book has been a keen reminder of the immense power of words, the possibilities that power offers, and the magnitude of the responsibility it entails.

Many episodes in this book concern misunderstandings and communication problems relating to language, and how people rose to the challenge of overcoming them on the ground. Retelling those stories has made us more aware of the difficulty of using language accurately. But it has also given us a new understanding of how words can be a tool for guaranteeing people's rights, changing countries for the better and transforming the world, for words have the power to light a spark in people's minds. And it has strengthened our commitment to working on a daily basis to support legal and judicial development overseas.

JICA's cooperation will continue to expand by building on past experience. We hope that after reading this book, more people will take an interest in legal and judicial development, aspire to become involved, and ask themselves what role they can play.

The JICA Law and Justice Team
December 2017

The JICA Law and Justice Team Editorial Committee

Akimitsu Okubo
Miha Isoi
Mitsushi Edagawa
Koichi Kato
Makiko Arai
Ayano Matsudo
Satoko Yamamoto

*The original version of this volume was compiled by the Editorial Committee of the Law and Justice Team, Governance Group, Industrial Development and Public Policy Department, JICA.

Further information on JICA's cooperation for legal and judicial development is available at the following sites:

The JICA website
https://www.jica.go.jp/english/index.html

JICA-Net Library "JICA's Cooperation for Rule of Law Promotion"
https://youtu.be/mWblPKO3RXI (Full ver.)
https://youtu.be/fFQSxOUYRRA (Digest ver.)

世界を変える日本式「法づくり」──途上国とともに歩む法整備支援

Japan's Approach to Legal and Judicial Development in Developing Countries: Building Trust and Partnership

---

2020年6月1日　第1刷発行

原著編者　独立行政法人 国際協力機構
英語版編者　一般財団法人 出版文化産業振興財団

発行所　一般財団法人出版文化産業振興財団
〒101-0051　東京都千代田区神田神保町2-2-30
電話　03-5211-7283
ホームページ　https://www.jpic.or.jp/

印刷・製本所　大日本印刷株式会社

定価はカバーに表示してあります。

Printed in Japan
ISBN 978-4-86658-130-9